Author's Note 5
Prologue 7

PART 1 | Getting Started Now

Start a Conversation 13
The Plan for Building a Plan 23
Tender Topics 31
The Nitty Gritty 35
Financial Inflow and Outflow: Finding Your Numbers 39
Answering Medical Questions 49
Who?? Naming a Power of Attorney & Medical Surrogate.... 55
Need a Cure for Overload? 63
Stage Four: Action (Going Legal) 67

PART 2 | Living With A Plan

Maintenance 87
Early Years 93
Life Is Not a Dress Rehearsal 99
Family Reactions & Dementia Concerns 103
Emotions and Relationships 115
Sea Change 119
January 2008: Shoes Dropping Into Gray Matter 133
Bend In The Road 137
Time For Help at Home 147
Life Lessons In the Trenches 155
On Guard: 2008-2010 167
A Plateau of Sorts 175
Caring for the Caregiver: Facts, Fatigue, and Leaning In 191

Late Middle, or Early Late Stage 209
Mindfulness.. 215
A Sentinel at Work 221

PART 3 | Almost Home
The Journal... 229
Epilogue 315
Resources as Red Bull 321
Bibliography 323
Final Inspiration and Encouragement............................... 329

Author's Note

Thinking about managing your own senior future, or helping an aging loved one? This book is our success story to guide you forward. Whatever the motivation-- love, compassion, necessity, responsibility, it is possible to build a successful personalized life care plan for traveling the senior highway with dignity, confidence and respect.

In the beginning, Mom and I didn't have a name for what we were doing, but we had intentions to figure out how to allow her to finish living life, her way. With lots of iced tea and conversation, we put ourselves ahead of the curve for her final emotional decade on the planet. We mapped her self-directed route before she needed it with an end of life care plan.

If you worry about losing control of decision making in your senior years, too much paperwork, family squabbles, or troubling reports of stress-filled caregiving, we are proof that you can learn to navigate. Walking with Mom offers step-by-step instruction and guided tasks combined with anecdote, insight and suggestion to help readers succeed and prosper with life care planning and living.

Learn how to prepare, protect, maintain and live your way. Use our daughter-mother experiences to gain an insider edge. Optimize senior living, enjoy respected and cherished final years by creating a self-directed life care plan like ours, and then read about what happens when you use it!

If you are a senior who needs a plan for the future, or a caring loved one who wants to help, did you realize that by reading this far, you have already begun?

Walking with Mom is a partnership of love. Woven throughout our story are lessons learned, the transformation of effort into ultimate privilege, and moving on. Being there forever changed us. It was supposed to.

But I'm getting ahead of myself.

As the one who remains, I get to tell both sides of the story. You know those childhood books that allow kids to choose their own ending? This is the adult version.

Get excited about the opportunity and an uplifting sense of accomplishment as you build plans for an awesome and best senior future.

Choose the ending you like best.

Bon voyage,

(and Jean)

Prologue

"The journey of one thousand miles begins with a footstep." - Chinese proverb

I hear Mom jangling the car keys. Lulu's ears perk and I pull on my Keds. My sisters and I pile into a station wagon, the destination a forest preserve--nature trails, scurrying leaves, ponds, tadpoles below and red tail hawks overhead.

I see Mom packing tuna sandwiches and lemonade into a cooler. A hot ride takes forever through city streets, until finally, we are racing across blistering sand to cool toes in Lake Michigan.

I see Mom in fur-trimmed boots, an excited Lulu at her heels. We load sleds and saucers, headed once more to forest preserves and a snowy afternoon gliding down a slippery slope.

Time spinning away in the endless seasons of growing up. It

feels like yesterday and simultaneously like ancient history. The last dozen years or so got in the way. It is months since I said goodbye one hundred or one thousand times.

At the end, we were closer than either of us had probably imagined possible. Years beyond diagnoses that clouded daily life and lifetime events. Years beyond plenty of angst. When words were gone, her eyes held mine, reaching into the depths of human understanding. When her eyes no longer opened, handholding was the touchstone between us. We had plotted and planned, made a determined effort to reach a grace-filled Autumn morning on her terms.

A fine art of hanging on and letting go. We had mapped what was important to her and held on for the ride. Somewhere in the middle years, we reached the day we had planned for even when we could not see it, the day I began to act for us both.

It was not perfect, but it was the best it could be—her choices, her directions coming face to face with life events, family personalities and the ever-present elephant in the room—Mom's final curtain call.

Eighty-five years and 106 days in a successful run. A plan that allowed Mom to live as she wanted--made possible by forward thinking that plotted her self-directed footsteps (and mine) along a winding senior highway. As dry leaves skittered down her street, Mom reached the natural bottom of a final slippery slope, moving on to her next nature preserve date alone.

But she did it her way, because I was there to help see that happen.

PART ONE
Getting Started Now

"Without ambition one starts nothing. Without work one finishes nothing. The prize will not be sent to you. You have to win it!" - Ralph Waldo Emerson

Today, there truly is a wealth of information for families and individuals seeking input on planning for and living out senior years. Higher life expectancies continue to generate rising interest in extending knowledge and skill to manage life in those extra years. There are books, pamphlets, the Internet, attorneys, estate planners, health care managers, and more who offer advice and option.

Go to any financial advisor office and find recommendations about savings, investing and using assets. Go to a local senior center workshop on wills and trusts; find a webinar about advanced directives. Estate planners and the Internet have boiler plate versions of legal documents that form the foundation of senior planning. Google senior care options for your home town. Check out vast resources at AARP--a library full of elder information, caregiving data and frequently asked questions across the realm of senior living and senior care. Browse "retirement" shelves at your local book store. Even Hospice, which most people associate with end of life care, can be a place to begin the discussion of senior decision making for future needs.

The circumstances are different for every one of us. Some people actually choose not to plan for their inevitable future. Others, despite best intentions do not or cannot make their own plans and the rest of us end up leaping in to assist at an emergency.

Why does this happen when at nearly every level, we ask ourselves to plan? What are we doing this Friday? This weekend? We schedule the carpool, a family picnic, a week of meals. How many times in your life have you asked yourself, your family or your buddies, what's the plan?

Planning is the seminal task to optimize our later years but doing so means looking at death.

Dr. Atul Gawande, author of Being Mortal, acknowledges that confronting mortality takes insight, acceptance and possibly medical assistance. Gawande suggests the normal wind down and conclusion of life needs attention and thoughtful consideration. Gawande urges readers to spend the time, to think consciously about the end of the road.

Does clarity now about "later on" make sense? Envision a personal GPS, directions and route. Why not plan how to best spend the last of our mortal lives? Shouldn't we each want to lead the decision making? Shouldn't we each want to be our own personal advisors for the final trip of a lifetime? Shouldn't we each want a say in controlling our future?

There are four important documents that form a working foundation of senior living, tools that offer direction, guidance, reassurance and confidence for that future road: A Last Will & Testament; Durable Power of Attorney declaration; Health care surrogacy document; a Living Will. How to create and use them requires time and thoughtful exploration.

For us, it began with lots of conversation and time for thinking it through. Mom wanted a plan and my help. I wanted a plan for her. We were not going to be caught unawares. Neither of us wanted to find ourselves at some future serious moment without her instructions for how to proceed. Together, we wrote Mom's plan based on her choices and decisions, and then put the pieces to work.

Whether you are the loved one who needs the plan, (and let's face it, we all are going to need a plan), or the significant other family or friend cast in the role of helper/caregiver, we all have reason enough to think about, talk about, and create a plan. Pre-planning cannot control events, but helps us manage our responses to circumstance. It offers insight, provides direction and eases a path. Don't be the person without a plan.

Here is your first **Assignment: Think forward, envision planning a senior future.**

1

Start a Conversation

"Do not go where the path may lead, go instead where there is no path and leave a trail."
- Ralph Waldo Emerson

You might think that conversation sounds rather undefined, but if thinking about a senior future is a first step, conversation with yourself and others is the logical, next step.

Initially, all conversation between Mom and me was NOT about creating a life plan, but more like tossing sand in the air-- Mom and daughter life chats about aging and everything else. Eventually, the grit in the wind produced a grand pebble, the vision most of us have—to live happily and independently for as long as possible. How to ensure "Mom's terms" for that unfolding future was where conversation started ramping up, and that eventually lead to creating Mom's plan.

Start a conversation. With yourself, with a loved one. Explore what you want for your future. Right now, when everything is fine! Whenever you are thinking about it is precisely the time to power up a clear head and investigate your perspective about those later years. Start the process. There are choices.

Old age care has evolved across the last 100 years with the advent of pensions and Social security, nursing homes, and burgeoning home support providers and assisted living options. Some cultures promote multigenerational living where families care for their elderly, and some seniors want the privacy and independence to live and die in their own home. There's plenty to think about.

Consider the octogenarian buried in the Mount St. Helens' lava--he was comfortable with his long full life and would not leave home despite a spewing mountain. Or my great grandma, who reached old age 100 years ago, living with her daughter's family in a Chicago bungalow, awaiting final days in a back bedroom.

Choices.

Pause to imagine how wonderful it would feel to guarantee optimal senior years. Imagine a confident, comfortable and secure future. That kind of successful senior life can happen with early planning. How do you get there?

Gawande wants us to accept personal responsibility for our mortality and he believes the medical community should offer thought leadership. There are doctors, professional groups, attorneys and councils on aging enthused by the idea of embracing a personal understanding of senior living and dying. There are public service announcements reminding us to start thinking about the future. Pre-planning is an industry and a profession. But what do you need to know?

Go to your computer and check out any of multiple sites out

there today. Here are two:

www.Lcplfa.org/about-life-care-planning
www.n4a.org

When Mom and I began walking toward her future, neither platform was operating. Today, however, all offer encouragement and ideas. Consider www.aplaceformom.com as a clearing house resource, check out www.homeinstead.com for other topics that might jumpstart a conversation. Try www.caregiverhomes.com

What is your motivation? If helping yourself remain in control of your future isn't enough, consider how many other people you will help along your way. Your children, your families, friends, medical people. Even your banker.

My husband and I recently revisited our own future planning, a conversation that began when he became self-employed. For us, future planning has been percolating. It feels early, but my experience helping Mom and a sincere desire to ease into later years with as much confidence and as few surprises as possible, has pushed us forward. With research, honesty and effort, conversations are turning into concrete plans to manage those coming years our way. We are worth it.

Explore your own thoughts and ideas. Go where conversations take you. What are you and your loved one(s) thinking about for a future that ultimately unfolds for us all? What do you want?

Happy and independent is a great starting point. But how and where? At home? Living with your children? In a senior community?

Get the idea? There is a lot to think about, and plenty more to talk through.

If you are encouraging someone else to plan, discuss the importance of ownership. Does anyone really want to leave these life decisions to others? Does anyone want to ignore making their own plans?

Mom and I grasped the sensitive reality of that inevitable finish line. But more important was how she wanted to live between now and when she reached it. Her terms.

If we could not foresee specifics of time and circumstance between now and then, we wanted, somehow, to secure her idea of how she thought it should be.

Talking through her vision was that giant first step. It was undeniable groundwork for all that came after. Our path through those following years had emotional and bumpy moments but the most difficult times were tempered—always--by the plan Mom put in place. (Did I mention my eternal gratitude for that plan?)

Getting Serious a About a Plan

"To make a difference in someone's life, you don't have to be wise, rich or beautiful. You just have to be there when they need you." - Personal development author, Steve Aitchison

---

Mom's Story—The Kitchen Table

Mom's planning conversations evolved through several years. Living alone for the first time in 50 years after Dad had died, she was handling details with a family lawyer and the good fortune of an existing Will. I was what the AARP had coined The Sandwich Generation, the adult child, dividing myself between an aging parent and my own family. No urgency, no big questions, but life without Dad meant adjustments. We would sit at her kitchen table, a 70-ish Mom and her eldest child, chatting away. She wanted validation that she was AOK. I wanted to reassure us both! Learning about her everyday was how we began to look at her big picture.

How was she doing?

Personally? "Pretty good," to use, perhaps, her favorite phrase. The beach, card games, eating out. Singing in the church choir. Shuffleboard. Water aerobics. Occasional dating. Managing her house and a rental property.

Financially? I accompanied tax filing visits, the whole thing straightforward. My role was what I thought every child was supposed to do when asked—be there with a stamp of approval. Going much deeper wasn't on the radar.

But our mutual reassurances felt good. In some faraway corner of my mind was a blip of gratified ease — "So, this is what it's like? We're here? Not so bad!"

I was in my late 40s, with a professional life in community services, a traveling husband stepping up in his career, and my own complicated household--three kids--one in college, another graduating in a few months, and the last one moving through high school. My BIG picture.

Over time, I flew south every few months to chat, learn more, and help Mom organize paper. Mom called it vacation. Three or four-night stayovers, good opportunities for one-on-one visits, a bit of file management and a reward day at the beach. Mom was comfortable and my learning curve was on the up. Ticking boxes, I learned about her Social Security, pension, health care, lingering certificates of deposit, a little stock, changes in widow benefits. Monthly banking. Real estate taxes. Our open chats were mother-daughter collaboration over her orderly folders, which reassured me with her efficient household operations.

When she inherited money and role of executor for her oldest sister, my youngest ran the paper shredder to clear out Marilyn's clogged filing cabinet, and our conversations veered toward details beyond every day. Settling her late sister's estate was a task that percolated for us both, while she remained happy, efficient and independent. Until one day something changed.

Overnight, she was a giddy, 75-year-old widow with a boyfriend. She was nervous, embarrassed. That new relationship was the catalyst that made Mom build a plan for her future. Entering a serious personal relationship required Mom to think further out than the next hot date. I listened up.

I wanted to help. What she wanted hadn't changed. Privacy, separate finances, protection for herself and her assets. She wanted her independence, to continue calling her own shots about everything including living arrangements, and yet feel protected from any and all future what-ifs. She wanted to guarantee herself peace of mind by having everything in order while she enjoyed stepping out in romance.

Neither of us comprehended the extent of "everything in order," but I remember my initial emotional jolt-- how serious she must be about the romance, and how calculated she meant to be to protect herself. Mom was seeking confidence that leaping into couplehood would not jeopardize her status quo. Security in order to play.

> Can you imagine having this conversation with your Mom???
>
> We both thought she could have fun and security, that life could happen her way. We joked that she really wanted an office manager, a Girl Friday to track details while she inhabited her own senior playground. We adjusted our leisurely mother-daughter perusals of her present operations to cast a futuristic wider view. As guardians of her future, she wanted a widow's risk management formula to play safe.
>
> I bought a notebook. Made lists. We shared a common goal—her happiness and security--trusting that together, we could figure it out.
>
> She wanted both my understanding of her intentions and my purposeful oversight (which she mostly already had), but I wanted more than conversation. I wanted a how-to-proceed manual detailed to her specifications. If she wanted confidante, major domo, trusted helper, and farther out some as yet undefined life care manager, I wanted written instructions. I insisted her ideas be committed to paper.
>
> I have profound gratitude for all that chatter. It's how we fine-tuned her choices for life planning decisions.

But what about you? **Your turn to speculate, whatever the reason.** Watch for the opportunity. It might be one of those everyday moments, a holiday gathering, an unexpected visit to the ER, a day when your loved one suddenly looks older than you remember. Couples should talk about this stuff. Parents and adult children should engage in a chance to start a conversation. It is the first step.

If anyone sounds reluctant, keep asking. Get to the kitchen table, now when it is not urgent.

Be there and engage in this vital conversation, whether doing

it for yourself or helping a loved one. Envision that future and <u>**start talking**</u>. **Senior self, spouse, limited partner, son, daughter, friend, listen to your loved one's ideas for the future. You'll hear interesting things.**

Mom and Frank Sinatra

Mom's specifics emerged as she settled on a time frame she thought reasonable to protect. A decade or two to keep hold of Mom's innermost dream: that independent life, unfettered by day-to-day details, protection for herself for whatever lay ahead, and all of it *with the boyfriend*. A proverbial *have the cake and eat it*, with her kitchen in order.

She wanted me as business partner, for her "life" business. Someone to accept her decisions, respect her choices. Someone trustworthy, credible *and* willing. But someone who would sit back while she played away.

Respect extended in both directions.

Whether family history, intuition or just because it seemed the right thing to do, I remained adamant about getting it formalized, something more than her askance and my verbal promise. Could we legally ensure Mom's independence along with safety, privacy, security, and a boyfriend?

What legal authority could help me orchestrate what she wanted and make it last? With a fast-forward vision to a time when she might be unable to make decisions, might no longer be driving, might not manage a checkbook, we had a hunch about the importance of our goal. We became that two-person risk management team, working to secure her future with precision.

The breadth of topic required time! Time for reflection, time to pose deliberate answers for what and how-to. Examining all the specifics—money, medication, living arrangement, end of life actual medical care. And yes, confronting mortality.

Consulting an attorney was on the horizon.

> Sometimes we were uncomfortable. From my side of the generational divide I recognized a pivotal moment: my mastery of today's tasks was the toehold for the future. Her choices today would become tomorrow's written documents, a blueprint for her future.
>
> We stayed open and honest. We trusted each other. My notebook filled with details. If A happens, do B. Etcetera.

Mom was impatient with my extra slog of thoroughness. You hear strains of Frank Sinatra crooning "My Way," right? But we were almost there. Maintaining confidence that a critical layer of her intent could be embedded, we got ready to formalize Mom's decisions. Time to write her Last Will and Testament, The Durable Power of Attorney, health surrogacy statement, and a Living Will--those four foundational documents, created with an attorney.

My mother and Dad had a will that needed some tweaking, but neither she nor I had done any other documents like this before. We did not know the magnitude of authority and reliability a formally written plan would provide. But we learned through all that followed, that tremendous strength and credibility was the result: Mom's official game day playbook with all her answers would become a reality.

Take as much or as little time as you need, thinking and putting it together. But put it together.

A Future Forecast?

Ask any attorney. Read excepts from family intervention counselors working in elder care. Read 'Family Conflict as a Mediator of Caregiver Stress," research from University of California-Berkeley that attempts to quantify the emotional toll of family dynamics (conflict) on caregivers. Visit any elder care blog and read personal comments on the daily mess of families coping through senior care in their families.

Did Mom foresee flies in the ointment? I don't know. We never went there in planning discussions, talking instead about what would make her happy, what she wanted and how her plan and her trust in me to honor her choices would put her at ease now and for later.

We assembled her answers for the future. I assumed her sacred choices would be honored.

You know the thing about assumptions? They derive from the word assume. As in making an ass of u and me. Did Mom know something I didn't? I never thought anybody could disrespect her wishes. But it happened. (More on that later, when we were living with her plan).

For now, assuming success was our best hope.

Assignment review: Planner, carer, significant other. Loved one. No matter who you are, start talking. Envision that senior future, gear up to create a personal plan. Buy a notebook and begin to create an organizational road map to optimize future living.

The step-by-step process of changing someone into a person with a plan is outlined in the next chapters.

2

The Plan for Building a Plan

"When you have a great and difficult task, something perhaps almost impossible, if you only work a little at a time, every day, suddenly, the work will finish itself."
- Isak Dinesen, author

How does planning happen? Does it sound like a simple conversation? A breezy task? This chapter discusses building a plan from ground zero, where one never existed. It offers a social science-based look at how humans maneuver through various necessary phases to complete the efforts involved in planning.

The Stages of Change

No matter what our age, psychologists say the human process of change means developing plans and that requires a lot of thought. Social scientists have gone so far as to suggest the idea of change may begin *before* you start thinking about it!

In the 1980s, James Prochaska was a psychologist studying how humans worked at eliminating risky behaviors like smoking. Prochaska theorized that although successful individuals start and stop the behavioral change process multiple times, a number of concrete steps were intrinsic to the process. A bit of going forward, a bit of going back, a route that involves thinking, re-thinking, preparing, doing and possibly **re-doing, and finally maintaining the new behavior** comprise Prochaska's theory to explain what steps are involved in change.

Forty years later, social scientists continue using Prochaska's 6-part Stages of Change model to describe how humans succeed with change. As a culmination of stages, Prochaska's model can demonstrate the steps in life care planning. After all, the point is *changing* from someone without a plan, to the individual with one. Have a look at his "formula."

Stage One: Pre-Contemplation

A tiny passing blip of thought is the actual onset of change. A spark, neither light bulb nor lightning bolt. If somewhere, someday, once you wondered about what the future might hold for yourself or a senior loved one, congratulations! It doesn't matter what triggered that passing thought about the big unknown entity called your future, Stage One is complete the very first time you wonder about it.

Stage Two: Ongoing Contemplation

When that initial blip has turned into a tumble of ideas or observations, bingo, **Stage Two**. Whether you are watching aging parents navigate their later years with rising concern, or you are thinking about your own later years, this is contemplation. If you are of an age when retirement is shutting some doors and opening others, there is reason to think ahead to the future. Many people who have raised their families might look at senior years as time to relax and enjoy life, but empty nesting and retirement create their own questions. Released from daily responsibilities also means released from major earning power. There is reason to think about finances and many other life topics. The brain begins to shuffle and categorize ideas. (Your friends and loved ones should be doing the same thing.)

Contemplation takes a while. This is personal involvement, a pro-active approach exploring how you or a loved one is going to meet the future. Contemplating, the circling around an idea, is normal, necessary and frankly, a logical pre-cursor to taking action.

Contemplating senior life planning means you care about your future self. Regardless of how little or much contemplating has been done, compliment yourself for the effort.

There is no time limit. Contemplating is mental action that eases your way into a shifting mindset toward behaviors that will change you, (from no plan to plan), that will allow you to be thought leader and manager of your own future.

On the plus side, each individual brings personal expertise as witness to the multigenerational aspects of their lives and family to contemplating. Participation in the circle of life, each life, the span from infancy to death, has its own needs and requirements.

Same with senior planning. Use that personal experience, and contemplate based on it.

If you are the adult child, raising kids *and* concerned for aging parents, you stare toward their uncertain future and your involvement in it, from the middle of a very busy place. There is plenty of data about carers caught up with responsibilities on all sides. All the more reason to encourage that loved one to get ahead in the process, right?

Change is underway, whether you think so or not. Continue to mull. Jot down ideas. The point is that it never matters *how* you got to Stage Two, but that *you are here,* thinking about the future, yours or that of aging loved ones. Unknown, unwieldy, or enormous, that's okay. This is Prochaska showing how change works.

Major topics—money, medicine and support—the meat of contemplation, need exploration. Specific questions and tasks about money, medicine and support personnel are described in coming chapters. This data is necessary consideration for the next stage of change: preparation.

Stage Three: Preparation

The process. Over time, contemplation naturally expands into deeper thinking pertinent to personal circumstance. The ruminating that swelled Prochaska's Stage Two contemplative nuggets leads to preparations.

Preparations, by nature, are bigger than thoughts. Stage Three represents another big part of life planning. It too, will take some time.

That is Stage Three: time for thorough fleshing out personal details. Remember: **there is no time limit to preparation.**

Stage Two and Stage Three are what you are doing while reading this book. They are critical background work for taking action. Prochaska's notion about the back and forth nature of thinking (contemplation) and preparation (action) demonstrates why the process requires time. A bit of going back and forth is necessary to build enough validation to move on to the next stage.

Stage Four: Action

Stage Four transforms preparations into definite plans. Ideas get formalized through proper paperwork. Those documents mentioned earlier—which I affectionately call The Fab Four, are now finalized. The power of attorney, a living will, a health care surrogacy statement and a last will and testament will become cornerstones of any Life Plan. **Action** produces the documents, the map, the guide, the rules for a future life plan. Stage Four Action *changes you into a person WITH A PLAN.*

Stage Five: Maintenance

When your plan is in effect. When you use the plan that has been created. **Maintenance**, like other stages, takes however long we need to be there with one major difference: unlike the speculation that dominates preceding stages, you are finished figuring it out! You are now the person *with* a plan. Maintenance encompasses the *use of your plan,* for you, your agent and loved ones. **This is you (and/or your agent) executing and using a personally directed plan that manages** living senior years with pre-ordered directions. The way you want them to be.

Nothing guarantees maintenance will be easy, but thoroughness to date offers the best possibility to maintain according to your wishes. Maintenance can last from only a few days or months, to years. It is while you, your loved ones and your agent LIVE LIFE, while freely and purposely relying on the previously created plan. Does anyone say NO to this?

*Are you wondering about **Stage Six**? That is completion. When your plan is no longer needed. That is when you and your agent finish, when your plan ends.

***

At this point in reading, mark yourself at Stage Two, the process of contemplating. You have thoughts, ideas for those four documents and a need for more detail. Feel good! This kind of thinking has you in the driver's seat, or riding shotgun as co-pilot.

A few (final) words about *motivation*.

Prochaska's formula for change describes developing a life care plan as behavioral progression, *something doable*. We humans thrive on making all sorts of plans. If you are skeptical or worried about *all* the details, this is still how it happens.

Life planning is neither sprint nor marathon. It is an organized series of tasks to create personal answers to senior living questions which ultimately will allow someone to remain in charge of their own life.

Maybe you are deciding right now to think about all this later, because, well, you're busy and the future is just too far away. Or, maybe you are the carer, the go-to agent, a daughter like me, and the months or years in someone's future when you could be on duty, seem really far, far away.

Uh, maybe, but not really.

Trying to convince someone to start working on a plan?

That old saying about "leading a horse to water" doesn't mean you can make anyone drink. But helping a love one understand that using pre-planning is a viable way to "maintain personal control" of *their* future (with an assist) may be one of the best arguments for it.

Someday we all are going to need a plan. Everyone. The circle of life always closes at some point--how we get there is what's at stake. That full circle generally portends an end a lot like the beginning—complete dependence, when other people are taking care of details. Setting up one's own list of details for managing that time should make *motivation* crystal clear.

Using a systematic step-by-step process to create a life care plan is how to "control the future." This is how to get your life affairs in order. Pre-planning is honoring the self. It ensures your qualified voice from the past will be providing procedural instruction in the future.

Sounds like the perfect reason for everyone to want a life care plan.

Get motivated. Find courage to be open, honest and very aware of the conversation--in your head, at the table, and during the process. Whether it is your worry over aging parents, retirement, something more serious, or you just are a pro-active planning sort of bloke, choose preparedness as the motivator. Plan for a plan.

Repeat Assignment. Engage in the process. Discuss the what, the how and the when. Participate. Incorporate Prochaska.

3

Tender Topics

"Nobody gets out of here alive." - Jim Morrison

What are the questions for Stage 3 preparations? How did we think, contemplate and talk out everything in order to build a plan for Mom's future? Over time.

Death and dying are tender topics where feelings are front and center. After those bits about happy, engaged living and independence for as long as possible, Mom jumped to nitty gritty end topics, despite the uneasiness. She had definite views and needed to share. For example, she said she wasn't getting plugged in anywhere, ever.

I heard *what she said,* and then we had to *determine* how to guarantee that. We openly shared mutual discomfort about the *idea* of confronting the inevitable end of her days on the planet. It was a normal response from our emotional selves.

This discussion topic might weigh heavy on your heart or hit you in the pit of your stomach. It might make for some anxiety. Each and every life planning conversation requires acknowledging the inescapable. We were feeling it. Are you?

Tremendous! Woohoo! These signals are the human body on alert. Emotions which surface when talking about death are real, important, and worthy. The pastor of our church maintains that anything important should feel this way.

Take a deep breath. Realize--

One: Feelings of unease or nerves are the body's way to say, "Listen up." That tummy flutter is a lightning rod message from body to brain, a signal to pay attention. Translation: what you are thinking about is important.

Two: Discussion of death is not only about the end. Translation: discussing one's demise is always <u>about how you get there</u>. Reflection is good for the journey.

What will make your days easier? Who do you trust to help?

Mom's Story

> As Mom and I began planning, there had been a long running family legal battle in Florida over a woman named Terry Schiavo, who was, for 15 years, in an irreversible persistent vegetative state. Her parents wanted control and care of her completely disabled destiny, while her husband, also her guardian, campaigned valiantly for Terry's wishes to die with dignity and be sustained no longer. After a grueling time in the media and courts, Terry's feeding tube was removed, and she died.

> Mom and I talked about Terry Schiavo. Mom was definite about not lingering. She was fishing for how I might handle her "no plugs" edict, awaiting my unconditional willingness to do things her way.
>
> Weighty topic? I say easy answer. It is Mom's right to choose, not mine. I said I could do that. We moved on.

Stomach flip-flopping usually diminishes during plan building. But acknowledging discomfort is important for another reason. Potential health care surrogates and powers of attorney may also feel discomfited by the weighty management of follow-through, but these people are NOT making choices. They can admit discomfort, but know they follow instructions, respecting the wishes of their loved one.

Discomfort is vital to life planning. Get beyond it to envision living to the best of one's intentions in the months and years before the finale.

Reminder: You are worth it. You are on your way. The plan will evolve, and your comfort level will return.

The Comfort Factor—A Mental Exercise

Imagine that completed plan in your fist. Everything in order the way you want it. You have built a remote control. Device in hand, reassured, relaxed about stepping into the future. Confidence in the form of a legal how-to guide. Feels pretty great, right?

Some of us may get thrown into an uncertain process of helping ourselves or our loved ones with life care questions when we are at an emotion-charged moment we didn't anticipate. Instead of readiness, we find ourselves playing catch-up with one issue or another, or with no plan in sight. Talk about stomach flipping!

If you take nothing more from reading our story, try not to be victim of that misfortune. Try not to play catch up because coming late to the game incorporates crunch time, a reality which takes away the luxury of time for contemplation, and makes a series of tasks more complicated, harder to accomplish and more emotionally charged.

4

The Nitty Gritty: Real Questions

"All the guys who can paint great big pictures can paint great small ones." - Ernest Hemingway

Our generation of baby boomers is heading into senior years with that hearty information bank. Unless you have been living under a rock, general information on just about any senior topic or trend is readily available. If the process starts by thinking about what you want, then use whatever means necessary to gather information.

Decision points for anyone thinking about senior life fall into three main categories-- **finances, health, environment.** Use the Big Picture context: all personal feelings, facts and ideas are collective considerations. Said another way: money, medical treatment and care, personnel and support are details required for anyone's Big

Picture. Do the research for your own particular situation and environment.

- Go to a financial advisor for recommendations and a plethora of options about using assets in retirement.
- Go to a local senior center workshop on wills and trusts.
- Find a webinar about advanced planning.
- Google senior care trends or home town options.
- Check out a library full of elder information via AARP, a giant resource for frequently asked questions across retirement, senior living and senior care.
- Visit a local hospice. Although most people associate hospice with end of life care, hospice can be a resource for pre-planning that offers specifics within your community. Hospice has sample care documents and information about advanced directives and home health support costs.
- Contact a council on aging. Same reason.
- Learn about Medicare. When you reach the Medicare age in the United States, there are multiple considerations. Understand the term "aging in," a phrase that refers to exploring options for receiving basic Medicare coverage and supplemental medical insurance.
- Tour an "over 55" community, or a tiered, assisted living facility as part of thinking through housing.

Ask yourself some questions.
What do you want to do with your money? How much medicine will you want to take? How much does it cost you each month? How

long can you live on your own? Who will help you?

Where will you live? Who do you want to help handle your affairs? What are your thoughts on death and dying?

Answers will fuel decisions and planning for future care.

Building a data bank within these three categories is the assignment, but a quick glance at the above questions highlights what could be viewed as a major complication: all three categories are interrelated. All three categories have moving parts. Decisions or details in any category impact one, the other or both.

Don't let the overlap feel problematic. Seriously. Life in general, is made up of moving parts, for all of us, and about everything. Divide and conquer is a good approach.

<u>Start by taking notes.</u> Make those general statements about your wishes and use those wishes as perspective. Concentrate on questions or facts *within each category* as you jot down your thoughts. Environmental questions—housing and costs vary with various housing choices and available options. Medical health and care choices will impact other categories. One answer could lead to another question or category, but after a few minutes of categories and questions, you probably have realized that finances impact everything.

Determining the answer to finances, is one way to start formalizing a plan. It worked for Mom and me.

Perform the Inflow/Outflow Exercise in the next chapter to build a personal financial data bank.

5

Financial Inflow and Outflow: Finding Your Numbers

"Money doesn't grow on trees." - Common idiom

The big worry: is there enough money? Will assets match what might be required? Is there enough to fund the forthcoming yet unpredictable future? The common anxiety that the money runs out before you do.

How do you figure this out? **Inflow vs. outflow**. Financials, lifestyle and choice. An exercise to determine your financial bottom line.

Getting Mom organized required that she project herself into the future with a consideration of today's well-worked bottom line. Mom's life style would be impacted by her health and her choice of accommodation, as well as who could help her, but as we compiled her big picture vision that bottom line kept popping up.

Mom's assets *in relation to* funding *for how many* years demonstrate the **moving parts of life planning.** We didn't *know how much* she might need, nor for *how long*, but we knew we had to start by looking at here and now. We would not let uncertainty or "moving parts" be reason to stop planning. Instead, her bottom line was necessary to guestimate future expenses, *based on what we knew.*

Note: This kind of calculation is important no matter what your age.

For almost every one of us, life is about living within our means, right to the end. Unless money is no object, you have a rich uncle, plans to win the lottery, already received a giant inheritance, or are the next billionaire inventor, your cost outflow by necessity, needs to be covered by income inflow. Anything extra you may have saved along the way, becomes an asset, insurance for any shortfall.

Bart Astor, author of The Road Map for the Rest of Your Life, offers charts and computations in his book, demonstrating how to spend down assets while living out your days. Bart's dollar figures are samples, and he's an interesting resource for zeroing down. Try out his formula, but even Bart can't tell you *how long you can expect to be here!*

Which is to say that a financial "bottom line" number is essential, **but only as a beginning**. Comparing income and outflow might produce a sigh of relief or a gasp of concern, but that bottom line is the essential status report, a dollar number critical to any considerations made for the future.

How Much Does It Take to Fund a Year in Your Life?

Projected Income and Outflow Calculations

Every year or so, the media trots out an alarmist version of "America's aging population," a feature story highlighting everything from rising medical costs and housing inflation, to crumbling pension plans. It fuels the mystery about caring for ourselves in the future.

The media aren't the only folks crying about uncertainty for seniors. Financial planners might offer a formula but even they admit getting a handle on a precise number is sketchy.

Whether media or expert, the inconclusive conclusion about how much money is needed, is that there is NO right answer. Certainly no one size fits all. No wonder the finance question seems tricky!

Wondering about money today vs. tomorrow might be where to *begin an internal ponder, or that life planning chat with your spouse?* It also might be when people get really bogged down and quit the process.

Step-by-step, please. We can get into the ballpark for future speculation. This is best done by calculating with current data.

> **Inflow**—Sources of income. Social Security, IRA distributions, pension payouts from previous employment, wages. Dividends. Interest income. Government returns?
>
> **Outflow**—Expenses. What is the monthly, annual, cost of your current lifestyle? How and on what is money being spent.

Additional assets such as personal property, real estate or the money in the mattress are worthy of notation, but comparing inflow to outflow is first. Arriving at today's figures is real progress, but the proverbial dilemma remains:

Will You Need More, or Will You Need Less?

The answer is a mind bender: Yes, you will need more and yes, you will need less. For example: you may travel less, you might sell your car. You may eat less. You might move to a smaller residence or move in with family. But you also may need more money for unforeseen health issues, and you might want to purchase long term care insurance or home care support.

Adjustments are a normal part of every life. Truly how life works, and definitely part of an overall look at any financial drill. By acknowledging that spending needs will fluctuate, we can put that notion to the side, for now.

Stay calm and carry on with plotting today's financial status report because understanding today's numbers is the starting point, the only place to gather key **financial information** for a future time frame.

If you have been making ends meet today, this is a good sign. If you are not making ends meet or have significant debt, there might be other books and research before continuing with the life planning endeavor.

For now, consider a budget, high, low or in between. Examining the inflow/outflow details is a step to determine if present finances could accommodate *what you predict for your future*.

You do not need to be an expert at Medicare, Social Security, estate planning, or banking. You just need to be thorough and pencil in your numbers. Get that current annual number.

Using What You Know

When we began thinking about Mom living in those future years, it was natural she wondered *if* she had enough money--and *how much* time she had. How do you answer one without answering the other? How do you project an expiration date?

We used *what we knew*.

What were her bills vs. how much money was coming in annually? How big was her savings account? AND: How long, how many more years forward did she want to talk about? At 72, forecasting for how many years would make her feel comfortable?

Both her parents had died in their early 80s. She decided that 15-20 years out was good conjecture. Twenty years would put her in her early 90s.

Everybody has to start somewhere.

A yellow legal pad is good for a two-column comparison—costs vs. income, both sides of this equation. Find those numbers. It is Stage Three preparation. Can you add and subtract?

Make Your Own List

Step One: Inflow

List all income amounts, then tally. Any pensions? Your Social Security monthly checks? Is there other anticipated retirement income? For example, do you own rental property? Stock dividends? Do you draw on an annuity? To your best ability, add up today's monthly inflow figures and multiply times 12 to get an annual income amount. Write this number down too.

Step Two: Outflow

Write down all your expenses. Categorize now or later. Basic categories should include taxes and insurance, utilities, household operating, and daily living.

How much does it cost you to live in today's dollars, for your current life, in any given month? It will take time and a stack of bills but figuring this out is doable. What is spent per month to maintain yourself and your household? List dollar values on your costs--food, utilities, your car, your lifestyle, your phone, your church tithe, credit card payments, cable television, internet? Clothing? Pet care, lawn service? Memberships. Car payments? Subscriptions. Medicine. Homeowner fees, auto insurance. House insurance. Garbage removal. Charitable giving? Tuition? Long term care enrollment. Do you support the local arts community? The cost of any supplemental health plan. Anything and everything you spend money on today.

Total the costs list and multiply times 12 to find average monthly outflow for a year.

Second, add up expenses that don't fit with weekly or monthly bills. Property taxes for example, or Christmas spending, other annual bills. Maybe you take an annual trip to see your grandchildren?

Add those expenditures to the 12-month outflow amount. Write down that number.

By the way, if you are still employed, calculate your income taxes as another expense.

Step Three: Compare Inflow and Outflow numbers

Are they close? It is good if they are, but you are not finished until you consider other additional assets.

Are there other assets? Tally up savings accounts, a nest egg, money in the mattress. Real estate? These are assets beyond liquid income *could be available for* later. This number is sometimes called the "float."

Example: If you have $10,000 in your savings account, and you project living another 10 years, you could say you have an additional $1,000 annually to supplement your inflow.

You don't add this number to the inflow, nor do you need to spend it. But you should know if it exists.

Three numbers. Together they provide insight to **your baseline,** a financial annual bottom line starting point.

Mom—By the Numbers

> Mom wanted to stay home. She liked her current lifestyle. She owned her home. She was not going to resume employment. She was not planning to remarry. She had Medicare medical insurance.
>
> What was her income from pensions, social security, investments, rent?
>
> Roughly $28,000 annually.
>
> What were her costs this year? Last year? Next year? Everything we could think of, and then a few more costs popped into our figuring—like the annual insect spraying (utilities) we didn't think of the first time through, the newspaper subscription (household operating), her yard maintenance (utilities), and an additional sum for surprise household appliance repairs.
>
> Roughly $28,000 annually to live as she was accustomed.
>
> In fact, Mom's expenses were presently slightly below her annual income. She had discretionary cash for a new hat, a swimming pool heater, and other desirables without touching savings.

> For the foreseeable future, Mom's income level appeared to meet predictable outflow calculations.
>
> Did she have any savings that could/would supplement the government supports she qualified for? Yes, and this was especially comforting. She had a savings account, two annuities, two Certificates of Deposit, and two pieces of real estate. All those assets were available if Mom's daily living costs increased at some point.
>
> Did we think Mom had enough? *As best as we could see.*
>
> Hear that sigh of relief? We decided that this was such a good exercise, we would review her costs to income ratio every year if we wanted to, checking numbers to see what changed. <u>Adjust</u> as necessary. We acknowledged the dynamic nature of her financial portrait and would keep checking as life unfolded, but she was okay for now. We checked Mom's money question off.

Assemble Your Known Costs and Known Income Figures—Get Your Bottom Line

Date the computation sheet and store it safely. This financial snapshot is a resource essential to life plan considerations. You will come back to it. Congratulations! You are on the way to filling a personal toolbox for the trip of a lifetime.

Now, let your brain wander over how you *feel* about these intriguing future considerations:

- In retirement, do you expect to live differently?
- Will you live independently in your own home? Do you rent? Own? Live with family?

- Are you thinking about a senior care residence?
- Will you sell property, will you downsize?
- What about your car?
- Do you have a nest egg or retirement savings? Will you rely on savings?
- Do you expect to rely on your children?
- Might you access public aid? Veteran's benefits?
- Will all your costs continue? Will some increase? Will some decrease?
- Are you willing to change your lifestyle?

Feel good about the inflow/outflow exercise. If you have not done it already, go out and buy an accordion file. Then take a deserved break. There are more questions, and more details for other categories.

6

Answering Medical Questions

*A*rmed with the current financial baseline, your fact-finding preparations move to the remaining two categories—your personal considerations of current medical needs in relation to care and treatment. Cost and personnel/support for your health status.

Does it sound comfortable? No, but discomfort equals importance, remember? Mom and I dug in. It was necessary to answer life and death questions we had been dancing around. Time to "brave up" and push ahead.

How to proceed?

Like the exercise for that financial snapshot, current data is where we began exploring any medical care future. The concrete facts included building a **personal medical history** document which describes current health conditions. This is another status report, a medical baseline, the starting point to anticipate what might be expected or needed healthwise for your future. This is also where Mom would be answer what kind of medical routine she wanted, how she wanted to be treated later on and who would help her.

Does it sound powerful? Provocative? Yes.

Break bigger tasks into smaller ones.

To make decisions about future medical care, we chose again to divide and conquer what was required. We began with that baseline medical snapshot. Plus, we listed things we wanted to talk about in this category. Mom's care choices and end of life decisions could come after that.

Organizing Mom's medical history was an eye opener! It created a thorough past and present checkup list, another valuable worksheet, a **medical status page.** We broke Mom's details into seven areas and collected data. It fit on one typed page.

- Contact information and Social Security Number. Medicare ID info. (also, a place to identify health care surrogacy)
- Current conditions. A short narrative of her health that allowed for observations and diagnoses.
- Personal medical history. Mom's medical conditions, operations, etc.
- Family medical history. Doctors always want generational data to "see" a complete picture. For example, in Mom's case, heart disease, and osteoporosis ran in the family.

- Medications. A list of current prescriptions and dosage.
- Doctors, pharmacy. Identity and contact information.
- Consider listing hospital preference if this is important to you.

Date the finished page. This life plan toolbox item will be updated as life unfolds. It will be a go-to sheet for medical information that you and your supporters refer to time and time again.

You have created a Medical History Data Sheet. File it in the growing collection of planning documents.

Once the **Medical Information Data Sheet is complete,** consider what these facts mean for the future. Envision choices for treatment in future medical circumstances. Future health care you may require has a lot to do with how you want it to be. When you are healthy is still the **best time** to talk about and make health care decisions that you want.

Itemizing choices in this category eventually will form a *Medical Directives* document. Answers and decisions have far reaching implications. Directives become essential care plan components for a *Living Will,* another document that will be created.

You might once again feel that internal twinge. Yes, how you feel about these things is important. Reflect and gather your thoughts as you ponder the following:

- Did your medical history sheet include conditions that are progressive illnesses?
- Will you need more medicine? How many more pills are you willing to take? For what outcome? For the rest of your life, or, is there some point in your future, when you want to stop taking medicine?

- Would you agree to extensive medical procedures, experimental treatments?
- Is there a time when you want to stop treatments?
- What is your stance on heroic measures? Resuscitation?
- Ideas about artificial respiration. Under what circumstances?
- What about treatment for incurable illnesses?
- Do you want to be fed? Hand fed, tube fed?
- Would you want palliative, comfort care when there is no hope of recovery?

Working through each topic provides a foundation for individual medical directive decisions. Your decisions will enable you to choose your road ahead. Remember Mom and the NO Plugs rule? That was her Do Not Resuscitate edict.

Discussing beliefs with loved ones is important and may have an added bonus. Soon you will need to identify a certain someone who can/will support your medical care choices in the future. For now, however, *focus on how you want to be treated, and what you think about all these questions long enough to master the medical decisions for your future.*

If you are a family member or friend who has been helping discuss and explore medical topics, respectfully remember discussion is valuable currency, but **all choices about medical care are decisions which belong to the creator of the plan.**

That's why medical care decisions require legal form. The *medical directives* are the plan creator's *personal choices* for medical treatment. The plan creator also is required to name the individual charged to carry through with those decisions for the plan creator.

If it hasn't happened already, identifying WHO becomes the **medical surrogate** should happen now. Unless you already have this person concretely in mind, consider taking a breather. Go for a walk. You can come back in a minute or an hour, a day from now, or next week.

An interesting phenomenon happens while away from the tasks. Your brain has this habit of continuing to think all by itself. It knows what you've been doing. It will congratulate itself. It will reinforce the importance of a medical plan. It will acknowledge the respect you have for yourself. Right now, your brain is probably running through a list of potential surrogates.

Here's more information on naming that surrogate.

7

Who?? Naming a Power of Attorney & Medical Surrogate

One of the best things about being older is having that lifetime of experience to draw upon while formulating a life plan. You are your first and most important resource.

Who else knows you really well? Have you been sharing this journey to build a plan with someone? Is there someone you trust to see a plan through? Is our story resonating with you as the adult child who wants to help a parent?

If the plan you envision epitomizes your lifetime of experience, beliefs and desires, the WHO to assist in carrying it out should be a trusted individual who can follow your directions. Pre-planning requires someone you trust to guard, support and carry out your decisions in the future. Who will be guardian for your plan?

That WHO is the medical health surrogate and/or durable power of attorney.

Predicting precisely when to activate this agent may not be possible. What that agent will encounter is also likely unknowable. But someone must be identified to carry out choices when the plan creator is unable to do so. The plan owner must decide who that person will be.

It involves making tough observations about love ones and others. Trust, comfort level, character and leadership skills are considerations when choosing a WHO, often referred to as a *second self*.

You might consider choosing one surrogate for health care and another person for other duties such as financial or household actions. Some professionals in the life care business recommend choosing **one and one only** to promote efficiency and minimize possible conflict, but others suggest separation of duties. Consider

- their overall ability to manage and direct
- their moral courage, strength of mind, sense of responsibility
- your feeling of confidence and comfort in their ability

The WHO will be the powerful and necessary link between choices today and implementation tomorrow. Someone WHO can step in and lead medically, and in all efforts on your behalf. The WHO should be a respectful, moral person to honor your plan, agree to be your advocate and lead as you would intend. *Your way.* The WHO takes you and your plan to the finish line.

As mentioned earlier, introspection and effort to date has possibly prompted your brain to run through a list of candidates. If your personal decisions and details have been fleshed out in company with a trusted loved one, a partner, spouse, friend or adult child, you may already have identified your health care surrogate or your DPoA. Your WHO. The identity of your agent, your second in command, may be the person you've been talking with all along.

Do you know already WHO you would trust to act on your behalf? Do you know WHO will hold your durable power of attorney, to back up your wishes for future medical care? If not, here is a quick exercise.

Envision a medical emergency scenario, when you cannot speak for yourself. Maybe you are unconscious, but decisions need to be made. Ok, that's uncomfortable. Now what? By imagining even temporary incapacitation, you quickly realize the need for a trusted agent. WHO did your brain *see* as the best person to help you through that incapacitation?

Boil It Down to One Word: TRUST

The legal responsibility, the authority to act for a plan's creator, will fall to this second self-person when the creator can no longer act for him or herself. Identifying a trusted agent is the absolute best chance for seeing a senior path unfold as the plan creator intended.

The health surrogate or DPoA choice is challenging and delicate. It involves their abilities, the plan creator's comfort level, family relationships and just about everything but the kitchen sink. Many different people will support, remain or enter those future senior years to assist in myriad ways, but the execution of intentions set forth in any plan will be the responsibility of the durable power of attorney. When some future event of physical, emotional or mental challenge makes a plan creator unable to physically, emotionally or mentally to call their own shots, WHO will call the shots?

Not to worry: having a plan means the shots already have been called. Choosing WHO can execute is what makes this decision so important. That second self-agent will be relied upon to advocate for the plan creator. The WHO will have work to do. The WHO will have to make tough decisions.

Another flutter in the tummy? That's right! Your gut should be involved. That twitching is letting you know if you're on the right track with one person, or off with another.

Considering the Candidates—Family Members and Others

Spouses, family members and significant others are obvious possibilities for power of attorney because these people are already involved in your life circle. But there is an undeniable truth--family doesn't always act on the same page. Probably, your brain has scratched names off the short list. Because you are entrusting your future to this person, this is about what the plan creator wants to happen, not about anything else. People might have hurt feelings.

In a perfect world, every family would be happy, healthy, and each member would understand and completely agree with the choices and views of the others. Is this your family? Will everyone accept your ideas, honor your plan? Would your family work together? If so, yours might be the gold standard of families with high moral character. Pick any one of those people, because they all sound wonderful.

But Google that catchy phrase "elder care family conflict" and blogs explode with complaints and challenges in families with emotionally charged circumstances. Chances are high that you are part of a family where people have opposing views, where a possible power play is occurring, where smoldering childhood rivalries are present, or where individual hierarchy, opinion, and maybe even greed, jockey for status. (Count yourself lucky if this is NOT you.)

In circumstances where family isn't viable or comfortable, some plan creators identify an agent of record, an attorney, or even a friend, creating a formal business-style arrangement. This may or may not diffuse family issues, because choosing an outsider could create its own uproar.

Whoever is named, this representative uses legal authority as a Power of Attorney, or Health Care Surrogate, to carry out decisions for your welfare, no matter the family or circumstance.

The phrase "one tough cookie" comes to mind.

Your Own Unique Decision

Social scientists can give you reams about responsibilities and traits linked with birth order. Generally speaking, the oldest offspring or the youngest is most often assigned responsibility and tasks of helping Mom, Dad or both as they reach these years.

That person may or may not be chosen. Or asked. But unless the plan's creator is an orphan, planning to leave the country or live out his or her days in seclusion, that WHO decision and the future will not fall outside family life, because even a non-relative will encounter family reactions.

The decision remains unique to each plan creator, family and circumstance, and what is known about the cast of characters. Naming a surrogate may or may not be sticky. Maybe it gets resolved with sensible family discussion. Maybe making your reasons known will clear the air. Maybe not. Regardless, naming this WHO is the choice of the plan creator.

At its very best, that named agent is an extension, the chosen surrogate "second self," not the unhappy unchosen. Any way you slice it, the WHO will have plenty of miles on themselves by the time the path is done.

The Acceptance Factor

Still with Mom and me?? Good. After polling a cadre of care support professionals and friends, reading the blogs, knowing

Mom's situation and spending my days with her, my armchair assessment about *acceptance* of any one person as agent is running 50/50. Some families rise to the occasion, at least half do not. <u>Hard feelings aside, choose the trustworthy individual with whom you feel most comfortable.</u>

Your surrogate or DPoA will do whatever it takes according to your wishes and will be accepted cart blanche` in medical circumstances. Ask for a promise from that person to follow your wishes. If you are convinced, if you are confident in your choice, move forward.

A Power of Attorney Final Review

If you have been that friend or family helping a loved one explore any of this life care planning, and you are asked to be that DPoA or surrogate, you must answer one big question: Will you honor and respect the directions provided? **The morally right, only acceptable answer is yes.**

***

Preparations for a personal life care plan are nearly complete.

- Enjoy some back slapping. Feel confident about your future because you have identified a trusted person, a sentinel, that second-self quarterback to carry out directives when you hand off the ball.
- Impress that potential agent with the absolutely essential requirement to respect your choices.
- Give the agent your support.
- Do not pick anyone who does not agree with your decisions.

Finally, understand that you do not have to defend or explain your choice. Openly sharing support for your surrogate may or may not ease their role. Only time will tell.

Assignment: If you don't have that WHO brain photo, take time now to bring it into focus. WHO can carry out your plan?

About Mom

Mom liked our working partnership because she had already jumped ahead to **personnel and support** by asking me to assist, to become her agent. I would be her WHO. We had tackled questions about money, living arrangements and other supports that sounded good to her, and she was making decisions about end of life care. She knew what she wanted and what she didn't want. She also had told me what she wanted from me later. We revisited four main topics: her day-to-day life, her money situation, options for her living circumstances, medical concerns.

We believed our conversational marathon of planning gave us an edge. By all our efforts, she confidently anticipated a future where her pre-planned decisions would be used. She trusted me to respect and support her plan, to be there, carrying it out when and if she was ever physically or mentally unable to participate.

She was ready for auto-pilot, my agreement *and* my distance from her current day to day.

Time to go legal. But first, we were going to the beach.

Assignment: Identify the key person who can be your surrogate, your future second self.

8

Need a Cure for Overload?

Almost Done

*I*f you are struggling with details or feeling overwhelmed with the scale of decisions outlined so far, or if you simply are not ready to finish, take heart.

Consider two analogies: Both begin (ahem), with a plan.

Thanksgiving Dinner

The menu planning. All that shopping! All the kitchen prep. Maybe a cookbook or two. Do you have utensils? The right pots and pans? All the cooking! Maybe another cook to help? Hours, days and maybe even weeks of planning and adjusting a menu before ever turning on the stove.

But you start somewhere. Make a grocery list. Select favorite foods. Identify kitchen helpers. Invite guests to the table. Set the table. Finally, there is the reward of an enormous spread of yummy goodness. You eat!

<u>Vacation</u>. You get the travel bug and plot an extended tour, visiting multiple places around the world. All that investigating where to go! All those ideas about what to see! Activities, maps, destinations. Choices. Costs. Time to establish an itinerary. Reservations. Packing. And then you are off!

Satisfaction (confidence) is directly related to time and preparation. Effort. Bit by bit. Tasks and requirements with multiple moving parts.

Life care planning is like this, dictated by desires, choices and impacted by economics. Even then, someone can't eat cranberry relish, or the museum is closed by a power outage.

Find the courage to be open, honest and very aware of what you want, what you can afford and who will help. Discuss things. Discuss them again. Use time to your advantage, as in NOW. Time for talking it through.

Life care options and decisions belong to the plan creator.

Finish up or finally begin. It is not too late to start.

Review: A Final Preparation Pep Talk

Part One is a read along/work along segment. If you are still *contemplating*, it is NOT a waste of time.

If you are helping someone plan, or if you haven't started your own plan, if you have only been reading about how and why, ask yourself if you really care about this stuff.

Life care planning is **not** one enormous challenge. It is many challenges, and systematic steps. Keep going. Be a warrior.

Plan creator or helper, you have given thought to the idea of life care planning or you would not be reading this. Keep thinking! Stay motivated and engaged. Design a plan, have a say to optimize that future. Seize this opportunity to prepare for later.

Divide and conquer. Take steps. Keep thinking and writing your way toward a completed life care plan of your choosing, one piece at a time. Anticipate the reward—an exemplary final chapter of life, your way, with a plan that supports and meets your wishes. Anticipate sitting back to confidently enjoy getting there to the best of your ability and for the best reason--caring enough to plan ahead to do it *your way*.

But if you are just *still thinking, still contemplating*, here's an idea.

Get out a notebook, a clean sheet of paper, or scribble in the margins here. Right now.

Write down one idea. Just one idea. Something that captured your interest in the preceding pages. Stop reading until you've done it. One idea.

Okay. Maybe you wrote: no feeding tubes, or look at budget, or write medical history. Maybe the identity of a possible capable mentor/advocate for this process entered your thoughts and you wrote down a name. Maybe you identified the person or persons who will respect your wishes and honor the directives of your unique life care plan. Maybe you want to start the conversation.

One little note to self on the margin or in your notebook, is you moving forward. The assembly of planning for that personal future *on your terms* has begun. That, my readers, is **Stage Three: preparation.**

Own it.

9

Stage Four: Action (Going Legal)

"Success seems to be connected to action." - Conrad Hilton, hotel magnate

"Action is the foundational key to all success." - Pablo Picasso

A quick internet search for "Estate Planning Documents" yields everything from advertisements for attorneys and specialists, to banks and financial advisors, magazine articles and boiler plate images of important paperwork…and maybe a blog or two or 2,000, from people like me caught in the process.

Acting to formalize your decisions, your course of action, to legally and clearly outline directives for the bevy of family, professionals and well-intentioned others who will be part of the coming years, is "Going Legal."

Completing the FAB FOUR

Estate planning documents are the finished products of your deliberations, the valuable, essential components which guide the senior future. These documents are a legal footprint of a life care plan. They formally state intention and choice, mapping instructions for future circumstances. They are the "rules of the road," the pre-planned tools and directions for how to step confidently into the coming days, and for others on your behalf.

Those four documents--The Fab Four: The Durable Power of Attorney, The Living Will, The Health Care Surrogacy, and a Last Will and Testament are the recognized major components of life care planning.

Forbes Magazine recently published an article suggesting not only the recognized four, but 10 must-have planning documents. Another "expert" says there should be five.*

Personally, I say, start with The Fab Four. These official documents are evidence of your decisions. The Fab Four are formal pieces that identify, support and outline choices and agents in a format that meets local law.

There are boilerplate versions of these documents available from various estate planning sources, the internet and books, to study and copy for your own purposes. Seek them out as samples. Some forms can be overly verbose while others may appear almost too simple. Certain states have specific language that must be included.

Each document is intended to stand on its own merit as

---

* #5 is a suggested Release of Information form for medical concerns, the HIPPA component. Most medical offices have their own permission forms which grant informed access to medical information. Generally, permission to release your information has already been detailed and granted within the durable power of attorney, the medical surrogacy and living will documents. But you can certainly add this document if you like.

instruction for specific tasks and actions. But the documents work as a team. Together they are a powerhouse.

If preparation has been thorough, a generic format can be molded to meet personal needs. Each generalized item can be drilled down to define and direct specific actions tailored to individual circumstance. Taking Action to complete these official documents creates your personal plan for your future. These cornerstones change you into the person with a life care plan.

They are important enough to list a second time (smiley face):

- a last will and testament
- a durable power of attorney
- a health care surrogacy document and
- an advanced directive document often called a living will

They are the written foundation for all efforts to care for yourself and to help others do it—on your terms. If you have answered what seemed an ungodly amount of overwhelming questions about how you want your future to be, if you have identified someone to help get you there, acting now to complete these four powerful essential resources to guide your future is required.

Attorneys and estate planners will gladly create the finished product for a fee. The final step is signing and witnessing the documents when language and intent meets your approval. These documents are executed with an attorney and witnessed, because signatures bind the authenticity of the documents.

The Fab Four documents are advance blueprints, the officially certified directions and decisions of a life care plan for the future. The Fab Four identify powers and agents who will use them to manage and direct actions you expect from your doctors, your family and all caregivers.

These documents are essential gear, the underpinning of a senior future.

Detailing the Fab Four—Your Way

#1. A Last Will and Testament

This document is used to describe how someone wants to transfer assets upon their demise. Identify who gets what, what the distribution should be, etc. It is a great starting point when creating your own FAB FOUR, and often can be the least complicated because it deals with specifics in a time frame when you are no longer here. Hence, the word "last."

A last will and testament is your opportunity to designate beneficiaries for your assets. A will commits bequests to others at the time of death. It is your opportunity to gift Aunt Alice the silver tea service, or diamond rings to your daughter. A will identifies an executor, tasked to handle paperwork and all efforts to manage the disassembly, disbursement and dissolution of your estate. It is a legal instrument that provides both specific and general instruction about assets and holdings that once belonged to the deceased.

Some estate planners may recommend revocable living trusts, or a life trust, in addition to a will because trusts provide additional distribution options, and specific protections while the principal, is still living. More time consuming to prepare and therefore more expensive to create, living trusts have advantages and protections for certain situations like complicated estates. Trusts are instruments which also can impact eligibility for certain government benefits.

> For example: Eight years into Mom's plan, we discovered she qualified for Veterans' survivor benefits based on my

> dad's service record but only if her assets were transferred into a trust. Qualifying would provide additional income to supplement Mom's final years. But Mom's plan was working without a trust, and there would be a cost to change over. Additionally, creating a trust at this point involved the larger tasks of disassembling her existing management plan and reassembly within a trust structure. It didn't make sense for Mom, or me. But it might make sense for you.

Life trusts are sometimes used when family inheritors need assistance in managing distributions, or when family dissension might create problems in meeting day to day supports. Trusts are not a necessity, and they can be burdensome when real property is included, but whether a trust fits your needs or not is something to discuss with an estate planner or an attorney versed in this type of law. Your personal circumstances, your wishes and needs, will enable you to make the right decision for yourself.

FYI, while you're alive and of sound mind, all wills and trust documents may be altered or amended as you like.

#2. Durable Power of Attorney

This document is the go-to legal instrument that identifies tasks and an individual certified, verified and charged to complete them on your behalf. An array of topics and needs which impact daily life can be outlined here. The identified agent and the actions that your agent is authorized to make are detailed herein as protection of your interests and their empowerment. A choice can be made to create different Powers of Attorney paperwork for financial asset management, and for other types of decisions, such as health care. Either way, the language used in this document covers a lot of territory.

Some Powers of Attorney documents attempt to describe every conceivable action possible to be taken on behalf of a client, and some go so far as listing actions which cannot be taken, or actions that require additional signatures. But some powers of attorney formats are simple. Whether general or overtly specific, the durable designation has the luxury of immediacy, and the comfort of permanence. This document should be customized to authorize actions for your specific circumstances. Finances, property, insurance, living arrangements and health (see health care surrogacy statement) are topic areas that come to mind.

A Power of Attorney instrument names an agent to be the decision maker on your behalf, without delay. As needed. Actions taken on your behalf may increase over time, but this document provides your permission--when the time comes--for your agent to handle your affairs. This document is proof to many public entities, banks, hospitals, and the government, that your agent can, in fact, make decisions for you.

While you're alive, this document can be altered, revoked or amended as you like.

#3. Health Care Surrogate Document

This document is alternately called a Health Care Proxy, or a health care power of attorney. In many cases, the health surrogate is the same individual identified as Power of Attorney and surrogacy paperwork extends and complements the DPoA's authority specific to medical care. Naming the same person as agent in both documents may be appropriate and efficient, but it is not necessary.

A medical surrogacy document is informed legal consent extending permission to the named agent to work with your medical team and make decisions for medical care and treatment. This document grants permission for medical agencies, doctors and hospitals, to share your information and access your medical files with the surrogate. Types of treatments, medicines, or specific care you wish to receive or wish to refuse can be itemized. Decisions regarding experimental medicines, or participation in trials can be spelled out or refused with explicit instructions.

This surrogacy document also obligates the agent to enforce of your choices in the provision of your health care. It can improve the quality of your care, as you wish it to be.

While you are alive and in good mental health, this document also can be amended, revised or revoked if you so choose.

#4. Living Will

Also known as *advanced medical directives*, a living will is your opportunity to make decisions for <u>final</u> care and treatment you want to receive when you have significant, terminal incapacitation that will lead to your death. It is enacted when your condition is recognized by two or more doctors, as something from which you will not recover.

The living will formalizes wishes about end of life medical support--treatments, comfort or palliative care, and decisions about prolonging life. This document can strengthen the position of your health care surrogate. It can grant permission for hospice care. It allows family, doctors and hospitals to know what care, tests, treatments or life sustaining measures you want or do not want in the final days. It is a last guide for personal medical treatment.

The creation of a living will requires the creator to make specific choices, to itemize what can be done and what should not be done. This document grants permission to refuse treatment, refuse food, to opt for palliative, comfort only care.

Sometimes referred to as a "die with dignity" letter, a living will is an individual's final answer for end of life choices. It is a declaration of intent, a place where one may ask others--family, doctors and carers who may not agree, to respect these pre-determined choices. Most importantly, perhaps, is its status as a final legal demand that doctors and family honor your wishes about the dying process and your part in it, the way you want it to be.

Like the others, this document also can be altered, amended or revised while you are in good mental health.

Finishing up the Fab Four

Don't worry if there is a rough draft or two before creating the perfect personalized FAB FOUR. Normal. All the preparation and planning that preceded their creation is being incorporated into legal form, as specific intentions and instructions, so a rough draft or two can be expected.

When completed and signed, these documents should be put into your files for safe keeping. But consider making several notarized copies of each because these pages will need to be shared with financial institutions, family, doctors and others at appropriate moments. Chances are quite high, actually, that you will distribute copies of these important documents more than once.

Think of them as the remarkable and comforting foundation, probably the most important documents since your birth certificate, your Social Security card and your driver's license. Think how you want to use and share them.

Other Organizational Tools

While the FAB FOUR provide the solid foundation of your plan, and literally hold up the house, other "preparation pieces" likely will make their way into the files over time. The additional pieces

Forbes Magazine suggested fall into the realm of enhancing organizational efficiency.

Operative thoughts here are <u>organizational efficiency</u> and <u>over time</u>. You don't need to do it now, nor all at once, but organizational extras can add to easier plan management. Placed in your files as informational cheat sheets, these pages are useful day-to-day data needed by you, your agent, your carers and support people. The pieces are handy operational short cuts that keep frequently needed details in ready form. Forbes suggests:

- a one-page resume of medical history information. (In Mom's case, this completed sheet was already in the file--a go-to guide highlighting Mom's personal medical details and family medical data.) Routinely updated and edited when medicines, diagnoses, procedures and family history occurred, this piece went with us to all sort of places. Repeatedly.

- A personalized directory of important people, doctors, family, financial, legal and their contact information. Your family members, your docs, the attorney, the person who cleans your house, your pharmacy, the lawn service company, the pension administrator. You can always look up a phone number, but doesn't it make sense to look them up once, make the list and have your own "Directory" at your fingertips?

- An asset inventory with complete digital access details. Account numbers, bank identities, contact information, passwords. Remember the inflow/

outflow exercise? Again, in Mom's case, we already had placed financial bottom line data with accounts information in the toolkit.

- Specific beneficiary pages. Lists of the persons and causes you deem worthy for specific items/your distribution of assets. Include contact information as available.

- A list of designated gifts, items beyond general statements, (Dad's baseball glove, your alligator luggage) to specific persons or causes. It can be formalized at any point as an addendum to a Will but keeping a list in your possession offers the opportunity to add or remove specific items and ideas as they come to you.

- Signed general medical release of information forms. Since most doctors require their own versions of this, medical information releases are usually completed at the doctor's office, so it may be unnecessarily repetitious (except for Forbe's followers).

- Funeral arrangements. Written thoughts and directions for your funeral.

Mom and I added a couple more. Her life plan toolkit file was a great place for an immediate To Do list, a calendar of appointments, and a Task List, things yet to be completed for organizational efficiency.

The value of the task list is three-fold: a concrete listing of items that need attending to, the ability to add to this list as we became aware of uncompleted tasks, and the satisfaction of being able to check off tasks when completed.

What type of tasks?

- Adding authorized users to your bank checking and savings accounts, or opening new joint accounts, visiting the social security offices, meeting your tax preparer, etc.

- executing additional affidavits when appropriate, to extend or prove that the aforementioned Fab Four documents remain in effect. Banks, pension programs, financial institutions will want reassurance every few years that paperwork and named agents of record are, in fact, still in effect. Affidavits do that.

The accordion file was home for Mom's plan. It was a secure place to keep extra copies of everything to use as needed.

In case you wonder, there are now eight pieces in Mom's toolbox. 1. The inflow/outflow projection worksheet. 2. A medical history information. 3-6. The Fabulous Four. 7. My do to list. 8. Financial account information.

Signing Mom's FAB FOUR

"We're all just walking each other home." - Ram Dass, educator, spiritualist

A kitchen table, soft Florida breezes whispering in through

open windows, overhanging greenery shading the patio, her small gardenia tree heavy with flowers, blooming and pungent. The big moment.

We had arrived at our personal **Stage Four: Action**. Mom, with her senior heart and desire to command her future, and me, the administrative minion, demanding organization—setting plans in legal space with her suggested timeline, and then getting on to what was really important: enjoying life. We were more than ready.

Her attorney, whose business was estates via house calls, was a lanky, soft-spoken legal mind Mom always described as her young Abe Lincoln. Eric had a history with our family, initially representing my grandparents. He had moved on to representing my parents, and he represents me now, a third generation.

Young Abe began with housekeeping, updating my parents' Last Will. But today was really about taking care of "everything else" Mom had in mind. Today would create her official FAB FOUR, legally securing her plan, and legally naming me as durable power of attorney.

A little extra family history: After a family reunion celebrating their 50th anniversary, there was a year-long foray punctuated by my dad's quick physical and mental decline to death. Dad's assets had passed seamlessly to Mom, but the caregiver stress of Dad's failing health included troubling memories—a guilt-ridden daytrip when Mom and a girlfriend had taken Dad to "visit" an assisted care complex, and permanently enrolled his faltering self. He hung out with a group of old guys in similar shape, who one day conspired to dismantle a window and escape, only to find themselves outside the building but fenced in.

Mom visited every day. Dad lived there six months, was hospitalized twice, and then died.

Two more family deaths followed--Mom's sister, Marilyn, and her longtime retired school teacher companion Mary. Both single professional women with school pensions, investments and a condo, slipping earthly bonds one after the other with cancer and frail health. These gals had orderly wills, but a slew of personal possessions and that overstuffed metal filing cabinet 20 years deep which kept us sorting, sifting and shredding (thank you Bry) for almost a year.

Fast forward: Mom wasn't ending up anywhere without her own list of do's and don'ts. Neither of us wanted another overflowing file cabinet. Most importantly however, was Mom's earnest desire to optimize whatever was left, unfettered by worry over possible future dilemmas.

She wanted that guarantee for later, and my shared responsibility. Eldest of four daughters, birth order or organizational whiz—we were in it together. She trusted me. I was named agent for all her life decisions, authorized to protect her future however she chose to live it. My sisters were listed as "seconds" on all legal documents, in case I resigned or wasn't able.

The youngest sister would be a support. The middle two were something else. Years ago, Mom had coined a descriptive nickname for them, exasperated by their unique personalities, categorical irreverence, challenging misbehaviors and off-color humor. She often referred to them by that snarky shortcut. (Remember having to make tough assessments about loved ones?)

Anyhow, Young Abe agreed wholeheartedly that NOW was absolutely the right time to formalize Mom's plan.

Execute with sound mind and body. Hold it in waiting.

We could see the finish line on planning efforts! With a legal mind well versed in the territory, discussion was driven by the reasons we had at the outset of planning—Mom's choices, what she wanted, and who she wanted calling the shots when harder days arrived. Eric explored financial protections, revocable trusts and the deed to the house, happy with our preparations. He also asked for more detail while offering examples, showing typical paperwork and validating what we had accomplished so far.

Everyone drank iced tea while from across the table, Mom's green eyes locked onto mine repeatedly, silently urging compliance, seeking agreement. My brown eyes returned her gaze, congratulating this effort to formalize her decisions. Meanwhile, Eric recommended we continue adding to our bank of shared household information, tidily incorporating anything necessary to handle whatever might come our way going forward.

"Will you do what I'm asking you to do?" she asked. "Will you follow my directions?" Eric was official witness to my affirmations. Except for one thing, and it surprised us all.

Eric had wanted to keep Mom's house, her largest asset out of probate, safe from inheritance tax, by using what is sometimes referred to as a "Lady Bird Trust." He suggested using this legal instrument to put the 3-bedroom 2-bath Florida ranch in trust now, with all four daughters named as owners.

I wouldn't do it.

Eric's idea might have been reasonable for some families, but I saw nothing simple about group home ownership, or the idea of getting four women in two time zones to work together over time and space to sell a house, much less securing four signatures for a sale, or any easy consensus on leaving window treatments or fixing sprinklers, especially in an emotional framework of grief. At a minimum it would be a cumbersome project that I did not want to tackle.

Buying and selling real estate was something I was fairly good at. By then, I had bought and sold ten homes as family relocations had gone hand in hand with an upwardly mobile husband. A brief and immediate consideration of family dynamics made it less desirable.

A few more words about my sisters. The baby was a 30-something lovely, spiritual character with a penchant for abandoned cats, orphaned coyotes and personal causes. Tee could be a fine co-owner, but the middle two were those unpredictable, impudent characters. Singly, they were troublesome, but together? Together, their deviousness magnified and kept sisterly relations permanently off kilter. I had hurtful memories I didn't want--their frightening disappearing act one afternoon with my toddler, the ungrateful return of a gift box full of favorite but well-worn treasures sent from my children to theirs, nasty note included. Enough sharing.

Anyway, I announced I would give up my one-quarter future ownership, no Lady Bird arrangement for me. Let the other three work it out. I appreciated the thought but didn't want the work (or the torture, depending on perspective), no matter how equal Mom was trying to be.

She didn't like my refusal. Denied her equal four-way distribution, she was frustrated and openly disgruntled about any additional delay created by my impasse.

Did Eric have a suggestion?

After a minute, he counseled foregoing the trust, recommending instead an alteration to the present deed. A paper change filed with the county would allow Mom to name an additional "homeowner" <u>as Remainder</u>. She retained complete ownership until she died. The property would then transfer to the "Remainder," avoid probate, and allow a single agent to sell and disburse equally among four. What did Mom think?

It was a reality check. Critical thinking and formal thought laced with iced tea in lengthening afternoon shadows. Mom knew I had more real estate experience than three of them combined. We had trust and honesty, and the luxury to say what needed to be said.

"Do you promise?" Mom asked. I promised.

The Remainder would be me.

Mom and Eric would reconvene to sign and witness final documents. Daughter and lawyer would hold down Mom's fort, an information and legal partnership headed into the future.

We were relieved, elated, exhilarated. We offered each other congratulatory hugs. Parent, child and attorney, tucking away prepared instructions until whenever Mom's journey required using them. No more talking, no more planning.

A sunset ride to the beach was called for.

Within a week, the documents were signed, but there was an unsettling glitch: Mom had refused to share beyond me and the attorney. This was her right, but I protested, fully expecting that sharing what she'd created would add credibility to her plan, thereby helping me when I might

> need it.
>   She flatly refused, remained adamant about privacy, defensive when I campaigned against stealth. No one else needed details, she said, only her lawyer and I needed to know. Widow in charge. She had done what she had needed to do for herself. She would not take another minute to share, much less explain to anyone else. She trusted Eric. She trusted me. She was finished.

Memories of the day's soft breeze play on my skin whenever I recall that kitchen confab. We had worked out her grand plan, secured my required legal endorsements, protected her for how she wanted her future to be. Mom's Fab Four documents were cornerstones, the outline to guide us, starting now. Other operating data would/could come over time.

We had launched ourselves into **Stage Five: Maintenance**. Young Abe and I would have it in our hands, and it would be years before I realized how strong a foundation had been laid.

Remember the big picture. If you are the one making the plans, bravo for you, and your forward thinking. If you are the loved one doing the assisting, bravo for you, your support and your forward thinking.

Oh. Are you wondering about that cheeky life-long nickname Mom lavished upon her two middle daughters? Devil Twins. I rest my case.

PART TWO

Living with a Plan

10

Maintenance

"When the winds of change blow, some build walls, others build windmills." - Chinese Proverb

It is one of those things about living our lives isn't it? It just happens. The progression of days from childhood through adult years to older age is natural. One day we were kids, the next we graduate. We get married, have our own families. We have full calendars, busy lives, bodies in motion, maximizing our earning power and often burning the candle at both ends to do it all.

Probably most of us haven't spent a lot a time thinking about our senior years. One day we are surprised by the face in a mirror or a visit with our parents. Our kids are older. We wake up startled and find ourselves at the middle years facing west.

One of my angel friends says life's overall rollout should have prompted at least some forward thinking for our future older selves. Great, if that's you. But who has time?? Most of us don't get to thinking about *later* until much later when the crazy busy early years are finished, the kids are out of the house, and we've finally had time to take a breath and see that face in the mirror.

Maybe that is more natural. Our lifespan cycle offers us TIME after the kids are out of the house. Maybe we have to collect enough years on the planet to begin wondering about the future. We do all get there.

As an adult child looking beyond my own high energy operations, and not aware of my own future planning needs, at all, I was slightly surprised to feel the shift--I had become a watchman of my mother. Wondering about *"what's next?"* For her and subsequently for me. I was an official generational observer, looking at the preceding (or receding) one.

Do my adult kids watch me? Probably. I am aging too. But the day I realized I was "watching Mom" was when my brain began trying to think this life continuum through. What happens next?

My husband just complained about all the re-writing and editing as we work to finish our own Fab Four. A first meeting with an estate attorney, (not Eric, who has since retired), produced draft documents with what we gently label cumbersome language and an overabundance of legaleeze. Both broad and specific considerations written in awful, run on sentences.

Ugh! We had hoped for thoroughness *and* simplicity, but realized after that first go-round, that our documents were not ready. We thought some paragraphs completely unnecessary, and some content difficult to decipher. The hub was frustrated because more time and effort would be required to complete what he was paying an attorney to do. Didn't sound right, he said, until I gently reminded him that it was our lives we were talking about.

> Bob: "These are boiler plate. I knew it. This attorney doesn't know me. He didn't write about us. How could he after just a few questions? The papers he sent just aren't us."
>
> Me: "I think a lot of it **is** us, but these drafts need our touch. We need to customize! Our lives, our money, our wishes. That attorney knows legal jargon, but he can't know everything about us. The basics are here. I think for starters, we simplify the writing. That's why I said we need to figure this out. For us. Our big picture. Exactly what WE want, and need, isn't necessarily the same thing as boilerplate for Everyman."
>
> Bob: "So each of us has to read through these, and then go back to the attorney? I guess I'm frustrated because it is taking a lot more time and effort *from us!* I guess it just takes time."

We are on Draft #2, in the process of becoming *people with a plan*. Leaning in, (thank you Bob Seger). Get the idea?

A non-scientific poll of my friends revealed that some of them have answered their own future life management questions, exploring retirement options, thinking about where to live, guestimating *how long* to plan for and if they have money enough to make the end game. One friend admits she just cannot get her head around *all of it*.

Aging continues whether we are paying attention or not. Our bodies, these amazing machines, are altered by simple passage of time. Our joints complain, some parts get replaced, some hearts wear out. Some of us sleep more, some less. We adjust, we compensate. We renew efforts to stay busy and active as long as possible, and dream about dying in our sleep!

But if we pay attention, we know our situations are evolving. We should be thinking ahead.

Learning How to Maintain a "Long and Winding Road"

I found myself and Mom living with her plan. Have you ever heard someone say, "If I only knew then, what I know now?"

It speaks to hindsight and the trove of wisdom gained through experience. Perhaps that is precisely the point. **The hindsight lesson for me is all about gratitude for living with Mom's plan across months and years that followed.**

Finishing up that breezy day, neither Prochaska nor maintenance were on the radar. The goal had been creation of a plan, not whatever would come after. With Mom's FAB FOUR as foundation, I simply continued doing what I always had done--visiting, checking finances, keeping an eye on a loved one's health. A daughter caring about her mom, a sounding board if asked, but giving her privacy she wanted.

For a good while it was ordinary, day to day, mundane, exactly what needed to be, living the status quo, with that plan in the wings for Mom's future date with destiny. We felt good about going along with a written strategy for her future, and not needing it. (Yet).

Mom happily enjoyed her days, independent, continued to manage her own money. Traveled. Kept her own schedule. Drove around. Lived a personal life with her new friend, away from her children. This was real comfort to the whole family.

But we had to feel our way through information sharing.

As Mom's partner/agent, my status had begun with that unforeseen complication. Struck by a challenging conundrum--believing communication was vital and accepting Mom's unwillingness to share. Her plan said nothing about communication beyond Eric and me, but at a minimum, all parties should know about a plan for the future, right?

The news received mixed reviews. Explain or don't explain, Mom's life ambled along, but the *journey and process of handling circumstance or issue* prompted grumbling. Family emotions and personalities were like windy weather, forces that rattled trees along Mom's path.

That was early "maintenance" --best times accomplished with ease, and nothing to do about grumblers. Mom and I had a high comfort level, a written guarantee for sorting through her future with the benefit of pre-planning.

Today I know this is NORMAL.

But as years passed, there was more exertion in maintaining Mom's plan than either of us could have anticipated! Which is only to say that maintenance was another giant learning curve, and it made an impression!

Not an *if* question, but that proverbial *when* question. Despite no real needs early on, plan maintenance was still an ongoing gamut of organizational activity and emotional response. I watched, listened and kept pace. I knew I was watching for *when* my loved one is no longer able to perform certain tasks or make decisions, much less remember to open the mail, go to a grocery, balance a check book, get dressed or use a telephone. But I didn't know maintaining was also going to include *when and how* to use the plan *when* others don't approve.

Not a warning, but a weather forecast. Prepare for a rolling out of everything over time. Anticipate validation, dissension and possible exhaustion, hopefully not all at once, and sharing information, communication, plays a role.

TIP: If you did not work through Part One, **con-**

sider going back. Build a plan. Or keep reading to see how working with Mom's plan unfolded.

11

Early Years

"Old age isn't for sissies." - Audrey Hepburn

My uneventful visits seemed a sure sign that Mom had created her life plan from a vantage point of good health and reason. We had good beach days, meals out. Conscientiously checking in at least three times a year, I had chosen to share news of my visits with family. I had ongoing apprehension over Mom's steady boyfriend, thirteen years her junior, and I shared that too, but the family chuckle remained an inability to get her on the phone.

She was her busy private self in those days, relishing the boyfriend as near constant companion. On my visits, she would send him home and make time for me. She repeatedly dismissed my uneasiness about his character, intentions, or trustworthiness, blowing off any worry I had by telling me the pairing was "good for them both," he was "so positive, never negative," she was "having a good time," and she didn't mind being the banker. She delighted in his attentions and after all, this was *her* life.

Maybe he was harmless. If his steady presence erased Mom's loneliness, I hoped I would grow accustomed to it.

The relationship had altered her social butterfly calendar with her sister, Susan, and best girlfriend, Joan, taking a back seat. Couplehood also altered the stream of contact…Mom never spoke of Dad anymore, or girl outings, her days filled instead by adventures with the thrice-divorced guy and his positive attitude.

But she also admitted her friends weren't as active, less inclined to be out and about, and dying off, an offhand admission of change even a boyfriend couldn't replace. Almost smug by comparison, she was this merry widow. Amused friends likened it to a high school crush.

I stubbornly promoted her old circuit, made social calls to see remaining pals, kept up with Aunt Sue. That wasn't going to change, but growing disengagement from what had been a norm of family, friends and activities, poked at my thoughts.

Did it mean anything? Was she pulling away? Was this normal Senior Relationships 101? Was it simply life evolving? Were we jealous of the new guy's time? I couldn't tell.

Their relationship continued, and we all adjusted.

A few years into the relationship and the plan, Mom quit choir after singing for more than 50 years. She stopped playing shuffleboard. She no longer taught water aerobics. She stopped going to church. There was little interest in grandchildren. Conversations were still highlighting what she and the boyfriend were doing.

"We are good for one another," she repeated.

And the life care plan said nothing about this either, <u>except</u> that Mom was living her life.

***

Partial Truths

One day, Sue tells me Mom is having trouble with pinochle and their card group is disbanding. Card games had been family legend and now might be the latest victim of Mom's flagging interest in activities not boyfriend-related. When asked, she said she was quitting pinochle because one player had died, and several couldn't keep game details straight anymore. Sue's version was nearly the same, except that Mom was one of the confused players; the hefty kitty of coins that comprised the card group treasury, too hard for her to manage.

Wish I had witnessed one of those last games! Giggling girlfriends quitting cards! Both Mom and Sue were telling the truth, with differing vantage points. Whatever was happening, card playing was history, and the pouch of leftover coins bought ice cream one night.

The devotion to the boyfriend grew deeper, and I had not been able to shake a nagging discomfort. How was Mom not interested in her family, her grandchildren?

When they weren't gallivanting together, he found ways to keep busy and spend some of her money. She allowed him to decorate her house with second hand mirrors and colorful pottery Calavera sinks. He installed a concrete walking path to border her landscape beds. He planted random vegetation, or spent hours chopping it down. He built a shade gazebo, bought odd trinkets for the garden, installed recycled kitchen cabinets in the garage. Together they fantasized a kitchen remodel and a new roof.

Where I might see unnecessary projects, he saw my interest as intrusive oversight. We butted heads more than once over questionable schemes combined with his distinct disinterest in property upkeep. Mom allowed it all, ceding to his proprietary companionship. I did finally get him to stop hacking down the hibiscus, despite his declaration that cutting them was always her idea, by announcing complaints from the garden service. Interior festooning, however, seemed open territory, Mom unwilling to put the kibosh on his decorating. This was her life.

All right, already. Annoying yes, but beyond the few dollars spent, major assets were protected, as she and I had secured away everything but the few thousand dollars in her checking account, what I had been calling her daily operations fund.

But I began to sense weird competition upon my arrival in town. The twosome was a fixture and, maybe this was his style? Insinuate himself in her affairs, rank his relations above mother and daughter? How did senior love affairs operate? How would I know?

Whatever it was, he was never shy with opinions, happy to tell me *how it should be.*

I did really want to like him for Mom's sake but attempts to befriend him had me confronting a blustery motormouth, a cavalier carefree manor and a major interest in enjoying life, mostly on her dime. I found the incessant chatter tiring. Visiting Mom now meant listening to the boyfriend. Work to get a word in.

Our family history? He already knew it. Talk about your vacation, he had been there too! Mention any home project, he had done it. He could numb you with random dialogue, cause a listener's mental shut down with faded out-of-focus photo albums. A jack of all trades, an everything you can do, I can do better guy, with an I've already done it personality.

Did he clean? No. A family friend/housekeeper helped Mom do

that. Did he cut grass? No. There was the garden service. Did he shop, cook and eat? Yes. Did he sleep at Mom's? Yes, although he never moved in completely, keeping a mobile home nearby.

My daughter stayed with Mom between her midwinter college graduation and employment. She was creeped out by his appreciation of her 22-year-old figure and by bathing suit catalogs addressed to him and arriving in Mom's mail. I cautioned distance as my own creep meter ratcheted up.

Was this really a beneficial relationship for two senior citizens? Was I a good judge of character, a picky daughter, or both? Welcome to Crazyland. He wasn't leaving.

My mind sadly worked overtime comparing differences-- the age gap, his nonexistent resources and her financial stability, their lengthy cocktail hours. Skepticism had me hoping it would end soon. Mom tempered my concerns, she had no interest in remarrying, his staying power was balm for being alone, and by her own admission, she was happy. No matter how annoying to me, he was there in Mom's big picture, a cheerful companion for an attractive, financially stable widow.

I worked to unstick my craw, tried to put aside his dismissive attitude toward my daughterly interest in Mom's days and his general disdain for Mom's plan. His own suggestions about how she should live never ceased, while I knew my resolve as her protector would not waiver either. If he was staying put, it didn't matter, I had been here forever.

Did I mention being my father's daughter too, a stubborn Italian girl?

Ultimately though, I stepped aside of their day to day as much as possible, schooling myself to let small things go and maintaining the eagle eye on the overall, a daughter watching out for her Mom's big picture.

I put my foot down on bigger issues. He might glue up mirror tiles, but he did not replace the water heater. Mom did not need repurposed 1970-style anything, nor more thorny roses or garish lawn ornaments clogging her tiny garden, but those were small potatoes in the grand scheme of Islander Court. I wouldn't look at every day. He called me once to resolve a broken central air conditioner, but there would be no new designer kitchen.

I tamped my frustrations mostly by purposely diminishing contact with the guy, scheduling time with Mom during his absences and sharing various absurdities with commiserating friends. For a decade, we tolerated an uneasy shared circumstance through limited contact. Dashing in and out from my own hectic life, I planned to last him out.

Tip: Sharing quirky details lightens a load.

12

Life Is Not a Dress Rehearsal

"You cannot travel the path until you become the path itself." - Buddha

During one Spring Break, Mom and I hosted Easter dinner for her friends and our family. Sue and Joan were invited. My college kids traveled from distant states. I expected one of those big holiday gatherings reminiscent of our past. No.

Mom had invited the boyfriend's family and her social time was spent with them in another part of the house. She did not cook, did not serve. She spent zero time with her sister, ignored the grandchildren; the college kids remarked on the "unvisit," put off by Grammy's persistent lack of interest. With the luxury of hindsight, my oldest is convinced this was the red alert. Welcome to Crazyland became an inside-my-head joke.

Mom continued to frolic, and I continued to manage those short duration occasions which limited the conversation free-for-all. Tasks and details were Mom and my responsibility, and we persevered with our routine to maintain her household. My visits ticked boxes on organization and safety, and Mom's medical stuff stayed in her own hands. We handled financials timed to the boyfriend's absence.

We went electronic, consolidated accounts, simplified deposits and withdrawals, added my name to records, updated and signed Transfer on Death instructions, completed routine household repairs, grocery shopped. We distributed Power of Attorney paperwork to pension agents and insurance companies. Paid taxes and annual bills, updated her driver's license. Got online banking for long-distance access. Created annuities. Made and kept routine doctor appointments. Catalogued, monitored, reviewed. Kept up with Young Abe, tweaking paperwork as needed.

A note to self from those days: "Apparently I move like a spinning dervish. Mom calls me a human tornado. 'They' notice my pace, but I'm not hyper about anything more than my little window of opportunity to get things done during a visit."

We refined operational bits and pieces and added them to the tool box to maintain her life map. We continued to poke away at her pesky blood pressure issue, finally finding a regimen to hold her numbers in safe range. I got acquainted with bankers, doctors, and her accountant. Beach afternoons continued to be rewards.

She was looking good, taking great care with her makeup, her clothes. She had a sparkle in her green eyes.

About three years into maintenance of Mom's plan,

things began to change.

Mom and I were still ride along partners on errands to the bank and beyond, but she was slacking off on management between my administrative visits. I would arrive to a pile of mail, bills to pay. The refrigerator was often a museum of old food and white Styrofoam takeout boxes. Newspapers and paperbacks were piling up in the garage. The yard again was a victim of faulty gardening.

From my view, she was safe and secure, comfortable and absolutely able to be unconcerned if she chose to be less involved with these kinds of details, but I made a mental note to keep watching.

Our days out had a deadline—home by 5 pm. Time with the boyfriend was a daily routine eclipsing everything. Keep him happy. Keep him around. Take him on trips. Keep a full refrigerator. Stock the wine and margarita cabinet. Go out to eat or order in. Relax together and watch night time television. Repeat.

It was working for her, and even if I was an obsessing, organizing oldest child, I still did not know if this was what to expect for a healthy senior in love or not. No experience in senior living! I'd never been *here* before.

If Mom's life was charted on some quirky silver-haired tsunami path, we still had her desired road map created years ago. I tried hard to keep frustration under control, despite being unable to shake my worry that Mom's dwindling interest in anything not boyfriend related might be cause for more concern.

Regular update letters to my three sisters and Mom's brother were sprinkled with details of keeping a senior widow ship afloat, as well as the subtle differences I continued to observe. The baby sister and Uncle Jim always said thanks for being in the loop. The other two categorically dismissed the updates, disputing my concerns.

They were their snarky selves, they did not "need" my reports because "Mom was fine." They had decided for themselves that the boyfriend knew her better than me. They didn't care if I was concerned. That hurt my feelings. I wasted energy and emotion worrying about their negativity.

Thank goodness the internet proved I wasn't alone. (Consider that earlier suggestion to read a caregiver blog about family!)

Tip: Try to not waste time worrying what others think. Instead, Google *elder care family conflict*, read blogs about family dissension and toughen up. It's part of the territory. I believed Mom's subtle drift away was a warning. But read those blogs. Not everyone is on the same page.

13

Family Reactions & Dementia Concerns

"If He cannot turn their hearts, may He turn their ankles so that we may know them by limping." - Indian saying

Communicating with my sisters ignited their growing campaign to divide the lines. Rebuttals escalated from short notes and pissy phone calls to angry letters, cross talk and arguments that repeatedly mocked my worry. They vehemently denied Mom's disinterest, lack of follow through, or that noticeable dependence on the boyfriend. They were his fan club, defending him as a devoted Godsend who filled Mom's days and nights. Blatant disregard for my observations had them loudly flinging insults at me instead. I was an alarmist, paranoid, nuts.

My sisters' visits to Florida were unlike my own. They went on vacation, partied with the merry widow and her guy, and needled at discord. Their dislike of Mom's plan and my part was evident. They even attempted an unsuccessful bid to change Mom's plan to a voting majority of daughters, by inviting the youngest sister to join them for a 3-to-1 "voting majority." Tee refused. I lost additional points by reminding them Mom had made her own decisions and there would be **no voting**.

Despite the rancor, I wanted them in the information loop. There were nagging differences in the Mom I had known for a lifetime. I felt this ongoing slow drift of Mom's senior citizen years and I visited more frequently because she made less and less contact, increasingly out of character.

What was going on?

I was in the process of change, for months and years, over what my observations might be trying to help me realize. Prochaska would say there was lots of ruminating going on in my head as I worked to decipher whether it was Mom's devotion to a man not my father, or was my contemplation more problematic?

I heard a tiny bell ring.

Maintenance Tip: Pay attention to your gut.

Parameters for Dementia—Today's Short List of Warning Signs:

- Memory
- Communication
- Basic Reasoning
- Concentration
- Visual Perception

In the last decade, research has been directed toward identifying markers helpful to determining early diagnosis dementia. When

Mom and I put her plan together, there was no checklist. I wasn't looking for danger signs. Today, the list is a go-to early warning system.

The parameters for dementia today suggest that difficulties in any one of these skill areas can be an early warning sign, alerting loved ones. Okay, but I knew subtle changes I witnessed would have been imperceptible to a casual observer.

But I *knew her* and what I saw didn't *feel* right. Apply these latter-day parameters? Mom was less attentive. She was quieter. Less chatty. Less social. Even with sisters who consistently put off my worries as paranoia, **communication** issues rang that tiny bell.

Taken further, it seemed Mom's **concentration** was off. She was actively ignoring household responsibilities, waiting for my assist instead. Did failure to use a cell phone or any phone mean a lack of **concentration**, a disinterest in communication or both?

She certainly ignored changes in home décor! Did those goofy mirrors bother her, or was her **visual perception** off?

As for the boyfriend? Later, a cousin would suggest to me that Mom getting involved with him was when her **basic reasoning skills** had first taken a dive. (Humor is medically proven to help)!

But whenever I would try to seek his opinion as Mom's significant other about her quieting, for example, his reply always was complete denial of anything amiss. (A mask in place or maybe his **basic reasoning skills** were also challenged.)

I had not observed **memory** issues. Doctor visits were up to date, and no professional appeared disconcerted. No one had seen any Big Sign of Trouble, but my overactive brain would not stop churning.

If my check-ins had always had dual purpose--enjoying time with Mom and providing reassuring oversight for us both, I was slowly convincing myself, preparing myself to believe--even without the list of basic dementia parameters—there was change in Mom. I just couldn't decide if her diminished participation was normal or something to worry about. And let's be real, here. Mom didn't seem worried at all.

What was I witnessing on those trips in and out of Florida? I was becoming annoyed by my CEO, who was assuredly becoming less involved, and who wouldn't buffer much less halt the boyfriend's interference or devil twins' acrimony.

But I saw no real risks, no safety concerns. No one in her routine medical community visits had sounded any alarm either. As far as I knew. If someone asked me to pick one word that defined what I was sensing in response to compassionate oversight, that word might be *dismissal*, in multiple respects.

Communication was *dismissed,* dwindling between Mom and me. Two sisters *dismissed* my concerns. Mom's boyfriend regularly *dismissed* my care and watchfulness. Mom herself, was more and more *dismissive* of details. Additionally, because I would arrive to a folder full of mail, I knew she was *dismissing* details in my absence. Broad dismissal, period.

But the decriers of denial had left their mark. If my gut was unsettled, it spoke only in a whisper.

Repeat Tip: Listen to your gut.

> I kept coming back to her kitchen table to watch and listen, expecting a noteworthy event, a major medical episode, a noticeable demarcation that would cause any observer (and especially me) to pull up short. Something more pronounced than this meandering, confounding slipping away over a goodly stretch of time.
>
> Was she comforted when he jumped in to answer

questions for her? Maybe she really did not have much to say anymore. Maybe she could not get a word in edgewise. I felt her personality shrinking, yet she seemed happy.

So why could I not let this go? Why did it feel so off? Because one night sitting at that table, intently taking in the whole scene--Mom's downcast eyes and withdrawn body language while he animatedly bustled around the kitchen and prattled on--I just knew.

The mother I knew would have smiled, gotten a word in edgewise, participated somehow, laughed. She did not. If a shoe hadn't dropped completely, it was falling off her foot. Mom's body language was all wrong. Those quiet downcast eyes while he chirped away were not normal.

We were inching down a changing highway. Boyfriend and devil twins to the contrary.

It was tricky. Even as she continued to manage, Mom was beginning to falter. The "human tornado," whirling in for a few days and then just as quickly out, could no longer deny what my eyes saw. I had to acknowledge, had to be honest with myself. She was slowing down.

We would adjust, Mom and I. Nothing needed to change her day to day path.

I could fly in, give Mom my love, do some tornadic paperwork, and adjust. I only wondered how to recognize when to wade in deeper, hoping I was in the room when it happened. I felt sadness and some satisfaction too, because I knew that moving forward, the rest of them would soon be unable to deny her fade.

But remember, listen to your gut.

The Shoe Drops

You know what it is like when you see a person after a long absence? How you notice a different haircut, a growth spurt, something changed from the time before? I ramped up visiting, but when I blew out of town again, I was back sooner than expected.

> A birthday call with my aunt revealed a new health issue to worry over. Not an "episode" but an announcement. Sue had run unexpectedly run into Mom, and subsequently was ratting her out. Mom had a secret. She was hobbling around, limping badly.
>
> Mom was not happy with Sue or having to tell me. The whole family had a history of osteoporosis to talk about, except Mom didn't want to chat.
>
> I started tagging along for her doctor appointments and *WE* needed an orthopedic doctor visit. If Mom wanted to play on two legs instead of from a wheelchair, she needed a hip replacement. The cat was out of the bag. Do something about it. Taking time for surgery would be on her calendar. That about sums up the conversation. I flew back in to consult with bone people.
>
> Surgery was scheduled for December. We made pre-op appointments. I flew home for Thanksgiving. She got clearance from her general practitioner, had surgery, and my sisters did post-op care while I attended my daughter's mid-year college graduation. The boyfriend hung out at the hospital, urged out each night at the end of visiting hours. I was told Mom went to rehab, dopey with morphine, hallucinating dolphins.

By the following April, there was something else. If you have had major surgery, you know about energy levels and recovery time. Although Mom was back on her feet and walking quite well, she was openly worried about not feeling great, concerned that she never got her pep back.

> I took notice of her openness. This was a change. To be safe, *we* scheduled a heart doctor visit for mid-May when I could return. I suggested she rest and continue physical therapy. I flew back home.
>
> Only a week later, the boyfriend calls an ambulance on a Wednesday. Mom went to the emergency room. He called my daughter, who called me. Then he disappeared. The ER run revealed something more serious than recharging from hip replacement.
>
> It was Mom's heart. Blocked arteries. Mom had been admitted, reduced to a weak patient who could barely breathe much less sit up. My very first thought was how had Mom passed the hip surgery pre-op only six months ago, if something was so wrong with her heart? Do arteries get blocked overnight?
>
> Within hours, Mom was referred for emergency heart surgery, transferred to a bigger hospital. I jumped on another plane, arriving to find her curled in a fetal pose, a frail figure in an ICU bed. A nurse was finishing a pre-op interview about heart surgery risks. I watched Mom sign the permission form.
>
> The heart hospital made room in their schedule. Her brother flew in. Uncle Jim and I sat connected to the OR by cell phone. Medical staff would text updates, reporting when she went on an artificial heart machine and when she came off. Emergency double bypass. Two major repairs for blood flow, and discovery of a third defective and inoperable

> artery, possibly a hidden birth defect. The doting boyfriend absent throughout, except for one 5:30 a.m. phone call the morning after surgery, asking me for a ride home from his own little overnight kidney stone ordeal?
>
> Really?? Did he know Mom had heart surgery? Yeah, yeah. He was sure doctors were doing their best.
>
> Mom hugged a teddy bear as she healed. It was a long hospital stay. I insisted the hospital remove a brutish Russian nurse from the rotation. My sisters visited. Again, Mom went to rehab before getting home where she continued to improve through a quiet summer and fall while family diligently visited. The boyfriend had returned, a presence in the home of a recovering heart patient, ensconced in his role as dinner companion, night nurse and television viewing partner.

Which is all to say that at some point, the senior and the caring agent should start going to doctor visits **together**. Use the health surrogate paperwork or the DPA to become more involved in information sharing with professionals. Those documents allow us to gather facts first hand for the best shot at seeing the whole picture.

> While recovering, Mom's communication skill dipped further. She would listen to a caller, but she was not responsive. Was it anesthesia? Was it post-surgery exhaustion? A mystery.
>
> Mom and the boyfriend decide a holiday celebration cruise would be a nice recovery incentive. Planning a winter voyage held Mom's attention throughout the six months she worked to regain energy as her heart mended. Pre-payment, ordering new passports, reserving their stateroom. With

singular purpose, she chose outfits and thought ahead to a fun vacation with her steady. The devil twins had decided to surprise the happy couple, just show up and join the cruise.

I was traveling far away when a call came from the departure port. Surprise is an understatement. It was the boyfriend calling to say there was a problem. Mom could not board and she was too upset to talk. What?

She wanted him to see if I could fix this. What?

She did not have her passport and he said *she* did not know how that happened. Oh, her passport might be sitting on that kitchen table 200 miles away, but the ship would leave port in the morning.

Didn't *they* drive over to that boat together? How did *they* forget a passport?

The boyfriend kept repeating that Mom was feeling so bad and was so upset that she could not talk.

I was nowhere near Islander Court, when her travel companion had called me for that Hail Mary. Time for resolution was running out. How does one leave one's passport (essential) on the kitchen table? Concentration? What?

The warning bell was ringing boldly.

Oh, she had a passport with her. The old, expired one. What??

Despite the arm of Homeland Security, a kindly cruise ship agent, who was not supposed to do this sort of thing, would make an unbelievable exception for a harmless little senior lady with an expired passport. Mom could board if she could produce a guarantee of citizenship. Really?? Could we find a copy of her US birth certificate?

I found myself imagining a day long filibuster by the

> long-winded boyfriend, a frazzled ship's officer, and the ultimate in problem-solving to get him out of her face. The solution required the boyfriend to call me.
>
> Produce a US birth certificate and she can board. I hang up and call Mom's friend Joan. After commiserating over our involvement, we do our own problem solving. A house key, a paperwork file. The local UPS store. A fax machine. Thank goodness for organization.

I hear she had a great time, surprised and enjoying the extra attention and company of the wacky twins and their children.

> *Confusion. Memory? Concentration?*
> There is a photo of her on that cruise, in a black glittery strappy dress more appropriate for a twenty-something headed to Vegas. *Visual perception?*
> A couple more months go by. She and the boyfriend take a Spring road trip to Nashville. Somebody's wedding. I get an intentionally vague chat several weeks later. Mom mentions falling in the ladies' room, smacking her head on the tile.
> Picture it? A tiny white-haired woman sliding across cold tile, ending up against a wall? No idea how. Blackout? Ministroke? Wet floor? Did it happen? Did she see the hotel doctor? No, no. Oh, no. She was fine, just embarrassed.
> Did the hotel even know?
> Meanwhile the boyfriend was signing her hotel receipts. I asked him not to.

Keeping Secrets and the Psychological Toll

> The head bump in Nashville is another unsettling notch in Mom's private life. Their secrecy adds to my worry list. The less I knew, the less I could respond. The devil twins complain loudly again, blaming overreaction to both Mom's little accident and the boyfriend signing the credit card.
>
> Now it's May and guess what? Eighteen months after the first one, Mom needs another hip replacement. A result of the fall? Bad bones? No telling.
>
> It is her third major surgery in 20 months. Another bout of rehab and recovery. I insist she complete physical therapy. She seems smaller, slower. I take into account strange episodes and trouble overpaying the gardener. I witness additional slips in tempo, mood, behavior and skill.
>
> Are Mom and the boyfriend keeping secrets? Her silence. His denial. Have they been teaming up to conceal real issues from the very person she asked to help her? For how long?
>
> I wonder if I am beginning to lose my mom *and* my mind.

My uneasiness was finally that dropping shoe. We were beyond routine efforts at book keeping and household accounts, doctor visits and follow through. Assisting Mom, upholding her privacy and her lifestyle had put us in unknown geography. We were not lost, but her path was entering the woods. There was too much going on that I didn't know.

> Like a darn light bulb blinking on, I realized that uneasiness over helping Mom deal with her stuff was my early warning system. Too many occasions dealing with what

was happening to Mom was taking a toll on me! Perhaps a daughter's natural role--monitor, manage, help with details, I had not anticipated the gut reports, had not considered the emotional psychological roller coaster caused by care tasks *and* negative affronts. The darn light bulb was illuminating the real crux—so much uncertainty and beyond control. An aching throat and tears pricked at my eyes.

The unknown. Real issues and secrets paving a bumpy highway that had me up at night. Mom and I really needed to talk. And our October review would be a perfect time.

14

Emotions and Relationships

"It is always the right time to do what is right." - Martin Luther King

The Traveling Attorney

Usually in October, Young Abe would come for that annual house call. We would haul out paperwork to discuss and review. The recap added confidence, set us at ease. Her will was in order. Distributions clear. Her income was covering costs, and major investments remained untouched. Good news after three serious surgeries in two years.

Five years beyond the signature date for Mom's Fab Four, and we were pleased to remind ourselves of the ongoing security provided by Mom's life plan, noting its operational performance, and mindful that it would continue to take her through whatever else might be headed her way.

It was October, 2006. Mom would be 79 in a few months, and she was healthy, perhaps finally over the hurdles of multiple recoveries. Both business and social, it was another afternoon at the kitchen table. Iced tea and cookies.

We had kept pace. Kept people informed. Used the toolbox. Managed. Enjoyed the beach. She could relate to that. But there were operational questions.

My sisters had begun asking Mom to give them certain items. Eric suggested she start that list of specific gifts to keep with her other papers. We wondered out loud if she wanted to set aside funds for any grandchild's college costs. No. She said her four daughters were her only direct heirs. Gifts to grandchildren would be their parents' responsibility.

Her comments were sparse. I saw Eric note her silences—how she appeared attentive but relied on us to carry conversation, a yes or no answer provided, but no repartee.

Eric returned my gaze. I didn't know exactly where we were on Mom's time line, but we were around the first turn. As I walked him out, Eric said he had observed Mom's vacant stare, her distance from some facts. But he remained very satisfied that his client's paperwork was in order and that I was assisting. The plan was doing what the plan should do.

Mom and I circled though the house the next morning, looking at everything. She made her list, designating certain physical gifts to each one of us. We put the list away in the ever-expanding file. I sent a copy to Eric and started outlining another family update.

My youngest sister Tee, and my aunt and uncle, again responded with support, sensitive to the changing picture I described. For Mom's sake, and blinded by my own moral compass, I remained hopeful that informative letters might someday work magic with my sisters.

But it wasn't working with them at all.

The devil twins continued to misread any communication from me in four ways: grandstanding my authority, unnecessary alarm, false concerns, and general intrusion. They didn't want me telling them how Mom was fairing or what I was doing. They were willing to give support to her, but not to me. Despite Mom's own choices, they had audaciously resumed their quest for a daughter voting system to make Mom's decisions.

They did not like my reminder that Mom already had made her decisions.

Festering negativity erupted by phone call and tightly scrawled dark retorts. I delivered information, they delivered diatribes, outlined my faults and demanded their terms, continued urging Mom to change her mind.

I was unsettled by these attacks, by the incessant browbeating. I was beginning to feel depleted, especially when I found my emotions stupidly caught up hoping for approval where there was none to be had.

Not for the first time, I shared my frustrations with Mom. I could see concern in her eyes, but neither of us had an answer. I didn't want to lose my sisters or their help with Mom. I could be angry, frustrated and disappointed by them, but I needed tougher skin (or Kryptonite), because this was a stalemate: no end to their complaints, and I would never veer from Mom's plan.

Mom was getting older. The slow down and heart disease were progressing. We moved along through her personal storm.

Tip: The trust between the plan author and plan agent is vital because relationships and emotions are at play in plan maintenance. Response to any circumstance requires work and effort to figure out, but family dissension exacerbates everything. Acknowledging the possibility of family dissension ahead of time will neither resolve it nor make dealing with it any easier but naming the right people to handle your affairs, to trust with your directives, remains critically important.

Fortunately, Mom and I both remembered that she trusted me. That was good enough.

Hindsight: Should have realized how I wasted energy hoping they would change. The definition of insanity is doing the same thing over and over and expecting different results. Sometimes, I don't like the gift of hindsight.

15

Sea Change

"The best way out is always through." - Robert Frost

We were past that long season of major medical issues and I remember feeling fortunate. But warning signs of disinterest, the chronic blood pressure and ever-present heart disease remained as Mom's energy dropped further. There was less gallivanting with the boyfriend. She was worrying herself. And me, across the miles. It was not exactly shaky ground, but a dynamic of uncertainty became our norm.

> A daylong visit to the emergency room for chest pains, a daylong interruption of my daughter's wedding planning, had my husband sitting in hospital awaiting proof of heart

attack. But around 6 p.m., doctors sent Mom home. But she worried enough that I flew back down again, while Dr. A took an outpatient-under-anesthesia look at her repaired and pumping heart.

He shared good news: nothing wrong with the equipment, all valves and vessels performing properly. Senior anxiety? Why was Mom convinced something was wrong? I had seen the increased fatigue and lethargy. Despite reassurances, happy days weren't happening. What was it?

Dr. A reviewed the BP meds to make sure the recipe was right. I openly speculated that my beautiful mother was simply disheartened by high blood pressure and heart disease, aware that life was slowing down. Observing that shrinking personal vivre, I wondered if the private party girl was having a senior panic attack?

Heart disease is a progressive health issue for plenty of seniors, and Dr. A agreed with my armchair thoughts while my brain rolled onward glimpsing the heart disease highway, slower traffic stay to the right. If Mom was edging into the slow lane, I just hoped she wasn't being forced off the highway.

It was a bothersome fly in her ointment and mine.

Right this moment, however, I was also trying to solve a money mystery. Mom had been having trouble with her checking account, and with cashing checks. We decided to make sure she had a petty cash envelope in her house. Enough dollars for incidentals. A family friend and my daughter were enlisted to add a few twenties and smaller bills every couple of weeks.

Mom agreed that I should switch almost all remaining billing into electronic disbursement. Yet still, her checking account had been overdrawn. Twice. She had received worrisome bank notices. The boyfriend made Mom call me, confused and upset.

"I'm out of money! How could that happen?" She sounded frightened, demanded that I explain. Not to worry, I assured her. It must be a mistake. Her money was safe. She was not "out" of money. With electronic banking, I would see it to rights and figure out what had happened.

There was a problem, and it was not Mom.

One of the twins had written and cashed Christmas gift checks. **About a month early.** There wasn't enough money in Mom's checking account to cover that. A couple computer clicks on my end, a swiftly executed electronic transfer from savings resolved the issue, but calming Mom down took longer.

She was stuck on the scare of being broke, and despite reassurance to the contrary, terribly confused and angry that she couldn't keep this straight. She seemed doubly upset having to speak about it. I was angry.

The overdraft had uncovered a glitch in our operations. Mom's operating account and savings security had been working grandly, privately, but only if other people kept their hands away.

Apparently, my check cashing sister, (let's call her X), would need to know more about daily operations (the money), no matter how much privacy Mom wanted. I had not expected to explain the minutiae of *how* we handled Mom's funds, but neither had I *imagined* someone else helping themselves. I was being forced into sharing financial details. I would have to explain Mom's budgeting "safety net," savings versus operating accounts, and paying bills. I

> would also have to ask for "hands off" to Mom's checkbook and explain about the problem she created when she helped herself. My jaw clenched.
>
> The gist was this: Mom and I protected her cash flow *and* supported her independence as follows: Mom enjoyed the comfort of some cash in the house. Only one credit card. Most of her money safely elsewhere away from the risk of spending whims by Mom and/or boyfriend. No news flash, I was already managing money, keeping tabs on the ebb and flow of discretionary cash, keeping that small sum in checking. Click a button and move money *as needed,* while Mom had enough local, personal control to feel in charge.

Like writing out Christmas gift checks, *in a few weeks.* The method had worked for years until now. I hoped my sister would understand, but my gut already said otherwise. I wasn't looking forward to the call. No real surprise, it was ugly.

Something like this:

> ME: Hey, you know, I'm helping Mom handle her expenses, helping Mom keep her money safe. We had a problem here. She got overdrawn. It was Christmas checks. Kinda wish you had asked about that. Mom's money is not all in her checking account. I keep it low on purpose. Mom writes gift checks at Christmas, not a month before. Mom's got a lot of anxiety from you writing and cashing checks early.
>
> HER: Well, I didn't know. Mom has money, no big deal, right? You just think you have to control everything. I was trying to help, to get this done early. You think I can't do that?

> ME (already aware X had cashed out herself and her kids): You did this about a month early, right? That caused a problem. The money wasn't there. You know that I'm helping Mom, right? You should have told me, or asked, but you didn't. It would have been better if you had asked. Did you even ask Mom? Sorry, but you can't be doing that kind of stuff.

Ouch. Neither of us are happy. But X didn't regret her actions or apologize, choosing instead to complain about my control.

Emotions and relationships. Deal and then remember self-care—go to the beach!

> **Tip:** As agent and carer, you must handle unpleasant moments. Keep eyes on the moving parts. Expect moments when you have to take charge. Recognize that maintenance responsibilities mean you may have to remind others of your job.

Another New Year—2007

> Longer daily naps. Her noted lack of energy. More complaints over the regimen of medicines. Never a welcome exercise, taking medicine had become a confounding difficulty. Irregular. Why? How had pill taking become problematic?
>
> At the height of Mom's senior pill taking, there were 9 different medicines.... two or three as a blood pressure maintenance cocktail, a calcium supplement, a water pill, a digestive aid, a potassium supplement, baby aspirin, and she was still wearing an estrogen patch.

But she would not, or maybe she *could* not remember the daily regimen. She was tired of taking pills, that was a certainty. We brainstormed how to boost her dedication to those daily doses, how to ease medicine management. What might restore her regular dosing?

We bought a 7-day dispenser plastic case. It had potential. Then we bought a two-week version and another 7-day, precision for an entire month. My daughter would stop in to refill the tiny boxes when I was away.

But even with organization, no one could make those pills jump from their tiny cells on the right days and into Mom's mouth. If someone was there—me, my daughter, her sister, my sisters--a Tuesday box could get opened on Tuesday, and if someone was urging completion, Mom would take Tuesday's doses. Left on her own, it didn't happen. The boyfriend wouldn't pay any attention whatsoever, actually telling me he didn't believe much in medicine anyway.

His attitude prompted Mom to share a childhood impression. Her father had been a mind-over-matter Anglican whose children "weren't allowed" to be sick. He had held a dim view of medicine, and Mom would chuckle and nod, insisting that taking pills was against family policy.

The boyfriend suggested protein shakes and 5 o'clock margaritas as the viable alternative. You know, he says, a nice relaxing glass of wine and stop worrying about pills. He tells me Mom doesn't want to take them much less remember to think about it. What a guy.

Had she consciously or unconsciously decided she didn't want to take pills? Did surgeries and anesthesia contribute to unwillingness or forgetfulness? We both knew prescriptions had been ordered for her overall health and she wanted to try keeping up unless someone said differently. We decided to take the dispenser boxes out of the cabinet to sit front and center on the kitchen table, hoping a visual would improve the daily dosage dilemma.

It did not. Some days one or two pills were gone, possibly taken, but maybe moved, switched, dropped. No rhyme or reason. Taken or not. Heard the same from my daughter—refilling the dispenser boxes was never straightforward. I reconfirmed with Karen to set them up anyway. For now. But I began planning for a pill-taking discussion at the next visit with Dr. A.

In the midst of helping her grandmother with petty cash and pillboxes, my daughter had been planning her Florida destination wedding, and it was requiring a fair amount of back and forth, judging locations, sampling food, getting to know the fiancé. My Florida time increased that Spring, responding to rising maintenance responsibilities at Islander Court.

Observable further declines in daily living activities, a marked disinterest in health care (pills). More delay, less precision. Home alone during the day, no cards, no girlfriends, no boyfriend between breakfast and dinnertime. She wasn't using her swimming pool. She wasn't gardening. I watched her wander through the house.

We kept doctor appointments, paid bills, renewed house and auto insurance.

Yes, Mom is still driving. There is insurance, for her short and very infrequent forays to the local beach and grocery store, and for her boyfriend, the other driver. She owns a senior citizen special, 12-year-old blue Buick sedan, with 53,000 miles on the odometer. Going nowhere fast. I am her chauffeur when I'm there. I'm told the boyfriend drives around her aging Buick just fine, but those middle sisters have demanded it needs replacing under the guise of safety? They want something newer.

I suggest they rent a car when visiting. They can be safe *and* reimbursed. There's more to the car story later. Mom is not buying a new car. I lose more points with the devil twins.

Another ping on the caution sensor, with a new forgetfulness peppering Mom's days. She needs me to repeat a lot of things. With my head swimming in wedding details, I wonder what I may have forgotten to share? Does she ask because a detail has slipped her mind or because it never got there? The answer is delayed while the mother of the bride concentrates on wedding plans.

My sisters are urged to attend the big family party. One twin declines the invite over plans for a trip to Spain. (I feel a slightly guilty moment of relief.) Tee is all excited to come to Florida for the wedding. She and X will be doulas, extra hands to help Mom.

I rent three houses, one for the wedding party, one for us and another smaller bungalow nearby to accommodate Mom and her crew. I create an important job for the boyfriend. He will be the official "driver" getting Grammy to the wedding destination. He is near bursting with excitement. I'm near bursting with relief that I have solved how to transport Mom to the festivities without having to personally manage her needs while hosting a 4-day weekend celebration.

Drive south and get this party started.

Lots of family and friends spend time at the beach that

first day enjoying down time before official events. Oddly, I catch sight of Mom in a lightweight pajama robe walking hand in hand with her boyfriend down the sand. They are coming toward us. They are within 15 feet, oblivious. They do not stop.

At the rehearsal dinner, Mom is happy to sit with family and watch the mingling and table hopping as family and friends catch up. I hear someone asking the boyfriend how he fits into the "wedding party" and I hear his answer:

"Well, haha," he blusters, "I guess you could say I'm the step-grampa." He is beaming, enjoying the moment, fueled by ego and who knows what else.

I lean into the table of friends to gently make a correction.

"No, no, not a grampa at all," I smile. "This is my mother's boyfriend and official designated driver for the Grammy."

Mom's boyfriend moves on to chat up the Midland Ladies, a trio of my long-time girlfriends. Under cover of wedding conviviality, he is attempting heavy poolside flirting. Ann says she's married, hubby at home. Cathy has lucked out, doesn't catch his eye. He pitches a 180-degree spin toward Nancy, who deftly puts him off.

I hear this story several weeks later, and today, the Midland ladies and I still chuckle about his approach, their politeness, and Nancy's firm push off. **Remember the tip about humor!**

Another memory is not so funny. I am visiting the family table when I see Sister X toss a glass of water into Aunt Sue's face. X informs me Sue is talking about weight loss over dinner, and X has taken it personally. Tossing a glassful is her idea of retribution. Alarmed, I'm wiping Sue's face with

> a cloth, and glaring at my sister. Really? At my daughter's wedding? Disrespectful. Bad behavior. A cue to take Sue and myself away from that table. I ask her to sit with me for the remainder of the night, distancing ourselves. Mom is fortunately not paying attention.
>
> Mom arrives late for brunch the next day, and they all leave early, the designated driver in charge.
>
> I catch up with Mom a few days later and am struck immediately by two things: overall silence and confusion as we talk. There is more repetition than I can ever recall.
>
> "You just asked me that," I say.
>
> "What did you tell me?" she says back.
>
> So it goes. **Memory** questions have arrived. Ding ding.

More Gray matter

By Fall, there are moments when we are out to eat, when Mom is not eating but looking around and voicing opinions about various people within sight and hearing range. Beyond ordinary people watching. Audible commentary. Observations you might *think* to yourself, but now a live stream of thoughts being tossed into the air.

> "Those are such cute kids." (Harmless)
>
> "Oh, just look at that lady. Do you see? I can't imagine how someone would let themselves get that fat!" (Visual acuity, but so completely inappropriate).
>
> "Would you look at all that red hair? It needs a good brushing! Why doesn't she have it styled better?"
>
> Yikes! I don't remember ever hearing her make these kinds of pronouncements in public.
>
> "Mom, please. You might have a point, but you and I

> can't know what is going on for these other people. Let's just eat our lunch."
>
> "Well, I just can't believe it," she shakes her head about another obese woman. I remind myself to discuss both unfiltered expressive conversation and memory concerns, at the next doc appointment.
>
> We have our annual catch-up with Young Abe, and the bottom line remains status quo, reassurances that Mom's papers and life are in good order. She is comfortable, safe and her income is meeting her outflow.

But 2007 was ending with wacky unfiltered comments, too many repetitive conversations, and moments when neither of us could believe she had repeated the same question five times. If slow down and disinterest had been first alerts to Mom's changing picture, they had been replaced by streaming chatter, out of context disjointed thoughts, and trouble hanging onto answers.

Mom and I chuckled —a tiny, teeny bit--about her memory trouble as a new inconvenience, an old age affliction joke, CRS. *Can't remember shit.* She brought it up, aware of the problem, all right, but with her wit intact. Thank goodness for small mercies.

A regular checkup was scheduled for late January and the topics list was growing. The sisters and boyfriend remained adamant that everything was fine, but Mom and I knew otherwise. Her gardener friend agreed. Mom had been trying to pay Joni every time she saw her. Joni's mom had her own set of aging issues, and I took over paying Joni while we commiserated our mutual concerns in a growing friendship.

> **Tip:** Having someone to talk with who travels the same road can offer validation if not comfort.

I started a table notebook and mounted a medium-sized dry erase message board on a cabinet near the kitchen table.

Financially, the year ends like the last one, another banking peculiarity. I see a $12,000 withdrawal. Bells are dinging like a five-alarm blaze.

I get on the computer looking for a trail. Money wired to Louisiana. Sister X.

Mom has wired her $12,000 big ones. Mom has a right to do this kind of thing, of course. But it is money and X in one sentence--a bit of déjà vu. I cannot imagine Mom deciding to do this on her own, nor accomplishing it without someone's help.

It is from savings this time, not checking. Someone had been listening to me last year, but I need to get clear on why, and whether the money was coming back or not.

"You gave X a lot of money? Mom?" I ask.

"No. It was a loan."

"That's a big loan, Mom. What did she need that much for?"

"It was something to do with school, " she answers. "I think, but I don't know."

"Well, nice for you to do that. You have money and you can do that," I say, "and there is no worry because you have enough in your savings. Is she planning on paying you back?"

There is a long pause. I give her a minute. She is quiet. Then I asked a second time.

"No, I don't think so." She says it with a slight grimace. "But she gets that much less...at the end." Mom has worked out a gruesome explanation. Had X suggested it?

"Ok," I tell her. "Thanks for letting me know. I'll put that information in your financial records."

Through the sister grapevine, I hear later that this is about a new car, and nothing to do with school unless it requires driving. The not-so-secret transfer is out, and X "gets that much less at the end." Yikes. At the end of Mom's road, if there is anything left, I will be happy to remind her.

16

January 2008: Shoes Dropping Into Gray Matter

"Cry a lot, but laugh as well. It's how we survive." Vonni, in Maeve Binchy's <u>Nights of Rain and Stars</u>

I have flown in after New Year. The sisters have been here. It has been two months, and I'm not sure how it happens, but the measure of Mom's forgetfulness is more pronounced. Her petty cash envelope needs a refill. I know her bankers pretty well, and I work with my computer to resolve a third overdraft. Mom is flustered, cranky and angry with the whole episode because she can't figure out why or how she has made this money mistake again.

Pill boxes are worse than ever. Perpetual evidence of confused dosing. But at a glance there is a new medicine I know nothing about?

Odd. That extra pill. Somehow in my absence, Mom had gone to her general practitioner. Disconcerting news. I doubt she went alone. The GP prescribed heart medication completely without consult with Dr. A, the heart doc, who is *supposed to be* in charge here.

How does that happen?

I hasten to make an appointment with the GP.

Once there, I have a rather strong conversation as Mom's power of attorney, letting the GP know another physician is in charge of heart disease management, and that prescription she added was on top of others already in place. In the lilting voice of island speak, the GP asks for Mom to complete a 10-task mental status questionnaire.

Questions Mom should know.

What day is it? Who is President? What year? What time is displayed on the picture of the clock? Mom shows me the paper and asks for answers. I say the doctor wants Mom to answer what she can on her own. I say it is ok to leave some blanks if she doesn't know.

"I have never seen this from Jean," the disbelieving doctor says to me, scoring the results. Mom doesn't know what year it is, has several wrong answers, blank spaces and signs her maiden name, something she hasn't used in 60 years.

"She has not ever been this way." There is surprise in the Caribbean lilt and concern in the brown eyes. Somehow this woman, who has seen Mom regularly for several years (and obviously within the last two months), and suddenly today, Mom seems different?

The GP is not happy I have questioned her treatment, but I am not happy with her observation skills. Until today, I believe she has missed the *real condition* of her patient. The doctor's concern is genuine, and the simple memory test a fail. With my added nudge, the GP refers Mom for a brain scan and a neurology visit. Mom agreed.

The beginning of a detective mission. I think I am the only person in the doctor's office who knows that Mom and I will never see her again.

I mention this and more to her heart doctor several days later, during that regularly scheduled heart status appointment. We embark on a long conversation of forgetfulness, the GP mistakenly involving herself in his medical plan for Mom's heart, getting a neurology referral, Mom's lack of filter and the overall slowing down. We unravel the melee of prescriptions. He is careful with words but says the newly added script is *not indicated* and could even be detrimental. He agrees to look at reducing Mom's medications.

Together, we hoped the neurology referral will give some physical explanation for the mental lapses, the confusion, the marked disappearance of her short-term memory.

I go back to Mom's, toss out the errant prescription and plot test dates on her calendar. We talk our business through, both wanting answers. An MRI brain scan, and EKG, a carotid artery blood flow test. The jargon of medical detective work. Mom did not look concerned, seemed to shrug off these additional appointments, routine or daytime filler, I'm not sure. It would fill her days, along with beach visits and reading romance novels, and the boyfriend would fill her night hours.

But I made plans for an extended Florida stay. There would be plenty to keep us both busy.

17

Bend In the Road

"The best you can do is to keep going." - Marc Chernoff

We had been using the choices and decisions Mom had put into her life care plan here and there as we maneuvered through those first five years. Our partnership in processing daily needs had been masterful, mostly private, and successful through major surgeries, beyond family stressors, and managing those uncomfortable, recurring financial glitches. Meanwhile, she and I had made progress over all that time in getting more detail into her operational toolbox.

I thought we might actually have arrived at that point in time that Mom's future plan had been written for. She wasn't handing off the baton, but we were holding hands on a route way past time when I was merely observing. Testing was the next pit stop.

The big lab was in a strip mall I had driven past countless times and never noticed. Comfy chairs, plenty of magazines, large art pieces, soft music, all a gentle counterpoint to the busy serious business I could feel in the atmosphere. A place where lives changed.

> **Tip:** Stay mindful and aware of what's happening. Learn what you need to know. Continue building the information bank and LAUGH when you can, but cry when you need to.

An Uptick in the Detective Mission

Mom and I were stepping further into uncharted territory. We had a good grip on the life plan, but *how* to proceed involved a dose of courage and more seat of the pants learning. Some people continued to ignore what Mom and I knew to be a shifting landscape, but we trekked on, gently navigating, conscious of our mutual need for follow through. I moved into Mom's seasonal rental that winter, hoping proximity would provide Mom additional moral support. Besides, I needed more than a few cyclonic intervals to see us through the laundry list of doctors, follow-ups, and waiting rooms. We held to an afternoon beach regimen, our mutual love of sky and water grand reassurance that life was wonderful, and we were still riding along.

We surmised that life with Mom's plan had been a waiting game until this point, and we'd been pretty smart, learning along the way. Her heart doctor contended that years of chronic high blood pressure rampant in the family genes, was the permanent marker for current issues. We were on that path Poet Robert Frost described as diverging in the woods.

TIP: Anyone on the care path must seek moments to recharge, as in going to the beach. Living consciously with joy and being mindful of humor wherever one finds it is an ingredient in the recipe for success.

> We visited friends, sat in the sunshine. We grocery shopped, Mom zipping through Publix in a motorized cart, disappearing aisle to aisle, enjoying the drive. If I lost sight of her whereabouts, I usually found her looking at wine, not produce. Why not? She was never too keen on veggies or too much fruit in her diet.
>
> Family visited. A friend stayed with me away from the snow and cold of Michigan while I worked at a weekly chore list and spent social time with Mom enjoying simple things—a haircut, pedicure, manicure, beach picnic. We were managing, but she kept asking the same questions and I kept repeating the same answers every day, multiple times. Getting past her confusion with these Q&A moments when she couldn't hang onto any answer, was a blend of compassion, coping and a few chuckles when we couldn't keep rhythm with it.....

Markers

> Life carried on. A trip to the store. New shoes. Changing furnace filters. I shared her paperwork and our partnership in new places as we waited for answers.
>
> I remember telling myself Mom's health status couldn't be too serious if there was no sense of urgency in the medical

community.

But I watched her tangled processing increase while immediate short-term memory nearly disappeared. I worked in her garden and listened. Topics jumped around, rife with questions. Mom wondering about her mobile home—did she own it? Did she still go there? Where were her sisters? Occasionally she wanted confirmation that my dad had died.

Each time she couldn't grasp an answer, I worried how to assist, working hard to be specific, truthful. If not pleasure, I felt satisfaction when, after four or five repeats, Mom's brain either snagged an answer, or she was comforted that my answers that had stayed the same. Calm repetitions assured her.

Meanwhile, her verbal filter was permanently in the off position--Mom had no problem telling me not to wear certain clothes ever again, how much she detested orange paint on houses we drove past, and how much she disapproved of my dark toenail polish. Some of it was downright funny.

Laugh! It Is a Healthy Reprieve from the Murk.

She continued spending nights with the boyfriend. I was living in Florida for weeks not days, providing myself time to update the general to-do list, keeping Mom's attorney informed, getting a needed affidavit, another opinion. I assembled her tax papers for filing and that appointment was refreshingly routine. She appeared interested and attentive, even if I did the talking; her familiar, beautiful penmanship easy and evident in her signatures.

Over the course of a year, Mom had been an emotionally distraught travel without a passport, repeatedly worried and angry about her money, confused by pills. She had withdrawn further, was repetitious, frustrated by short term memory challenges, unable to secure details that seemed to swirl just out of reach.

The milder temperatures of Florida Spring were softening the Gulf breezes when we finally waded into the test schedule that we hoped would provide answers and a fix. Then we finally had that first neurology appointment, hopeful about a detailed interpretation of test results.

The chief neurologist for a local hospital was our referral. If anyone had answers, he might. A soft-spoken man who shared his own family's experience with dementia, Dr. H explained Mom's brain imaging indicated damage over several years.

He says he is pleased to see Mom has me with her for support, her information partner. He acknowledges my "carer stress" about repetitive questions, processing problems and Mom's general lack of follow through. I sit to the side while he interviews Mom.

His consult notes are sprinkled with evaluative adjectives explaining the MRI array of red and yellow imaging. The mapping offers evidence of what had been happening-- multiple moments when brain cells were harmed by oxygen deprivation. Not destroyed but affected.

Ministrokes, over multiple years.

Collect a few mini-strokes and there is sensory impairment. The damage is physical proof which explains

Mom's recent memory issues, confusion with pills, time and money, and her unfiltered chatter. A lifetime of chronic high blood pressure and progressive heart disease did not help matters, raising questions about a daunting senior future.

But the scans show the strokes are tiny. Maybe as few, he says, 11 or 12, or as many as 20, but small tissue damage, a "medical measure" of small, much better than a big stroke. And that, he says, is Mom's largest future concern, the major risk of significant permanent impairment or death from something larger.

Causes? Natural course of health events in individuals with high blood pressure, heart disease.

Could they be dated? Yes. Within the last four years, after bypass surgery.

Is this because she has high blood pressure? Possibly.

Treatable? Not really.

Impacted by alcohol? A reduction in consumption couldn't hurt.

Is this because she isn't taking medications regularly? Or because she has too many medicines? Not answerable.

Is there a cure? No. But some skill recovery is possible, some memory improvement over time, *if* she could remember. Duh. Maybe brain game exercises.... maybe.

Will it get worse? Time will tell.

Final diagnosis? Mini-strokes, he says, not cancer. Nor will he name it Alzheimer's. Just aging brain functional issues. Monitor and revisit. Only way to tell if Mom was recovering would be by watching and following up. Put a mark on the page and check back.

High alert. All those little changes I had witnessed, had created what would be this new baseline. But there is some good news.

"General appearance: well developed, well nourished, in no distress. ...Mental status: awake, alert, oriented. Immediate memory normal, recent memory 2/3 with one intrusion, 3/3 with choices, remote memory normal, speech, repetition and comprehension normal, names fingers and objects well but slight trouble with parts of objects...Motor: normal power throughout; Reflexes: symmetrical..."

Diagnostic observations are specific:

"Assessments 1. Memory loss(primary) 780.93. 2. Small vessel cerebrovascular diseases – 437.0. "There is a wide differential diagnosis. Alzheimer's and cerebrovascular are #'s 1 and 2 statistically. The dilemma in a person of presumed above normal intelligence [Mom] is to be able to *document a decline.*" (emphasis added)

Translation: Mom is doing reasonably overall, for a person of her age and condition, while something else, possibly more serious, could be going on upstairs. A waiting game.

Gray matter front lobe losses to watch and investigate. Meanwhile, talk to a psychologist for a more complete understanding of current treatment methodology that might temper Mom's condition. Come back in a few months. Oh, and by the way, schedule PET brain scan to take another look inside.

We leave this friendly quiet office and do our own follow up in joyful life. Beach time. We sit in sunshine and sand, allowing Gulf breezes to blow away a downer of a doctor visit. We take full advantage of the shoreline to replenish ourselves, and to dispel, at least for these immediate moments, that sense of being lost in the fog on a winding

> road on a long dark night.

If I'd had that dementia parameter list, Mom would have been a close fit. Memory issues, communication changes, basic reasoning (tracking conversations and making sense), concentration and visual perception. We knew what had happened, but because we were managing, this chief of neurology had voiced no overt concerns.

I expected my level of assist would likely increase in all areas-- activities of daily living, finances, mail, household operations and care, bill paying, medical management, garden upkeep, even pool maintenance and fixing sliding glass doors.

But what did caring for her memory mean? For the short term, for every day, for the long term? Questions like how long, how much worse, could she continue to live alone flitted around my brain. We had a new reality of diminished brain function, an unknown calendar and I had a smallish knot of fear. Could she regain lost skills? Was there anything we could do? How much time did she, did we have?

Make a psychology appointment to learn more.

> As my gut squeezed up another notch, we had some good long hugs and I reminded Mom how she had successfully written her plan for just this time. She didn't have to worry. She had already answered questions about what she wanted, and she had her life to lead. I would be there. She could trust me. (But in the shorthand of texting, OMG)
>
> I remembered Robert Frost's "best way out..." being *through*, while I concentrated on Mom's personal comforts and home support. The dry erase board was getting daily use to share a smile or a detail, and the notebooks filled with a record of mundane day to day. The presence of written

memory aids helped to mediate symptoms.

We were travel companions on this uncharted highway, with indications that things might get bumpy, but there were four hands on the wheel. Mom was still driving, at least for now.

I did the dirty work of sharing the gray matter report with my list of loved ones, and the attorney, and made the psychologist appointment, another doctor to her health regimen.

Beyond Mom putting in her name and sometimes her address, I was filling out all papers at each doctor appointment and Dr. B, the psychologist, had a hefty sheaf worth. The referral to that psycho-social interview was another "senior aging" educational seminar. I held on to signs that testing had pointed to "mini, not major strokes." He talked to both of us, suggesting mental response testing for a behavioral baseline…doctor speak for a present status report.

Because my presence might be a distraction, Mom agreed to speak with him privately for the interviews and assessments.

Like Dr. H, Dr. B seemed a gentle, friendly soul. We took his calm and distinct lack of urgency as another good sign. His interviews with Mom might take a few sessions.

18

Time for Help at Home

During the months of doctor visits, brain scans and our experience with Mom's confusion, forgetfulness, task follow through failures, and erratic pill taking, I had begun thinking it might be time to consider adding some friendly in-home support, especially when I headed back north in a few weeks. The gardener/friend was in the neighborhood and could be counted on her to keep the house cared for, but I wanted another resource, another frequent set of eyes on Mom for safety.

I liked the comfortable *feel* of professional in-home support. A personal assistant could be both support and diversion for Mom, and impartial observer for me. I shared this idea with Sister X who surprised me with a rare endorsement. She agreed immediately that this was "a good idea to get Mom used to having people in the house."

Was that actual progress with my sister? Adding supported home care was already my goal but it felt even better as a family agreement.

There are plenty of agencies and people who do this kind of work. Mom and I were fortunate to find a local home care placement agency just blocks away. We had a visit with their care marketing person who discussed levels of available supports and scheduled her first home help, a four-hour time block to try it out. Tess, a sweet-natured Filipina certified nursing assistant, would start as a one-day-a-week companion, a driver and a general all-around household Gal Friday. Tess was taking nursing classes. By law, she could not administer meds, but she could remind Mom about her medicines and more importantly, be a warm body household presence.

> I left Florida at the end of six weeks feeling relieved. The boyfriend was there, I knew my sisters would visit now that I was gone, and Mom's new care initiative had begun. Mom would have that helpful visitor each week to assist. Tess would take Mom to the series of psychological assessment appointments and I would return for the results consult in a few weeks.
>
> An unsettling thing happened. The devil twins tried to intercept evaluation results before Mom and I had our follow-up. Tess had made a heads-up phone call to me because she knew it didn't feel right. (I'm not sure which twin was in the doctor's office trying to get Mom's results). It was a disturbing intrusion. I knew Mom did not want what one of them was trying to do. For the first time I

waved power of attorney and medical surrogacy papers in a doctor's office, (well, actually over the phone, long distance), but sufficient to intervene on Mom's behalf.

Wasting my own energy and emotion, I tallied a distasteful list of "sisterly dissension." Cataloguing my necessary intervention was like bumping an already sore bruise. I had said no about buying Mom a new car. I'd made financial corrections. Keeping them informed upped their anger. Foiling their attempt at securing medical data was unpleasant. They had resumed badgering Mom to change her directed giving. Or maybe they had never stopped. Tess heard them.

They wanted Mom's diamond rings, for their daughters. They had told Mom that Tee, for whom those rings were intended, was planning to sell them on the internet. (Tee never had these intentions, by the way.)

It seemed if I thought things were hard already, those girls had managed to raise the "ick" bar. Was it their true nature to meddle and make things worse? My sisters cared about Mom, but I failed to understand how a sneaky attempt to steal her psych evaluation, coupled with this repeat campaign to grab Mom's rings meant "care." It all left an ugly taste in my mouth. I didn't like feeling this way, sadly aware that these middle sisters seemed committed to making an already stressful job more difficult. To say I was frustrated is an understatement.

I would raise my guard, again. Further. I asked Mom's attorney to send a message, add his reassurance for Mom's plan, the legal voice at Mom's back. I wanted them informed and on the team, but on Mom's terms, not theirs.

***

The rescued psychologist's report was a 3-page neuropsychologic evaluation, a narrative incorporating neurology notes, our discussions, Mom's private interview and psycho-social assessment results. Multiple scales--like Wechsler Adult Intelligence, a geriatric depression ranking scale, the California Verbal Learning Test and others. Mom and I met with him in August to go over results.

Dr. B delivered that descriptive baseline, but he shared it gently, an honest conversation that focused on abilities, not deficiencies. Our meeting was devoid of *why* or *how,* instead gauging the present state of Mom's mind. I read along.

He had found her "fluent and topic focused" but "depressed and tearful...she worries about her future." Sounded pretty normal if you ask me.

Was it strokes, or because she had bumped her head as a kid in an auto accident, or fallen in a Nashville restroom? Was a past habit of cigarette smoking, which she couldn't remember, causal? Did hip surgeries and heart surgery and anesthesia contribute? But "how" didn't matter.

"She is noted to occasionally repeat herself...direction is often needed," but Jean appears "free of hallucinations, delusions and thought disorder." Good news.

His summary incorporates this impression: Jean is "experiencing mild but significant cognitive impairment... she performs poorly on measures of orientation.... some measures had to be discontinued due to confusion....in conjunction with reported history of progressive decline and maternal history of Alzheimer's...is unfortunately suggestive of an early Alzheimer's dementia."

There it was. A doctor putting the dreaded A into Mom's

> diagnosis. If that wasn't heavy duty enough, I had one more page to read followed by the sensitive task of additional private talks with Mom.

Wait a minute. Did my grandmother have Alzheimer's Disease? Had my mother mentioned that to Dr. B., or had he seen this single word descriptor listed along with pneumonia and heart failure on Mom's family medical history sheet?

Did it run *in the family?* Why didn't I know more about my grandmother's circumstances?

Probably because Gramma had died almost 25 years ago, when I had been a young mother caught up with a new baby, a four-year-old and a third grader, busily packing up for another relocation. I remembered hearing that Gramma died from pneumonia, but nothing about memory problems.

That was back in 1985, the year the Alzheimer Association was founded.

> Here was a psychologist suggesting Mom could be genetically predisposed to Alzheimer's. Yikes. My brain shot forward like a bullet. Would I be the next generation? It cranked up my own worries as I returned to the third page.
>
> I read through the recommendations:
>
> - continued neurologic follow-up
>
> - a repeat cognitive evaluation in one year
>
> - the suggestion to join a local support group
>
> - directions that Mom's "daily functioning may be best if she follows a simple, structured and predictable routine. She may enjoy activities that draw upon preserved skills.... "

- Unfortunately, "given her significant confusion, she is considered unsafe to drive."
- Get her hearing tested.
- Consider an anti-depressant to the extent that depression continues.

The foggy brain would not get better, it would get worse. Results stated what I already knew: we had been living through initial decline, all those vague little unsettling signals for the last five years.

We had an answer we didn't want, a sobering bottom line. And, yet despite the doctor's pronouncements, Mom said as always, that she felt "pretty good."

I smiled, grateful for that. We were okay for now. We could hold on to that.

As for getting behind the wheel? Dr. H was definite: Mom needed to stop driving herself around. Period. I had been driving her myself for years, and I'd been worried about her forays behind the wheel in my absences. I had dreaded, absolutely dreaded, asking Mom to hand over the car keys. I was emotionally drained by the topic and depth overall but gratified the doc's authority had saved me from being the bad guy about driving.

How did she handle it? Without challenge or complaint. Just. Quit. Driving.

Then Mom added she would be okay "playing Miss Daisy." Overly moved by her clever comeback, I savored that sweet compliance. I would promote the psychologist's suggestion for a "simple, structured and predictable routine," and I could also add more home care support time. Mom's income would cover the additional cost. The security it provided was a bargain. What a day!

Continuing Onward

With the well-seasoned Fab Four holding us up, I started looking for a nearby seasonal rental that would give me my own space and proximity during the coming winter, taking a lease on a small bungalow that offered yearlong flexibility to come and go. I predicted doing that more and more.

Mom continued living happily and safely at home. She had the boyfriend and a second home care support day. I was so thankful that her assets allowed for this safety.

19

Life Lessons In the Trenches

*N*ancy and Patty Reagan had it right. In <u>The Long Goodbye</u>, a daughter's intimate accounting of the prolonged slipping away of her father, you can read about their daily witness to the former President's lessening intensity of thought, diminishing physical ability, and the constant of increasing care responsibilities. President Reagan had Alzheimer's.

> With the neurologist one day, we found ourselves in a waiting room with a jovial man who kept trying to talk with us. His speech was clear but his conversation was a confusing jumble of thoughts and disjointed sentences. Mom was

visibly unnerved by this, so I switched chairs and engaged her face to face, blocking the visual swamp of fragmented chatter, glad to perform as human shield. Her own doctor visit noted additional decline in brain functioning, but at least she wasn't talking nonsense with strangers or driving herself home afterwards.

What day was it, who was president? What did you eat for breakfast today? How are you feeling? Did Mom want to try out some memory drugs? Mom nodded as he described the puzzle. Three available drugs, and a suggestion to try them one at a time. Each drug had shown *some* success in *some* patients by offering *some* stabilizing of memory, *some* lessening anxiety and *some* delay in disease progression.

Key word: **some**. Plenty of patients had found the side effects too much.

"I'll give it the ol' college try," Mom quipped. Hooray for wit and humor, a glimmer of her old self. Yet I could not possibly imagine adding another prescription to that troubled pill regimen.

Dr. H also suggested family and friends could benefit from reading more about what was happening for Mom. He knew one book that really laid out all sorts of symptoms, issues, frustrations and data for patients and loved ones. It was pretty lengthy, not some quick read. Was I interested?

Yes. I bought a copy of <u>The 36-hour day. A Family Guide to Caring for Persons with Alzheimer Disease, Related Dementias and Memory Loss.</u> And then I ordered four more copies for sisters and boyfriend.

Drive me to the beach, please!

More Pill Problems

Those smiling television ads of success to the contrary, Mom's endeavor to add memory drugs to her pill regimen was replete with very difficult side effects. There was no memory upgrade, no smile. Confusion and anxiety actually grew. Mom had bouts of debilitating vomiting, diarrhea and general body malaise. Those drugs might buy time for some people, but they were not working for Mom. Adding extra miserable moments was not acceptable.

One dreary winter morning, as Mom valiantly tried the final drug option, I arrived to find her in a dark house, pale, weepy, miserable. For starters, I couldn't believe the boyfriend had left her in that unhappy condition. But hey, remember, he wasn't into medicine?

She looked awful, her skin sallow. Stricken, worried. Said she felt horrible. I could see the furrowed brow, her already small frame sinking, disappearing into the middle of the sofa. Fear stared back at me from watery gray green eyes. I prayed silently for a day sooner than later, when she might lose the awareness of this awful part of her road.

"What is happening to me? I don't understand it." She began to cry.

Then her bowels let loose, as if everything released with my arrival. Her overall upset, the mess and our somber mood matched the gloomy weather. I helped her up, supporting her carefully, walking slowly into the bedroom, my gentle arm and calm voice masking my own quaking insides. It looked pretty bad to me.

"Come on, we'll get you cleaned up," I said, cheerfully as I could muster. "We can fix this. Hot shower, and you will feel better."

She was nearly immobile. I helped her undress and clean up, painfully aware that Mom had dropped down several rungs on anybody's comfort scale since attempting these drugs. There was way too much mental anguish, zero improvement in daily confusion, and rocketing anxiety.

Definitely not the quality of life she wanted. "We" would stop trying these memory remedies.

There was a near immediate turn in mood when Mom went off the last trial medicine. She was back to happy even with a faulty memory.

But everything was getting more complicated. My expanding file was growing. I worked to keep up, once more updating the medical information sheet, removing medicines I had put on the list just weeks earlier.

I scheduled the care company to add another weekday block of time to Mom's care schedule. I asked the gardener friend if she wanted to add household cleaning to Mom's support and I knew it was time to remove Mom's biggest complaint. She would be happiest to stop taking pills. All pills.

I thought about how to do that while packing up my Pennsylvania house. We were moving back to Michigan.

Growing Dependence

I left Florida in late Spring and Mom's annual anxiety about her heart health ramped back up the charts. Chest pains prompted a hospital admittance and just two weeks later I flew back. Real or imagined, indecipherable anxiety in Mom's challenged brain had taken her to the emergency room seeking relief or reassurance-

-a hospital checkup might provide what her own brain and my absence could not.

> Dr. A performed a heart catheterization to check the equipment. I arrived at the hospital and noticed a nasty L-shaped wound on her leg, held together with a clear bandage. A purple gash that looked like it should have had stitches. She shrugged me off, saying something about catching it on a car door. Ouch!
>
> All function was normal, so what had put her in hospital? Phantom health concerns? Anxiety over increasing brain fog, or me leaving the neighborhood? The upswing in unease was becoming a regular spring event. I also knew the boyfriend and my sisters were in her ears. Had those messages added to Mom's mental havoc?
>
> Mom wanted to go home, resume her life at Islander Court. I wanted her to go home too. But it was clear Mom was having troubles during my absences. And I couldn't stay. We brainstormed the dilemma.
>
> I wanted to be there for her, and I was, but I lived most of my life 1,200 miles away. Neither of us wanted the upheaval of moving her somewhere for more support. Frankly, if a stranger asked Mom about her life, I was certain she would rank living at home with her boyfriend as most important, no matter what. And just maybe, my oversight happened to be her comfort factor.
>
> I found Dr. A after rounds, hoping he could weigh in about how to proceed.
>
> Mom's ongoing complications with heart disease and Alzheimer's would continue, he said, adding that she would die one day from one, the other or both.
>
> I had questions about what could be done for additional

safeguards?

1. Was he willing to become her primary care physician since this was so much about her heart, despite the Alzheimer's? I watched him think this through. He agreed. (You know that term: flooded with relief?)

2. I apprised him of side effects and failure with Alzheimer's medicines, plus Mom's overall dislike for pill taking. I recited her wishes against being over-medicated; he had his own copy of Mom's medical directives. I noted her primary resolve for comfort care and her standing order to put quality of life above prolonging it. I watched him think through what I was getting at, but he agreed to systematically terminate Mom's drug regimen, pill by pill, down to zero.

3. He noted "family interference" on top of health questions.

4. I asked if he thought it was time for hospice.

"Hospice usually won't get involved unless a patient with these kinds of diseases has six months or less to live," he explained. "I think your mom has more than six months, but I think we all could benefit from their evaluation. Hospice monitoring and support can be a good thing. I think making the referral would be ok."

I brought Mom home from the hospital with the understanding that Dr. A was requiring additional home support for her to continue living independently. Hospice could provide that. We met with an assessment team and Mom signed herself in. I co-signed her paperwork.

As that meeting finished, I had a first glimpse of hospice reality.

"Boy, you're good," said Nancy, the social worker, patting my shoulder. These hospice social workers are touchy feely people, and she was complimenting how I had explained adding hospice involvement to Mom's home team. Reassurance for everyone. I told her it was nothing but the truth. Seriously.

For Mom to live at home right now, after her latest trip to the hospital, Dr. A wanted someone regularly checking in to assure her heart was okay. I wanted someone in there, too, especially after I went home. No matter what the idea of bringing in hospice sounded like, we all should think of it as extra help. Mom could rest assured, relieved by hospice's additional care support.

I told the social worker that Mom was in charge, but how we both appreciated the add-on care for our comfort levels, no matter if this sparked disagreement or problems with her boyfriend or other family.

Nancy answered with a voice seasoned by experience. Her eyes were smiling kindly.

"I've seen a lot in almost 15 years of hospice work. All kinds of people working through all kinds of situations with their loved ones, and you did a good job here. Your mom understands just what we are doing. Supporting her, like you are. That alone will help her feel better.

"But difficult people?" She laughed. She laughed??

"They're just part of the territory. They don't get better

in difficult times. Although wouldn't that be nice? Nope," she concluded, closing her folder, eyes twinkling. She cocked her head to look me directly in the eye. "They just get worse."

Not exactly the news I was hoping for! I needed to stop nurturing my deluded, ludicrous hope that Mom's decriers, actually my decriers, would ever come around.

Here was a professional *in the business* shooting it through with holes. Cringing, my heart knew she spoke the truth. If a difficult situation worsens, why should anyone expect that dealing with an already difficult person would get easier? Absurd question.

But for the next 90 days, at least, I would spend summer up north while Mom got a lot of individualized personal home care. Reinforcements for support. A boost of comfort, security and relief for us both from private duty and Mom's newest health support team member, hospice.

Pay attention! Feel the aah! I left Florida without that sick feeling in the pit of my stomach. Mom's private care management hours and the extra oversight from Hospice was already helping me breathe easier. I would check once more in June, when Bob and I had planned a brief visit to move into that pet friendly rental bungalow before my own summer respite could begin in Michigan.

> **TIP:** do whatever necessary to bring comfort and calm to hard days.

Changes in the Terrain

Eight weeks later, we were driving back to Florida hauling a trailer of furniture, when I got one of the most eerie sensations, a telepathic alert. It was Aunt Sue, somehow, front and center. In my consciousness. So weird. I was really looking forward to seeing her in a day or two. Was that it? She wanted me to call her and I was planning on it.

But why the sudden urge? Should I? Now? I would be there tomorrow. I didn't call.

We had been on the road for an hour the next morning when I took a sunrise call from my daughter. Bad news. Terrible news. I would not be talking to Aunt Sue that day or any other day except telepathically from now on. I was too late and it was incredibly sad.

My dear aunt had quit her road, ended her life with a suicide bullet to the brain. Worse, she had driven to my mother's house, to finish herself on Mom's front porch. The awful story had me wondering if Sue's heartbreaking finale was in order to be found sooner, instead of rotting silently in her condo.

Karen phoned from Mom's house where she was finishing up with the sheriff, the boyfriend and her confused grandmother. Deputies had draped the scene. When investigators left, Karen hired a medical cleaning crew. I needed to call my cousin in Colorado, and Mom's brother. We would arrive in hours.

I could not remember the last time they had seen each other, but now Mom's baby sister was gone permanently. Did not want to be a burden, the note said. On my last visit, Sue had lamented her aloneness, acknowledged losing too many important people to death or couplehood.

I knew more. I knew about sharp sibling dynamics in Sue's generation. Sue's childhood moniker had been Sassy Susan. (I guess the family had a thing for descriptive nicknames.) It hinted at Sue's manner, yet I catalogued a lifetime of Sue's personal survivor moments and kindnesses towards me. She had endured loss in childbirth, persevered after divorce, lived through estrangement and reconciliation with her children, struggled with aging parents, conquered breast cancer, had grieved the loss of two sisters (one still living), and battled, but perhaps not beaten, depression.

How had she come to this, how had she rationalized her final act? It wasn't fair to anyone, but I could only get my head around it one way.

Sue had decided to be done. Finished. She was in the wind that morning as we crossed the Florida border....a strong lady decidedly choosing her own departure date. She had put her affairs in order the preceding Fall, reconciled with adult children. Said I had too much on my own plate to worry about her. Told me she felt good about all she and my cousin had put together. It occurred to me now, to wonder just when she had begun planning her exit.

I yelled at Mom's boyfriend for calling my 27-year-old daughter to identify the body. I yelled that he did not call me when they woke up that morning and stepped outside to retrieve the newspaper. It was grief yelling, and I was exasperated.

I picked up my cousin at the airport. He had work to do, get his two sisters to Florida, conclude an investigation, speak with American Burial, plan a memorial luncheon.

Quietly, I did my own detective work. The weekend

before, Sue had visited old haunts, seen her circle of friends. The few people we had in common thought she purposely had made a weekend goodbye circuit. From the route, it appeared she may have looked for me. My heartache became a reminder to pay attention to telepathy, that timing is indeed everything.

I was close enough to believe I recognized her determination. I knew she had no intention of waiting to finish like her mother or older sister in a nursing home, nor as victim to any gamble with disease, especially not the dementia currently entangling her sister, Jean. Her terms, I thought. If it could help at all, I would share that thought with the cousins.

Purposely keeping the boyfriend uninvited, Bob and I brought Mom to the memorial. We remembered Sue through stories, laughs and photos while a summer storm raged on the bay, sheets of rain battering the big windows. I described the strength I had always seen. The spirit. My genuine pleasure for our connection. It was what I could give them, and myself, in such tragedy.

A group of us took the dissolvable urn, hidden inside a cooler, for a last ride to the beach. The all-day soaker had finally quit, leaving behind a summer wind, choppy waves and tumbling clouds. Cousin Steve carried Sue's remains waist deep into rough water, coming out empty-handed a few moments later. Glowing golden rays of sunshine chose that moment to streak down through cloud breaks, the dark sky ablaze, reflected in shimmering chop.

We all saw it. A joyful reception from the heavens. Sue's daughter thanked me and my family for being so connected in Sue's life. Said I had been the daughter she couldn't be.

> Sue was gone, but oddly enough, she was with Mom now, more than she had been in years. Almost daily Mom spoke of her sister, wondered where she was, the elusive truth swirling at the edges of Alzheimer's. The tragic finale remained out of reach in the tangled synapses that kept her asking for Susan's whereabouts.
>
> No doubt loss was there, and we missed her. But I think she was already hanging indefinitely with Mom, there in the realm beyond human experience.

Hospice helpers came in to the house all summer long and called me in September with a good news—bad news conversation: Ninety days of support were nearly over. Mom was too healthy to continue their oversight. Hospice would terminate visits, with a strong safety recommendation to step up private duty. I could comply.

I learned that people do, in fact, "graduate from Hospice," sometimes more than once.

Thanks again, Nancy.

20

On Guard: 2008-2010

"If you are going through Hell, keep going." Winston Churchill

We were trundling along as Autumn arrived. Hospice support and increased daytime care was my Linus blanket--keeping Mom safe, clean, engaged. Cared for. And yes, Mom's boyfriend gratefully covering her nights.

But summer respite ended with Hospice stepping away and storm warnings from the private managed care company. Private care had been the lead, "managing" in my absence, and was now reporting something sinister going on inside Islander Court that definitely did not model the "simple quiet routine" Mom's psychiatrist had prescribed.

The aides and the nurse manager overheard disturbing

exchanges: my sisters boldly badgering Mom about property and plan. No longer surprised by what had become regular drama, I am simply saddened by continuing reports about people who bring malcontent upon a sick woman.

Mom endured this unconscionable war against her status quo—the sisters have been heard urging Mom to change her will, fire her attorney and fire me too. Put themselves in charge and it was still about gifting Mom's rings to their daughters. They complained I'm too bossy, home care levels unnecessary, and that Mom's attorney was not doing a good job, all while lauding their own wonderful selves. They have tried, directly and repeatedly, to get care staff *and* management to side with them, especially over the rings.

It is their most atrocious low to date.

The care company owner telephoned to warn me of a takeover plot! As a veteran of too many care controversies that sometimes necessitated her testifying in court, Ruth says she's had an alarming run-in with Mom's devil twins. She believes her agency's defense of Mom's rightful and long-standing personal choices, especially about those rings, has soured already poor relations with my sisters further.

Ruth echoed my worry over what damage their cruel verbal dialog might be adding to Mom's emotional state and warned of a double whammy--unhealthy consequences for Mom, and a serious load of grief for us all, if it cannot be stopped. She wanted the attorney involved *yesterday,* and Mom's car gone pronto.

Because, she says, loyal ears had picked up something else. Whether despair by disease or mental barrage, Mom had announced she wants to go into the garage and turn on the car. Carbon monoxide. By law, Ruth had to share that.

> Two pre-emptive strikes are urged. I lean on the paper foundation and call the attorney alerting him to the care owner's story and requesting speedy legal intervention. Eric is worried on Jean's behalf. Aware of the decline, Eric believes his client is vulnerable--not mentally able to pursue making changes in her will, and insufficiently clear headed to manage without me. He would put a few words together. I was hoping for a strongly worded "cease and desist" letter.
>
> Ruth said Sister X had also requested an independent evaluation and we could diligently comply. We both believed an independent medical consult, overnight surveillance at Islander Court, would document Mom's disease and significant incapacitation. An independent onlooker would totally support our stand against any changes to Mom's legal plan, an outcome that would backfire on the sisters.
>
> I talked with Mom about the trust between us, and our confidence in her plan made long ago. We don't have to worry about daughters who disagree or want changes. I told Mom I don't like how my sisters behaved, or the lies they've told about the rings.
>
> Then I reminded Mom to feel safe and secure. She nodded when I said that. It has always boiled down to Mom's decisions and our shared mission. We are in sync. I knew she trusted me. On task, Mom quipped some little thing about watching out for devil twins, crinkling her eyes, laughing in the face of outrage.

I'm serious. How could I make that up? I drafted Eric a few talking points:

> "Due to recent difficulties, I want a strong tone...try to halt

future problems with my sisters who jeopardize my mother's care plan. Please draft a letter……detail…..

1. HISTORY AND LEGAL RIGHTS: Dated and legal documents prepared for your client, Mom, designating living will, medical surrogacy and power of attorney when she was a healthy senior citizen.

2. A statement addressing the legal binding nature of these documents and Mom's client contract…. all which cannot be altered, rescinded or replaced, because she is no longer competent—as cited in documentation from three doctors, and an RN nurse advocate….

3. Information on the sale/disposition of the car as a safety concern…and as a liability…..

4. The availability of transportation…….other sources: home health agency, transport service or boyfriend's vehicle.

5. Communicate that Mom's resources can/will be used to rent vehicles for future family visits which include home care/support….

6. Communicate the professional/medical recommendations of her Life Care Plan:

a. Keeping her home with additional daytime support and care management. Resources adequate for 5 to 7 years……

b. Asking all family and the companion to withhold from Mom their own personal disagreements with the Power of Attorney, toward the plan, one another, or the situation, because of the emotionally damaging risk to a person with Alzheimer's.

c. In the spirit of family cooperation to help Jean live out her life at Islander Court as she has directed: YOU, the attorney, recommend that all daughters, Jean's male companion, and other family keep the DPoA informed of travel plans or visits.

7. Your contact info…

Eric is an inherently nice guy who gently couched his legal opinion—"your Mom has experienced sufficient decline to render her unable to make decisions," and "she really would like to see her daughters get along."

His letter halts the purported coup but fans the flames of additional hostility.

Later, Mom and I drive her boyfriend to the DMV, await our turn to sign over the aging Buick with his word to keep keys out of the house (and hopefully, car out of the garage.) While waiting, he told me he won't keep her level of insurance, but I shrugged that off. I cancelled Mom's auto insurance effective immediately and take myself alone for restorative breathing at the seashore.

In an April update, I suggest we concentrate on providing the best care possible for an aging parent. I touch on recent

> unsavory problems, ask decriers to ease up on acrimony, and reiterate my intent to uphold Mom's choices. The letter is longer than I want, but it marks my last manic askance for if not support, a bit of compassion for Mom. From now on, facts only. There is no response.

Let me say something more about that beach. It could take my tears of frustration and dark clouds of angst and send them into the wind. Every time. I thank God for the peace it offered, the renewal of will and spirit to maintain the vigilance for Mom's sake. I don't know where I would be without it, because I already hate, hate, hate the hard task of keeping guard against those girls. So sad, right?

Tip: Find this kind of respite when needed.

A Last Swim

Early in 2010, Bob and I bought a 50-year-old Florida block ranch house, about a mile from Mom and we moved down for winter. I was in Florida more and more raising the shield for Mom's days.

Dr. A continued reducing the number of prescriptions while I added a few more hours to Mom's daily home support. We visited the psychologist to measure how Mom is fairing. It had taken several months to get on his calendar, and longer to get Medicare approval for repeat evaluation.

"The results…indicate…significant cognitive decline since she was seen in 2008…memory, basic orientation and speed of processing have particularly declined. She is observed to have poor awareness of her deficits……requires a supervised living environment… with in-home help or through ALF placement…"

Poor awareness is a good thing! Mom is actually pretty good.

Calm, content. There was no Spring hospitalization. Fewer drugs being taken. No acute worries. No tears. I am close by, stopping in almost daily to see her. I arrange flowers, work in the garden, talk with the aides, sometimes watch her sleep. She has in-home help.

> One good day we got on bathing suits and took chairs to the beach. Sandy shoreline, late afternoon sunshine and warm salty water beckoning us to do more than dip toes. Unplanned, we walked into gentle surf, feeling the motion.
>
> We floated for a while, buoyed by sensation and a shared memory of other days we had done this very thing. Water magic washed over us, hiding weakness, lulling senses, a delicious restitution. Caught up for nearly an hour, I noticed both turning tide and approaching dinnertime.
>
> "Do you think it is time to get out, Mom? It's almost five." I had looked back at our chairs, gauging the task of getting us back up there. The day was waning, our interlude pressing up against her routine.
>
> "Yes," she says, "he'll be waiting for dinner."
>
> We paddled and waded toward dry land, bobbing for balance, laughing, each holding the other against a receding tide, my arms wrapped about her, urging her to put her feet down when we tumbled into the shallows, eventually dragging ourselves on shore. Spent by effort, we rested awhile in the sand, stalling to gather oomph for the climb back to the chairs.
>
> How insignificant the human form even in gentle waves! Her eighty-plus years, my almost 60, our bad joints, and not enough muscle between us to stay upright against the tide. The facts hit me head on: Mom could never have done this alone, and I had neither strength nor legs to help us do it ever again.

> My nerves were up with the exertion and what yet remained to get us packed up and into the car.

I silently stored my realization in the tender memory of that final swim, grateful for our beach bond, carpe diem and the healing majesty of water. We would come back to the beach many times to enjoy the view, but her swimming days were over unless there was an army to help us both. She did, in fact, get home for dinner.

21

A Plateau of Sorts

Remarkably perhaps, the attorney letter had worked some magic. Troubled family wrangling been silenced. Mom's ease had been restored. The car was gone. We were enjoying springtime. Her gardener friend and I redid patio beds, trying to banish the boyfriend's surprised plantings. I had sprinklers converted to reclaimed water, the live oaks trimmed and entreated the boyfriend to chop down at least part of the overpowering banana jungle he'd created. The sodden trunks weighed a ton.

> Mom looks good, as good as it gets. Nurse Debbie tells me this is often the case with Alzheimer's. Enough decline to

notice actual evidence of disease, but then a month, six months, or even more when there are no further tumbles down the long goodbye. Mom is holding her own.

I walk into the house some mornings and hear her complaining to the aides, yelling at them for helping her bathe, arguing about brushing her teeth. They wash and blow dry hair. Help with makeup, do nails and toes. Guide reluctant limbs into sleeves and pants.

Sometimes they sing bits of old swing songs. Sandy calls Mom her "work of art," and Mom forgets her impatience with personal hygiene and morning rituals, enjoying the compliments and the songs as she gets put together for another day.

She watches her favorite television shows, takes drives, enjoys sitting in her shade garden, gets ice cream now and then, appreciates the changing floral arrangements we do each week as this calm plateau stretches before us.

It is another April in which Mom does not have a heart anxiety episode. There is no way to know why she is feeling okay. I don't leave town, she has forgotten to worry about heart disease entirely, and maybe there really is no problem. The disease is at a standstill. For now. Carpe` diem indeed.

Nurse Debbie says it will return.

I have started a computer log, the "Grammy File," to keep up a growing ream of correspondence. The expanding "toolbox" has been full of bills and medical paperwork for a half dozen years, but letters and legal materials need more space. Organization comforts me! I share the latest psychological evaluation with the attorney. Y comes to stay with Mom when the boyfriend heads west on vacation.

I complete the sale of Mom's mobile home and bank

the proceeds for her future. One less management duty. Meanwhile, I am considering financial gifts to four unmarried grandchildren, a devil twin request for equity, following Mom's wedding gifts to two now married grandchildren. A good friend, dealing with his father's Alzheimer's, says maybe parity for all grandchildren can be an olive branch. I think I laughed out loud.

But I sent checks with a short note of explanation. My oldest calls to say thanks for the nice surprise, but I never hear from the others. As far as I know, neither does Grammy.

Life remains a holding pattern against the backdrop of Mom's shrinking reality, another year slipping into the past, diminishing details and days. I keep thinking I almost *see* Mom shrinking too.

Together, she and I complete her annual family Christmas gift checks, her penmanship still pretty. I suggest that it might be nice to remember the home care aides for their devotion.

"Do I have enough money to do that?" she asks.

"Yes," I tell her, "you do." She nods, and I see a tiny, satisfied grin of pride and content.

I send a year-end family note, a typed half-page devoid of emotions: Mom declining, care costs rising but covered. Mom's next check-up is April, 2011.

All in the Details: We Keep Going—2011

Another year filled with Ds. I am immersed in <u>details.</u>

Daycare, decline, drug reductions, diapers, deviousness, diminishing, determination, directives, doctors, demands, decisions, distress, difficulties, disapproval, drama. Nurse Debbie says Mom's situation has "unique dynamics," an almost amusing way to add another D word about Mom's <u>d</u>evil twins and <u>d</u>ifficulties. There is one more D word in my conscious. Dread.

> Sister Y has retired and moved to Florida, physically inserting herself into the care schedule. She is living temporarily with Mom. She takes over grocery shopping and her presence means the table notebook is open season—a shooting gallery peppered with extra abuse for me, defensive posturing and cranky instructive commentary. Fix Mom's bad breath. Get Mom's eyes checked. Take Mom to the dentist. Do something about the mail. On and on. Whatever.
>
> The notebook isn't my concern. My visits with Mom invariably include updates from the aides on everything from appetite (waning), to time required to finish morning ablutions(increasing), to increasing concerns that the boyfriend is interfering when they've got Jean in the shower and using aide time for himself (nonstop chatter, asking for a haircut). The aides remain distressed by the chronic negative background noise they overhear from both Y and boyfriend. Coercion over Mom's diminished appetite. Exchanges like ordering Mom to eat or face the consequence of moving to an old folks' home.
>
> I decide to speak with the boyfriend, offer a refresher. I bring over morning coffee cake and put a few bite-sized squares in front of Mom. She picks one up. He makes a big deal to be sure I notice. See? See?
>
> I mention the increase in aide time and request his cooperation to let them do their jobs. I ask about his haircut. He says the aide offered, his answers refuting everything I've been told. Then he's out the door for the local Y where he takes classes and volunteers. I know this is where he

goes, because he has asked Mom, (via me), for a fundraiser donation.

Later that week, I have another *Groundhog Day* conversation with Mom's team. We commiserate, share our annoyance with the boyfriend's interferences. But we *tolerate* his presence as Mom's choice, acknowledging his devotion in the necessity of nightly security.

April 30, 2011

Hi all:

Wanted to share some information about caring for Mom.

1. Home care staff has added several new caregivers... Tuesday, Thursday, Friday, and Saturday have 4-hour caregiver slots. The schedule was adjusted so Y could take Mom on consecutive Sundays and Mondays. Joni and I often overlap on Wednesdays, for house work and when Mom and I go out. I check in on other days, visiting with caregivers, the nurse, working on home upkeep, the lawn, checking mail and finances.

2. FYI: Mom paid slightly more than $7500 in taxes for 2010, mostly due to income from the sale of the mobile home. The sale income supplements her SS income ($1354 monthly) and dad's pension ($1000 monthly) to fund living expenses, now running about $20,000 over income, but covered by her savings.

3. Mom and I recently met her attorney and nurse for a review. We discussed Mom's health and financial

status, care coverage and more. The nurse monitors Mom's meds, BP and things like pain, hydration, and emotional state. Slow mental and physical decline was noted but also adequate care and support from family, staff and boyfriend. No need to increase care hours unless changes in Mom's health or the boyfriend's overnight devotion require it. There is ongoing effort to reduce prescription medications and maintain Mom's comfort. The nurse described Mom's compliant disposition, but notes more personal confusion, shorter concentration, inappropriate speaking in public places, significantly lower hygiene skills and lower energy. Mom requires help walking any distance; she needs help dressing; her "reading" focus is down.

But her attorney was delighted to see how well Mom appears physically. As a matter of update, both home health and the attorney requested new address and phone information for Y in Florida.

4. Medically, Mom has terminal coronary artery disease, high blood pressure, a history of TIAs(mini-strokes), Alzheimer's, and she complains regularly about hip pain when walking. Her heart physician/primary care doctor removed two meds in April-- Trandolapril and HTCZ . He is keeping the Nitro patch for now, to encourage open blood vessels (arteries for a strong oxygenated flow) to mediate Mom's declining lucidity-- if possible. Pulse rate strong, her weight okay, but the doctor noted that gaining weight or "requiring her to eat" is not healthy,

mentally or physically.

5. Mom may live this way for some time. On a recent day, Mom complained to me that life is getting very hard for her at home, even with all the support. As always, I remain positive. I reassured her that taking care of herself is HER and my focus, and that her savings will support whatever she needs. For now, she enjoys her garden view, complains about the orange house in the neighborhood, asks Tess to take her out to look for men (!) and recently had lunch with cousin Arline and Bob.

6. FYI: The sprinkler system at Islander Court has been extensively repaired and will be converted to "green" cost saving reclaimed water next week. Any questions about anything, please call me. Thanks,

They never call. Then one more letter to the boyfriend:

I want to update you on the recent doctor visit and the change of medicine for my Mom—stuff I want you to know without having a long conversation in front of my mom:

1. Dr. A removed two medicines from my mother's regimen. He says she no longer needs them. Her blood pressure has moved into normal and low ranges, and she is not experiencing fluid retention.

2. The doc has kept the Nitro patch to help keep my mother's arteries open and provide more oxygenated

blood flow to her brain. He hopes this will improve lucidity, or at least minimize the rate of mental decline she is experiencing due to the Alzheimer's.

3. He noted her strong pulse, and good strong heartbeat.

4. While her weight is OK, he cautions about weight gain, counseling against urging her to eat. Both are detrimental to her mental state and her physical health. Added weight can create blood pressure problems. Both doctor and home nursing staff state that urging her to eat creates worry and emotional distress, even if we don't actually see that happening. Personally, I NEVER do it. I am not suggesting that you do, but simply letting you know—as the person who eats with her most often, that **appetite decline is normal**, part of aging and the several terminal illnesses she currently battles—coronary artery disease, high blood pressure and Alzheimer's.

5. Thanks again for fixing the garbage cabinet. FYI, the sprinkler system has been repaired—several serious leaks, multiple broken sprinkler heads, one buried, haywire timers. On Wednesday May 4, the company will be back to convert the system to reclaimed water. It is a cost effective green fix that should result in lower water bills and good pressure. Joni and I will be there.

Three Months Later

July 17, 2011

Dear Sisters:

As you know, Mom just passed her 83rd birthday with X and Y in attendance while the BF went on vacation. I want to thank X for coming to spend the last two weeks here. I sincerely hope that you both gained additional insight into Mom's declining condition.

I have left Florida for a few weeks. In my absence, the care plan is being managed by the owner of RMF Home Health along with Mom's attorney. I bring this to your attention for several reasons:

1. No additional care hours are required at this time. Noted declines in skills, mobility, communication and appetite are expected and normal. The nurse continues to evaluate safety, security and the overall home situation for Mom.

2. The nurse will continue to monitor Mom's blood pressure. After deletion of two meds in April, Mom's BP has stayed nicely in the normal range.

3. Mom has made a nice transition into protective undergarments, following aide reports about significantly wet and soiled undergarments, and soiled bedding as near daily occurrences. The use of Depends type protection enables Mom to maintain

her hygiene and her dignity as incontinence and loss of bowel control worsens; the protection gives Mom higher comfort and confidence when out and about. One aide however, mentioned that Y told her Mom didn't need to wear "diapers." This is Y's choice when she has Mom. The aides are not required to face the consequences or cleanup required by allowing Mom to be unprotected and poop in their cars, or in stores. FYI--We have begun using a schedule approach – a recommended 2-hour regimen to remind Mom to use the bathroom. (see your ALZ book about this)

4. Please remember to call the RMF care office directly or me if you alter the care schedule. There is a 24-hour answering service. Verbal contact with Mom's care management is ESSENTIAL SAFETY NECESSITY. (While X was here, she and Y moved Mom to Y's for several nights but failed to notify anyone. This would be a NON issue, if Mom had returned prior to a scheduled home care visit. But the return was late and there was no knowledge of the extended stay away from Islander Court--the aide was quite frightened and worried. She couldn't find Mom. She searched the house and garden. Had Mom wandered away? How long had Mom been missing? Where was she?

The aide placed an immediate call to the office for instructions, and a manager called me. I directed the OFFICE to call Y's house. Much later the aide saw a two sentence entry in the notebook: Mom would return Thursday morning. **But she wasn't there!**)

We're on a learning curve as evidenced by the boyfriend's hospitalization earlier this summer, <u>but the notebook on the kitchen table is NOT a place to leave schedule changes.</u> **A short telephone call to the care office about any schedule adjustment is responsible (and easy). Even when running late, a courtesy call to the office would have prevented worry. Please. This is a SAFETY issue.**

Mom asked me to be responsible, to <u>safeguard the procedures</u> which protect her at this stage of her life. Notes like this are unpleasant to write and maybe for you to receive. But please, for Mom's sake, direct contact with me or the office is necessary procedure.

5. My observation is both middle daughters remain hostile toward Mom's plan for herself. But many years prior to having Alzheimer's, Mom made choices, and entrusted me to carry them out. She insisted on keeping the administration of her affairs between herself, the attorney and me, specifically excluding her boyfriend entirely, and choosing not to share details further. I think she might have helped us all by sharing and asking you to support me. But she did not. Whatever. So, we all have been affected by her decision of privacy. <u>In a spirit of family</u>, I choose to share to the extent that I feel comfortable. I will continue to inform, and respectfully ask the same of you. I have benefited from your different perspectives but would appreciate real cooperation as I work to manage Mom's safety, health care, financial management, real estate, and her living situation--

according to HER wishes.

Though I am challenged by your disregard I know that I am following Mom's wishes to the T. It would be nice to have your support, but I don't need it to do my job.

I will return to Florida in early September. Mom has a doctor appointment. Thank you again, Y, for your help with Mom two days a week and your transportation efforts. Thank you again, X, for coming to Florida to help. And thank you, Tee, for your phone calls of support, and your conversations with Mom and me.

Recently, Mom surprised me by reminding me that her plan works because of the diligent efforts she and I make. Only last week, the attorney commented on Mom's "feel-good" ownership of her plan, her sense of security, and her comfort level. She has the best at-home assisted living possible. Her way. It surely is a credit to many people and I am grateful to all who participate.

Stay in touch as we go forward.

***

They do not.

A follow-up letter to Mom's attorney on September 20, 2011 shares ongoing care management details and results of a requested "second legal opinion" about Mom's plan and my administration of it.

- Mom's enrollment at supervised neighborhood senior day care (boyfriend thumbs up)
- Conclusion of doctor supervised removal of all prescriptions (Mom is drug free)

- Resumption of Mom's decline, (sundowning agitation)
- A dismissal of an option for revocable trusts
- A thank you for the attorney's efforts
- Researching and discarding the option to file for Veteran's Administration "widow benefits" as cumbersome
- And because both attorneys have now suggested it, my action to begin logging managerial hours beyond my inescapable 27/7/365 mindset

Actually, I am surprised how quickly I need a second tally page. Every day, there is a detail, or action beyond a mother/daughter visit. Some routine, some welcome, some not. The aides share status, the boyfriend regularly wastes my time. Check-ins at the house, a phone call or fifteen of them, banking, a follow-up, research, a new affidavit for her pension, day care transport notes, holiday staffing, schedule monitoring, locating equipment appropriate to her needs, including the hunt for an "adult version" for diaper disposal.

I had searched stores and online, opting, finally, for a deluxe Diaper Genie, a hard plastic lidded tower that promised airtight disposal into a plastic sleeve for "storage" between trash days. The slender profile contraption fitted nicely in her washroom. I also replace her shower chair with a sliding bench contraption that allows easier mobility in and out of the tub.

My hours add up ridiculously fast. I know why trust law requires trustees to take a salary. I don't because I work from love, but this is why, when a new acquaintance or a credit card application asks what I do for a living, I say managed care. It is a job.

If Mom was channeling Frank Sinatra singing *My Way* when she penned her plan, I now sing my own version, holding tightly to rare moments of Mom's clarity, like when she told me how hard it is to get through her days.

She is still here by God's grace, though we both know her vessel founders in murky waters. Her plan and my acts resonate to uphold the voyage, but increasingly, I stand on that foundation of paper as Mom slowly vacates the life she was famous for.

I buy a new washing machine, replacement for one that has seen too many loads of soiled bedding. I buy Mom a two-piece velour pantsuit with sparkles. She like presents, enjoys new clothes.

I try to stay healthy, but my knee, an old ski injury, is really starting to whine. A lot. I get an orthopedic consult and attend a joint replacement seminar.

The human tornado slows down a bit, walking with a cane for three months following knee surgery. The secret surgery had come on the heels of travel to funeral services for Bob's 88-year-old mother. No reason to alert any negative forces that my lead would be compromised for a few hours of anesthesia. There is one more letter to end this year. To the boyfriend.

"At Christmas time, I want to personally thank you for your continued support and affection for my mother as she brings us down the road of Alzheimer's disease. Your presence has been one of many factors which allow Jean to remain home even though she continues to decline. I am very grateful for your devotion and attention to her.

I want you to know also, that I appreciate your decision

to write personal holiday thank you notes to the aides for roles they play in my mother's care and support system. It is something I have done for many years. Sadly, aides brought to my attention that you signed your notes with my mother's name as well as your own. It is not appropriate for you to do so.

I know my mother's writing skills are nearly nonexistent, but as a matter of protection, I am her only authorized signer. It was very nice of you to extend your personal thanks to Mom's "employees" for the benefits you experience, but please refrain from signing "Jean," or for Jean in the future. This is particularly important with private care staff because there should be no mistaken appearance of your responsibility in management of Mom's care. Thanks."

I copy the home care company and attorney.

22

Caring for the Caregiver: Facts, Fatigue, and Leaning In...

Caregiving encompasses a broad range of activity through time, place and circumstance. It is emotional, physical certainly, and mental, and there are numerous online sites devoted to tips and helpful suggestions for keeping your head on straight through caregiving. Suggestions may offer comfort when difficult moments batter resolve or stamina. But caregivers are often too tired to do more than sleep! Good sleep is great self-care, but also watch for more self-care opportunities.

How you care for yourself is an important task that contributes to successful caregiving. It allows you to recharge, to refresh, to step away, *and* to therefore maintain optimum ability to care for your loved one (and not lose yourself in the process).

Trust me on this: SELF CARE IS NOT SELFISH. It is the right thing to do.

What more should I be doing about easing my caregiving 24-7 brain? Meditation, mindfulness? Xanax? Five o'clock somewhere?

I kept looking for *how to put it down* even if only for a tiny while, because caregivers must know this about their role: **caring for yourself is a necessity.** I willed myself to stay open to any and all possibilities, watchful for ideas that could create immediate self-care moments while storing additional hints that might ease my way.

My self-care tip list grew. Caregiving blogs, emotional health essays, advice from the experienced, as well as things for my enjoyment. Flower arranging anyone? Every possibility was worth consideration.

The charming bit about caregiver comforts? Their delightful ability to help your loved one too.

Anyone assisting on the life care path of a loved one knows this to be a hard, and sometimes troublesome place. Managing infinite details, carrying on with decisions, shouldering the load of support all while embracing a magnitude of emotions *and* the reality of physical exhaustion. *Because you care.* Label it stress from circumstance, but include effort, duration and the acute knowledge that we don't fix anything. We endure.

All along, I had been reading about caregiver stress, isolation and fatigue, unhappy to learn one Florida hospital claimed caregivers caring for a spouse are six times more likely to have depression and anxiety. What about daughters? Where were the rest of us?

Draining on its own, caregiving is always way worse with family dissension. That Florida hospital suggested something more disturbing: some of us could **lose as many as 10 years off our own**

lives from dealing with extreme situations.

Because Mom's slow mental and physical descent into foggy terrain had meant a corresponding expansion of my support and care management using her plan, we both were tired. I found myself wrestling with something I had heard years ago: that caring for someone with a terminal illness is harder on the caregiver than on the loved one. I wrestled, mostly because I remained unconvinced that our shared situation was hardest on me, because after all, she would not survive.

What can anyone do about it? I sought answers everywhere. I talked to professionals in the business, I searched the internet, visited websites and blogs for inspiration, information and strength. Gleaned a tip here and there. I went to church. I prayed. I tried to understand.

Five to eight years is average duration for Alzheimer's patients, according to research by people who track this stuff. But some stricken souls live significantly longer, up to 11 years or more. Three distinct stages with gradual increasing symptom intensity: mild (early), moderate (those middle years) and late or severe, termed end-stage.

I think Mom had reached some no-man's land of late/middle or early/end-stage.

In a frightening careen past all our years to date, my mind catapulted into the future. I worried about how much longer? How could this disease steal much more? How would Mom and I manage? What on earth was left? How could I care for us both? And how was I going to last as partner on the road?

Whoa! I called a time-out. For myself. I knew I had fallen away from the present. I wasn't staying in the moment. Needed to fix that!

So I re-focused. Chose **optimism**. I reckoned that **paying**

attention to all good days should be part of the care for myself. I thought hard about seeking out and latching onto the *pretty good--* Mom's catch all answer—for what was left.

Today, however, was not good. It was a downer. I took Mom home and ran myself to the beach, needing salty air for care of me.

Lectured myself on making a conscious practice of seeking good, and got back in the saddle.

I feast eyes on a sunrise in my east facing kitchen window, a peaceful rhythm in a world that keeps turning.

We smile at one another. I stay in each moment.

We spend a quiet afternoon outside. I watch her nap. We appreciate a good day. I bring in flowers. I like the flowers, Mom likes the flowers, a bright spot against all the rest.

We stay on the bright side as much as possible because things that help Mom also help me. Mom sits outside *with me* in the sunshine on a park bench. We drive off for ice cream, for a look at the beach. We watch ospreys soar and dive for their dinners, and marvel as a Great Blue Heron, my personal animal hero, struts the pier.

It is an endless tick of minutes, hours, days, but by **working to stay in joy**, we often find a piece of it. That could be enough.

Caregiver Comfort & Self-Care

- **Be honest.** From the start, Mom and I were direct and authentic with one another. There was integrity and candor in our conversations from early planning sessions right through to tough times. That moral compass gave permission to reveal true feelings.

- **Push beyond negativity.** We voiced reality in straightforward chats. She could complain, I could validate. We would acknowledge but did not dwell on difficulties.

  Why does this help a caregiver? Because even hard truths are easier than lies. You can be gentle and still be honest. It is delicate work, but tough conversations are eased by love and truth. Besides, nobody likes a liar.

- **Take time off.** Easier said than done due to the 24/7/365 nature of caregiving. But when my sisters complained that I didn't visit Mom and her boyfriend in the evenings, I could feel guilty **or** I could respect her privacy and appreciate my time off.

- **Economize your efforts.** If you find yourself repeatedly looking up phone numbers, or passwords, or account numbers, or forever going back to the files for the same information, *make a cheat sheet.* It will save time and help you ever after. Any shortcut that helps management is good self-care strategy.

- **Read plenty.** Nonfiction offered information and inspiration--Elisabeth Kubler-Ross on death and dying, C.S. Lewis on grief, Barbara Karnes, Hospice literature, others. Fiction offered escape, often with its own messages—Mitch Albom, Anne Morrow Lindbergh, Maeve Binchy, among others.

- **Turn on the music.** If you don't believe me, try singing along to your radio, or buy a CD of soothing "mood music." Music has power to heal. And who says troubadours don't carry messages?

- **Find your own special place, your own self-care spot.** Some people go to the mountains, some to a park bench. Readers already know how the beach soothed me, became an almost daily fix, a rejuvenating respite from rigors of managing care and heartache. To sit for an hour or a day, to walk the shore or not, to cry in the wind or laugh with seagulls, the beach was my recharging station. In rain and tumbling high seas, when I wouldn't even get out of the car, the water still worked its magic. Glassy flat water, gentle surf or pounding waves, the beach was a timeless, soothing presence.

Nothing was different when I left the causeway, but salty air had blown through my hair, sand had scrubbed away the day's hardships, just because I was *there!* I could be Bon Jovi's *rock, not just a speck of sand.* I could keep going.

- **Ask for and accept help. DO NOT DO THIS ALONE.**

- **If possible, find good, caring family to share tangible caregiving.** This is about my youngest sister, and yes, even Mom's devil twins, who took turns at the physical aspects of caregiving. This is about one sister regularly hosting Mom and her boyfriend for holiday dinners. This is about combined efforts to help Mom travel to the weddings of two granddaughters, and to be with us when the boyfriend was away. This is about post-surgery duty. This is about my daughter helping with pill boxes, my son constructing a television stand. Absolutely about *many hands* lessening a load.

- **Find or create opportunities for family activities outside the caregiver spectrum.** Anything works. As important as having family share tangible care.

- **Find someone to listen.** This is about easing an emotional overload. Sharing with someone whether in your trenches or not, can humanize the situation. This is not about asking for advice or a fix but asking for an ear. My friend Laura, once told me, "Just getting it out helps!" She is right.

A listener is recipe for release. Someone who will hear you out. The weight of policing Mom's plan came to me but being able to vent enabled me to discharge emotional strain and reduce my psychological hardship.

As much as possible I tried to minimize carer malaise at home, but because this was real time, my husband and children were the closest ears, and I know this took a toll. Immediate family was saddened by Mom's circumstances and what I was dealing with, unhappy with extended separations, discouraged that my sisters created so much dissension, but their acknowledgement held me up.

- **Receive support when it is offered.** My husband intercepted a deluge of hate mail, his voice affirming my determination to keep promises to Mom. He boosted my confidence by concluding I had done my best. His support gave me permission to accept that life at Islander Court was as good as it was ever going to be. It allowed me to let go of the worst of the stress.

This *lift* from family and friends is priceless. Sharing with people who cared about me, allowed me to "re-arrange" the mental load and *accomplish good living* on a continuum that included loving and caring for my sick mother, and tolerating everything that made it worse.

- **Hire professionals for advice, counsel, support, and ideas.** People do this for a living. They have experience dealing with exactly these situations. Not only can they guide us with methods, or be the calming presence affirming our efforts, they can provide much needed respite. *Ever hear this axiom: many hands make the work light?* Maybe not light, but definitely shared and thereby a little bit easier. They also listen.

- **Find a mentor.** There are always times of uncertainty in any situation, and you will find value in knowing someone else on the road, including professionals. A **mentor** is like having a **job coach.** It is as much about strategy and advice as about affirmation, a hand up to validate you and your path.

- **Remember to say thank you.** To everybody. Every chance you get. Mom had a series of professional in-home caregivers. Supporting Mom was their paying job, but I wanted these wonderful people to know how much I appreciated their partnership in caring for Mom and keeping her home. If you are able, those in-home aides sure appreciate everything from movie tickets, to dinner out vouchers, and a Christmas envelope is always a good idea. My gratitude reminded me how lucky we were for their presence.

When you don't hear thank you from your loved one, or those detractors, remind yourself to thank yourself. (See positive self-talk below)

- **Stay in the moment.** School yourself to deal with today. Acting on the here and now is far preferable to anxiety over what may or may not come next. This is about harnessing positive energy and getting things done. It works for all sorts of real world good and bad scenarios. By contrast, worrying about later wastes present energy over things that may not even happen!

In caregiving, the idea of operating in the moment has distinct advantages:

1. Conserving energy and emotion.

2. Creating awareness of unique experience. Being present provides opportunities to receive good energy and recognize the positive! I would have missed the joy of that awesome unplanned last swim, and never been part of that fleeting moment when Mom woke up clear eyed and fully present one afternoon, if I had been fretting about the future.

3. Being present is about nurturing ourselves, experiencing gratitude. Awareness equals appreciation, a gift for today. (Have you ever heard that you are right where you are supposed to be?)

- **Positive self-talk.** This is about maintaining an internal pep talk. Tell yourself that you are important and you are doing important work. It's the truth! You are good at what you are doing, and don't let anyone suggest otherwise. We all should do more positive self-talk!

- **Look for good news. For example:** I actively delighted in my low cholesterol and normal blood pressure, a reasonably active lifestyle, and my mostly reasonable food choices, especially *after* reading the care company newsletter about how positive lifestyle choices could optimize health and might decrease the risk for developing dementia.

- **Learn to accept and shut down your feelings.**
  Okay, this might sound impossible because after all, we are talking about feelings in a stress-filled circumstance. But this is not for the easy days, but rather, for low, sad and angry days, when you are not feeling your best and brightest.

Learning how to keep your feelings from taking over is what I'm talking about. <u>Accepting feelings and shutting them down is *how* to help yourself manage.</u> Feelings are normal. By acknowledging and then purposely shutting them down, you hit the bypass button, and get on with whatever you need to be doing.

When my aging Black Labrador became ill with a brain tumor behind her eye, my responsibility was compassionate euthanasia. I grieved her loss deeply and allowed myself to do so, but I chose to hardly speak about my sadness, so it would not define my interactions with others.

A friend told me this story. She watched two people she knew speak to each other at some distance. Suddenly one woman had raised her arms up over her head and began shaking her hands. Later on, my friend asked the hand shaker what that was all about.

The hand shaker said she had been getting increasingly upset by the conversation. That handshaking was a physical exercise to release, to swoosh her mental angst up and out. A physical act to fling away, to not let upset feelings take over. (You have maybe seen me using this hand shaking technique at the beach!)

Acknowledge, **but find a way to by-pass or shut down those feelings,** keep them outside your safety perimeter. Silence, flailing hands overhead or whatever your preferred method. Perform a conscious act to counter any attack of bad feelings. Free yourself to rely on habit (or autopilot) to move forward.

- **Insist on keeping your sense of humor.** With all the seriousness in Mom's house, we paid attention to lighter moments. We laughed. Example: Mom and I both thought the tourist-dressed flamingos her boyfriend stuck in the garden were appalling, but early on, Mom managed to drop one or two. Once broken, they disappeared. (Funny).

◦ While reading a local free paper in a waiting room, Nurse Debbie stumbled on a personal ad that sounded a lot like Mom's peacock boyfriend, extolling his personal virtues trolling for another squeeze. She checked company files to compare his home address with that used as a personal ad response box. Detective Debbie is right. (Funny)

◦ Mom told Dr. A she was a lucky lady because she had a young boyfriend who was good at taking care of her. Then she fist bumped the doc on the leg. He looked at me and smiled. (Funny)

◦ Mom does not like my clothes, telling me to "never, ever wear that shirt again." She rolls her eyes at purple toenail polish. (funny)

◦ I hear Mom asks Tess to drive her around so she can look for men. (funny)

◦ Like clockwork, any drive past the orange house prompts the expected critique of awful color choices. (Giggle)

◦ Catching sight of yourself in under counter mirror

panels installed by the boyfriend. (Hilarious)

- Clearing out two-week's worth of Styrofoam take-away mystery boxes clogging shelves in Mom's fridge? (Ridiculous work, but amusing)

- The twins dress themselves and Mom in matching orange outfits and snap photos. How do they not know Mom despises the color orange?? (stupidly funny)

- Giant red Christmas bows are taped to the breasts of Mom's mermaid statue. I did not do the decorating. (Theater of the absurd)

Humor is your friend. Humor helps.

- **Find your faith.** I'm not saying the caregiving road cannot be taken without it, but I am saying that you really should want a Higher Power on your team. A Higher Power can guide your way and keep you and your loved one in the arms of God. Those of us who have our spirituality intact, find that faith-based care offers comfort and confirmation. Faith promotes grace, inner peace, gentleness in the middle of a storm, a unique solace to thwart human angst. In fact, faith is deemed so important by the American Psychological Association, that a spiritual component is required these days for any proposed counseling plan.

Consider this verse, Isaiah 41: *So do not fear, for I am with you…I will strengthen you and help you…I will uphold you with my righteous right hand…"* Doesn't that sound like someone you want on your team?

Part of faith is also being able to ask for counsel through prayer. Prayers work, prayers help, prayers are as much gratitude as petition, hopes and wishes.

With God all things are possible. Matthew 19:26.

Just saying. *There is always hope, Psalms 73.* It is worth consideration.

- **Learn something new, just for yourself.** I put myself in graduate school. The brain exercise required by reading, writing and discussing psychology and mental health was stimulating, distracting *and* helpful. Subject matter held its own allure, a deeper exploration of family dynamics, environment and personality, but the real buzz? I was nearly 60 years old by that time and learning grounded me. Back inside a cohort of multi-disciplinary professionals in a virtual classroom was work, but it was fun. Learning as a key life skill rocks me every time.

- **Do something for fun.** Maybe you've always wanted to bungee jump or kayak. Maybe you want to visit a psychic or go to the opera. Maybe you want to learn to ice skate or cook Chinese. Now may not seem like the right time, and maybe you think you should wait until "later." But do it now. It may seem frivolous, but I assure you this too, is about self-care.

I tried to learn better Spanish, I remodeled two houses. Fun. Seriously, find something fun for yourself.

- **Find a support group.** A community of fellows on your same highway can offer comfort and understanding. You might hear practical tips, relieve your isolation, or simply find peace by hearing from others who do what you do.

Sometimes it can be about seeing caregivers with harder roads than your own and recognizing just how lucky you are! You don't have to become a life member. Do what works for you.

Sometimes it isn't a caregiver support group at all. For several years, I had attended Al-Anon Family Groups, a 12-step life care program for families and friends of alcoholics. I came away with a real gift. The Al-Anon philosophy promotes personal worth, spiritual faith, hope and doing the right thing. You may know this program for credible goals of serenity, courage and wisdom. It fosters valor and acceptance, perseverance, boundaries, compassion and letting go of things we cannot change, all helpful in the caring game.

I know you've heard the opening prayer, *God grant me the serenity to accept the things I cannot change, the courage to change the things I can, and the wisdom to know the difference.* Repeat. Repeat.

- **Keep your contact with others.** You are not supposed to isolate yourself from the world or the rest of your life in order to accomplish caregiving. In fact, doing so is downright dangerous. Family illness situations do not happen in a vacuum, life goes on throughout the process. While you may not be the full-time participant you have been in the past, do not stop participating. It is after all, life.

I got involved in a women's club with a busy calendar of options.

- **Keep a sense of wonder.** Any care journey will have magical moments. Depending on who you are or where you sit, this might sound grandiose or ridiculous. But wonder is key to enhancing the moments. The idea is this: being in the moment prepares you to be ready for wonder. Your mind is open to possibility. Therefore, you are open to wonder. If you are paying attention, your loved one will bring you closer to the other side than you can go alone. If you are paying attention, your journey alongside said loved one will be a conduit to experience you would not have otherwise. Read on to see more about what I mean.

- **Be ready for angels.** This is about human friends and spiritual encounters. On more than one occasion, a friend would share a story or take my hand in comfort, an angel in a bookstore would know exactly what I needed to read, I would look up to see a billboard of intuition. The glowing spirit of my deceased aunt came into my dreams late one night bathed in rings of golden light. She was radiating happiness, her bob hair shining and fabulous as she bent her forehead to touch mine and smile deeply into my eyes. I fell immediately to sleep, waking the next morning more rested than I had been in weeks. Not my imagination, Sue visited me.

There were other encounters. On one particularly very bad day, I had the distinct impression of being encased in a warm white peaceful place. I felt what I can only describe as a feather touch, a caress on both forearms, a hug of wings as I sat depleted at my desk. Utter comfort.

A dear friend's spirit leapt down from the rafters at his memorial luncheon, stealing joyfully and robustly into the body of his son I'd only just met. Jack gave me his very best familiar hug and kiss and used his son to do it!

I saw three softly formed gray shapes gathered behind a Christmastime speaker, and I bet they saw me looking, because they dissolved. They were there to listen in.

You should be lucky enough for this to happen to you. Energize your sense of wonder.

- **Exercise and eat.** Everything in moderation, right? A morning pastry was a guilty staple with my coffee, a comfort and reward that I knew I would not eat indefinitely. But for years, I ate away. (And, okay, I rode my bike a little.)

- **Take more photos of you and your loved one together.** You will be glad you did.

- **Make a note to self for later.** (Actually, make several.) As a carer, please commit to memory that you will have your own time again, when your carer days are done. Time will help you heal. By hanging on now, you really will be able to free yourself later. Time will help with that, and meanwhile, there truly is nothing like experiential learning.

- **Another mental reminder for your future self:** Promise to get your own Fab Four paperwork completed, sooner rather than later.

- **Know there are some things you just are not supposed to have answers for.** Permission to not know! What a relief! Tell yourself it is OK to *not know*. Some answers exist beyond our finite human experience. Perhaps, this is permission to be human. Accept it. Embrace it. Feel the aaahhh.

- **Know this will happen too.** When the intensity of trying to figure all of it out stopped for me, a switch flipped. Just do. Be. Do.

23

Late Middle, or Early Late Stage

I was not sure how it was possible, but it was happening. Mom's deterioration was back. She was inching her way downward, fading farther and farther away. Her appetite was off, words fewer, gait unsteady, daily hygiene completely in the hands of others, and after a few really messy accidents, everyone else finally had come to terms with the necessity of disposable undergarments.

My mental health breaks at the beach had increased in direct proportion to the escalating barrage of hate mail from my sisters. My husband cared for me by filtering the mail. Seriously, what I had to look at, or not.

Information from 6-month check-up:
Doctor Visit, February 15, 2012

1. Blood Pressure normal. Heart and circulation are great, although Mom called Dr. A "crazy man," and punched him on the leg. He has a sense of humor.

2. Mom's appetite is normal for her condition. By the way, she has never liked cashews.

3. Discussion of vitamins (at Y's request) result in Doctor labeling them "useless and unnecessary" for a person in her condition. We discuss the Whey Protein additive being mixed into Mom's breakfast drink: Doctor A's father, who also has Alzheimer's, is taking this supplement. Doc feels this contains beneficial proteins.

4. Regarding Mom visiting the dentist: I visit her dental office. The staff explains that risks to Mom for any dental work—even cleaning—definitely outweigh any benefit. Regular brushing is the only recommendation for a senior of her condition.

By March, Mom is pushing food away, not eating much at all. I smile to know she eats an occasional ice cream at day care, but never lunch. I know she does not want to eat. I know she does not want to be fed. Her doc contacted Hospice again for another evaluation. It is 30 months since Mom's "graduation" from that first round of hospice support.
Could this be failure to thrive? Could this be *it?*

This is NOT it.

Hospice re-opened supports but discontinued services after 45 days, based on Mom's weight gain. This is "late middle stage" or "early final stage." Slow, definite progression, but not severe, not end stage. Mom graduates a second time, mostly likely because the aides continue to watch both sisters and boyfriend put food in her mouth. (Y uses capital letters to YELL a list of all the foods Mom eats on days she is with her, into the table notebook.) Mom is lucid enough to tell me she doesn't like this, but she is too pliable, has no strength to refuse. I remind her it is okay to stop eating when/if she doesn't want to. She nods a hollow okay, and I accept that this, like so much else, is beyond the grasp of a moment. Nurse Debbie says Mom will stop eating eventually because the skills to do so will disappear.

Meanwhile, mobility issues abound. The boyfriend has mounted a grab bar for Mom. A good idea for balance and support, but he has installed it (not funny, ridiculous) on a glass window near the kitchen table. I remove it.

I have the exterior doors re-keyed after several mornings when he has locked out the aides. There are new keys for the care office, in my possession, and I leave one in an envelope for Y.

I walk in one morning to a horrible smell permeating the whole house. The aide and I throw open windows and follow our noses. The boyfriend has been using the Diaper Genie but without the plastic liner. In plastic gloves, the aide and I clear a stack of offending disposables to the outdoor bin, supremely grateful that today is trash day. We turn on ceiling fans, open doors, and reset the Genie with its proper internal bagging.

The table notebooks continue a daily record, mostly of complaints, but real communication continues between the aides, Mom's nurse and me in our one-on-one contact. The care company owner had always disapproved of table logs as suspect, mostly problematic records often filled opinion, inuendo and incorrect information from unhappy people.

She has a point. But the ability to leave a word has been meaningful to the aides. Glancing at the spiral bound pages, I gravitate to their short sentences, positive daily capsulized statements. *"Good day, we drove to beach."* Or, *"Jean resting comfortably after nice afternoon on porch."* Or, *"Jean has no appetite, but enjoys iced tea."* I chuckle at angry food intake lists and ignore the boyfriend's dinner time doodles, tossing each notebook in the trash as it fills up, but putting a fresh one in place. Keep the doodlers happy, I guess.

The normality of Mom's daily sail eventually hits another wave. I thought I had heard everything, and suddenly here's a new and utterly ridiculous wrinkle. In politically correct terms, it's about dress code. Apparently, the boyfriend has answered the front door in his birthday suit, exposing himself to an aide. More than once.

Nurse Debbie and I grimace and tell each other we would have howled with laughter if we had been "exposed to that." But this is serious. The aide could press charges. The care company management urges me to terminate the boyfriend's presence in Mom's home.

The aide must be mistaken, says Y. Says she spoke to the boyfriend who denies this happened, says he would never do it. Y believes it must be a language barrier, because the aide is a Filipina. This is a verbal problem, not a visual one?

Please be awake and be dressed. Avoid answering the

door without a robe. Be out of the bedroom as a courtesy to morning care staff. It stops or expect the order to vacate.

He said, she said. Regardless, they are forewarned.

No more undressed episodes.

Tip: don't forget to laugh when you can, theater of the absurd, whatever.

Life goes quiet again but not for long. I get wind of something new. The boyfriend plans to bring a camera crew into Islander Court, to video himself "helping." It is to be part of a short biography film that will be broadcast at an upcoming YMCA volunteer appreciation function. He is one of several honorees. Good for him, bad for my mom. I tell him no.

A week later, the morning aide says the boyfriend has ordered her to "have Jean dolled up and looking good this afternoon. Make sure she has on makeup...." because a film crew is coming to chronicle his three minutes of fame.

What part of NO did he not understand? I stop what I'm doing and go to the YMCA to take my concern up the chain of command. I sit down with an administrator, for straight talk from the power of attorney. My gut isn't even dancing.

No filming. My mom has late stage Alzheimer's. I do not care about showcasing a "wonderful Y volunteer." He has no right to invade Mom's privacy, was already told filming her is inappropriate. Besides, who exactly did this admin think was going to sign a photo release?

The admin cancels the filming. I offer a terse thank you, walk out to breathe in sunshine. I want to wash my hands.

The year 2012 ends as it began. Profound continuing loss of Mom's essence. Declining skills. More daycare. Chronically rising opposition to Mom's wishes. Persistent efforts by my sisters and the boyfriend to hand feed Mom. Nurse Debbie says Mom will have food put in her mouth until she spits it out or chokes. I will not remove these loved ones from Mom's life, but I stubbornly repeat her desire to never be fed.

I detest the wrangling but continue to defend the queen, saddened by circumstance, worn down by effort, depleted by the rigor of maintenance and response, most of which I could never have imagined.

But I think this is Mom's final Christmas. Call it intuition. I don't know why or how I know this, but I do.

24

Mindfulness

From Elderhelpers.Org, via Facebook:

When an old man died in the geriatric ward of a nursing home in back country Australia, nurses found a poem among his meager possessions. Its quality and content so impressed the staff that copies were made and distributed to every nurse in the hospital. One nurse took her copy to Melbourne and the poem has since appeared in Christmas editions of magazines across Australia, and in international mental health magazines. A slide presentation of these simple words has been created, and the old man, with nothing left to give the world, is now author of this anonymous poem winging across the Internet.

Cranky Old Man

What do you see nurses? ....What do you see?

What are you thinking…when you're looking at me?

A cranky old man…not very wise, uncertain of habit…with faraway eyes?

Who dribbles his food…..and makes no reply.

When you say in a loud voice, 'I do wish you'd try!'

Who seems not to notice…the things that you do.

And forever is losing…a sock or a shoe?

Who, resisting or not….lets you do as you will

With bathing and feeding…the long day to fill?

Is that what you're thinking…Is that what you see?

Then open your eyes nurse, you're not looking at me.

I'll tell you who I am….as I set here so still,

As I do at your bidding….as I eat at your will.

I'm a small child of ten…with a father and mother, brothers and sisters who love one another.

A young boy of sixteen…with wings on his feet,

dreaming that soon now…a lover he'll meet.

A groom now at twenty…my heart gives a leap.

Remembering the vows….that I promised to keep.

At twenty-five, now I have young of my own,

Who need me to guide…and secure a happy home.

A man of thirty…my young now grown fast,

bound to each other…with ties that should last.

At forty, my young sons…have grown and are gone,

But my woman is beside me…to see I don't mourn.

At fifty, once more……babies play 'round me knee.

Again, we know children….my loved one and me.

Dark Days are upon me……my wife is now dead.

I look at the future…I shudder with dread.

For my young are all rearing…young of their own.

And I think of the years….and the love that I've known.

I'm now an old man…and nature is cruel.

It's jest to make old age………look like a fool.

The body, it crumbles…grace and vigor depart.

There is now a stone…where I once had a heart.

And now and again….my battered heart swells.

I remember the joys….I remember the pain.

And I'm loving and living….life over again.

I think of the years, all too few…….gone too fast

And accept the stark fact……that nothing can last.

So open your eyes people……open and see.

Not a cranky old man.

Look closer….see…….ME!

More Mindfulness

"Be confused, it's where you begin to learn. Be broken, it's where you begin to heal. Be frustrated, it's where you start to make more authentic decisions. Be sad, because if we are brave enough, we can hear our heart's wisdom…" SC Lourie, dance teacher, writer, lover of life.

The holidays are over. I'm putting away Mom's familiar Christmas decorations, the ceramic tree, the four handmade paper dolls that represent us daughters. Mom is resting on the sofa, a usual pose. A soothing music CD plays while my mind wanders over the mile-markers in Mom's brave descent, our walk-along of more than a decade! Years of sustaining her chosen path, staunchly guarding the queen, but something feels different.

Status quo. Mom's path remains a downward trek, but I don't feel mired down in the worst of it. There is a tiny glimmer, something I cannot quite name. I feel something has changed. Something has shifted. I let my thoughts percolate. Maybe a New Year revelation? What is it?

Moving through familiar rooms reflecting on distance, effort, and some outrage, but viewing it outside myself, as observer, not victim. I still cannot quite put a finger on what this is. A breath of something, a wisp of calm. A truly strange sensation after all these years.

My nerves have eased against a mountain of challenge and negativity. Something has fortified me, touched my spirit, marshalled my resolve. It is more than my Christmas respite away.

It hits me. I think I have watched enough, been through enough, withstood enough, grieved enough, orchestrated enough, that I'm feeling the tiniest tingle, an awakening of serene self and it has rejuvenated the sentinel of Mom's path.

That tiniest blossoming inside, I realize, is satisfaction and confidence combined. Mom and I have done our best. I cannot see the end, but I have new energy, resolve. We will make it to her finish line, *her way, which also is mine.*

I take the box which holds the ceramic tree back to its place in the garage. I think the seed of something I feel is Peace.

25

A Sentinel at Work

"Life is amazing. And then it's awful. And then it's amazing again. And in between the amazing and the awful, it's ordinary.... That's just living, heartbreaking, soul-healing, amazing, awful, ordinary life. And it's breathtakingly beautiful." - L.R.Knost, author

January 4, 2013

As we head into 2013, I take this opportunity to wish you Happy New Year and update you on management of Mom's affairs and her declining condition. I have great compassion and distress for the increasing difficulties she experiences every day in her daily life. I appreciate your support of her in her home and thank you for your help.

I have to re-address several key components of the care picture, out of respect for Mom's needs.

The care staff has alerted me to time/schedule concerns

for day care mornings and the need for late day support due to sundowning, combativeness and agitation. I have added extra time on the end of care schedule days.

However, on **Tuesdays and Wednesdays**, as I've discussed previously, there is a real need to efficiently promote Mom's hygiene and her departure to Neighborly Center. Home health staff report delays primarily of your doing, and I ask/urge you to cooperate:

- A home aide arrives at 9 a.m. on day care days. On Tuesdays and Wednesdays, please be awake, dressed, and out of the bedroom before 9 a.m. to speed up completion of Mom's morning needs, her departure and yours. There is breakfast and lunch available for her at the center.

- Sadly, aides report you continue to hand feed my mother, that you place food in her mouth, and try to disguise this by sitting overly close to her at the table. I ask you again, please stop this now. You can cook, you should place food in front of her, you can cut her food in tiny bites and encourage her to eat. But allow her the dignity to choose to eat or not, as she is able. She deserves that we respect her choices, her directives and the natural process of her aging and circumstance. As difficult as this is for me, as difficult as this may be for you to accept or understand, Mom NEVER wanted to be hand fed. In fact, her directives specify that food and hydration be removed to NOT prolong her suffering. I beg you to respect her reality, her

> health status and her wishes. I know this means changes for you and your lifestyle, but if you cannot respect her wishes about food, let me know. I will make other arrangements for mealtimes and evening.

The **details.** I remind him for the umpteenth time about Mom's directives, my duty, the difficulties, and finish up by sharing Mom's own appraisal of these days.

> Understandably, Mom is not happy despite periods of singing. This is difficult to watch. She is supervised, safe and clean, but she suffers. She regularly addresses her condition and unhappiness, telling me and various aides how she hates living like this, that she wants to fall asleep and not wake up, that she wishes she could do something (like Aunt Sue) to die.
>
> ...I am copying the care company, Mom's attorney, my mother's brother and wife, and my sisters with this letter. It is important for each us to come to terms with the reality of what gets closer each day--a peaceful release that she deserves and always intended for herself.
>
> My sisters try to tell me and the private care company that Mom is too far gone to know what she wants. That she certainly couldn't know back at the beginning of planning, what she would want now. Their denial endures as the saddest disconnect, but they no longer insist everything is fine. I can shake my head, but don't try to fix it anymore.
>
> ***

I take myself for a slow waltz through Disney World, alone. A rare day away in early February for my own mental health. I get a phone call in the Magic Kingdom. It is Nurse Debbie.

Mom had gotten a slight cold and the boyfriend had ordered aides to dose her with cold medicine. The morning aide watches him leave and alerts Nurse Debbie.

A. He is not in charge of her health care.

B. The particular cold remedy he was dosing included an ingredient dangerous for high blood pressure patients.

C. B is why A comes first.

Nurse Debbie took over. She visited Mom, called to lecture the boyfriend. Called me. He will hear from me when I return from Fantasyland.

Debbie says not to worry, but she believes Mom has taken a step toward reaching her great beyond. Debbie has seen something, some change, some signal in Mom's overall flickering fade that makes her say this. Not imminent, she says, but movement.

Away, down, out, whatever direction you want. Mom turning into herself, in the room physically, but somewhere else. I know what Debbie describes because I have seen it. Mom's earthly form is a frail human shell nearly empty, the essence almost gone. She isn't always there anymore.

We have her regular check up with the unflagging Dr. A coming up. I'll ask for his perspective on what we have has seen.

The Checkup

Dr. A says Mom has stepped into in end stage Alzheimer's, her physical condition has worsened, her mental blankness a proof point. He wants to call in Hospice.

Hospice. A third time? Provide good reason for me to believe Mom will not be revived by the next round of force feeding that I know awaits her once the word Hospice hits the airwaves. Guarantee for me that Hospice will honor and support Mom's plan. Someone, please, convince me Mom won't be fattened up to "graduate" again, only to malinger in a manner she never wanted. Someone, please, please assure me that Mom is really ready for her final days.

I won't prolong her suffering with a repeat of last spring's food fest, and I don't need one more family fight. There are new food stories offering a telltale marker of disease gaining ground. Mom is pocketing food—in her clothes, in her cheeks, in her hands. One morning, an aide found Mom worrying something in her mouth, moving an object about with her tongue. The aide discovered an olive stone, from the Greek Salad yelled into the notebook the night before.

There is Mom's personal flatness, the singer mostly silent, swollen hands and ankles, observable anxiety, frowns, longer periods of sleep, extreme incontinence, moaning, incoherency, shuffling feet, significant shortness of breath with the least exertion. She is profoundly weak, sleeping more and more.

She has an erratic pulse and bouncing blood pressure. She's had several fevers and a urinary tract infection in the last month. More than once the aides and I have caught her up, interrupting a stumble, inches from the floor.

Not one of us believes the boyfriend's claims about Mom independently wheeling around the house with her tripod walker, much less successfully using the toilet.

I share the doctor's opinion with Nurse Debbie, the care company owner, the aides, my coyote sister, all hunters of the right answer. Debbie agrees with the doctor's assessment. Mom's doctor, her supporters, my mentors and advisors, bear witness that her clock is ticking toward a final hour.

It was what my intuition sensed at Christmastime.

I have begun praying at night for Mom to die. I have no guilt for this prayer, only peace, asking God to release my mother's once joyful spirit from the wreck of her corporeal self. She never wanted this so I'm down with inviting God to pull her plug *when He is ready*, to give her what she wanted for herself. She has had enough.

One more thing: Dr. A says the history of hostility and dissent fueled by the boyfriend is a serious deterrent to Mom's remaining time. Get him gone. The care company and I agree completely, but I remain trapped between what I certainly think would be best, and what Mom herself has asked for. I am reluctant to banish this last bit of her happiness, and I foresee an epic struggle with additional damage, to do it.

The twitch was not in my gut, but in my heart. Let's hear what Hospice has to say.

PART THREE

Almost Home

"You come to understand awe, strength, commitment, love and life in a way that humbles you." - Corinne O'Kelley, wife and carer in <u>Chasing Daylight. How My Forthcoming Death Transformed My Life,</u> by Eugene O'Kelley, McGraw-Hill, 2005.

At the end of more than a dozen caring years and a ton of paper--letters, emails, updates, instructions, legal pages, and medical record keeping, I finally began keeping a personal record. It was overdue, long pushed aside while immersed in the doing. Our story was coursing to its finish, and I needed a place to dump the heavy weight of diligence and effort, an overload of detail and exhaustion, as Mom and I faced what might be the toughest time yet.

I'd been writing one way or other since I was a kid and now it became a serious wellness exercise to unload a corrosive brooding spill from head to hard drive. Stream of conscious took over almost immediately. The journal filled with self-talk, a silent partner listening to my inner voice blow off steam, meditation and reflection of where Mom and I stood. Physical, mental and emotional, journaling helped to purge a chokehold of disease threaded with family turmoil right when I thought I couldn't last much longer.

Because, despite that touch of peace at New Year's, I was a weary warrior, and pounding detail and outrage into a computer reminded me we had done our best. Writing helped me reach within, find endurance and renewal. Cleared spaces in my brain began filling with affirmation and confidence, which is to say, it allowed me to sleep at night.

Somehow, I wrote myself through pain and frustration as Mom faded impossibly further. Bad behavior a `la devil twins and passive/aggressive boyfriend continued to escalate, but I was finding my stride, concentrating on commitment, its purity and strength of purpose. Ultimate self-care. I was the empowered protector, intent on fully living these last moments with Mom.

As we pointed ourselves toward her finale, I found a second wind, a third, a fourth. We had weathered everything. I could continue to do my best, and we would meet her finish line together.

I've edited grammar and spelling, added quotes meaningful to me. The rest is real time with Mom in her last days on the planet.

Oh, something else happened. Recording our final footsteps gave birth to this book.

The Journal

"Something else is going on beneath everyday life…another side of life we have yet to discover." James Redfield, <u>The Celestine Prophecy.</u>

March 15

Today is March 15. My mother has been admitted to Suncoast Hospice, for the third and hopefully, the final time.

Her road was mapped more than a decade ago, Mom looking into the future to answer questions and make directives, to choose for herself for these very moments. We are brushing up against her mortality. Serious times.

She has been declining with heart disease and Alzheimer's for a long slow time, but with support. A lot of support. Attention to details and a fortuitous expense account. Mom remains within the privacy and comfort of her own home, living days in a shrinking world, with less interest and more confusion, her nights shared alongside a boyfriend. There are visits from me, my sisters, her brother, numerous caregivers, nurses. I am hopeful that a journal can somehow strengthen me as we walk these last miles, helping Mom to the finish as she intended.

As daughter, power of attorney, health care surrogate and general care manager, I have been maestro for the composition, the one to orchestrate at her direction, including the privacy she scripted for a final decade-long relationship with a man, not my father.

Facing the end of her time. Terminal illness. Nearly at the final destination, nearly at a place we both knew she would someday reach. Her life. Her choices.

Others have helped along the way, they all care for Mom. Particularly when I'm absent. But a battle of control with sisters and the boyfriend has darkened the path. Professionals remind me over and over that this is the drill. ONLY ONE person can be in charge. One person must make the decisions, take the heat. Especially in this end of days.

It is a perpetual emotional quandary. Help for her. Hindrance of me. Beyond one brief grudging "I know you are taking care of a lot," their support for me as guardian at Mom's gate was missing from the start. The plan didn't fit what any of them thought it should be. Cruelly, repeatedly, in the face of Mom's escalating needs, one sister claiming I am mentally ill from the strain, badgering Mom to change. A volley of insults and reproach aimed low, aimed to break, hoping for a crack in armor that would allow for what? A takeover?

My focus has been Mom, and I have tried bringing detractors up to moral speed. But they have never seen it Mom's way. Respect for Mom's directives has never mattered to them. They make a tough situation worse.

Letting go of my responsibilities, this job for Mom, crosses my mind as refuge, particularly on really bad days. I've wondered if I can last. Bad behavior, lies and deceit strewn onto an already rocky end of life highway have me wondering why it has to be this hard.

I don't have the answer.

Sister X is half right: there has been great emotional strain. Pretty normal for these serious days, if you ask me. But I'm not mentally deranged. Disgusted certainly, sick at heart over attempts to deny Mom the right of her own choices. But in ways I cannot fathom, it has made me stronger. Filled me with kryptonite.

Poet Robert Frost just sent another message: Something about "miles to go before I sleep."

The sisters haven't spoken with me in ages, choosing instead to communicate by hate notes taped to Mom's fridge or left at the kitchen table, and tightly scrawled angry letters arriving in my mailbox. Dissent on the upswing, negativity, lying to professionals.

I did speak briefly with one of them recently, though, trying to explain about Hospice re-entering Mom's care. She raged--a long bout of hollering cross talk, final words something like:

"Oh, Mom doesn't know what she wants. She wrote that stuff before she knew what it would be like. She didn't know then what she wants now, and she doesn't know what is best now either."

My mind still boggles. What could this sister, who is a *nurse*, think the term "advanced directives" or "pre-planned life care" means?

So here is a disclaimer if anyone ever reads this: Mom is dying. She lives at home, because I have figured out how to keep this promise. There are four of us daughters. Two who honor and get her plan, and an angry duo who do not. We are near the end, a road that began with a demand for privacy and insistence on a paper plan. To use Mom's favorite status expression, the road has been "pretty good," for a long time.

But years passed, her health declined, her independence dwindled, and rancor grew while I assumed the role of protector. Senior aging, disease, escalating support, escalating acrimony, permanent vigilance.

It is complicated, but it has worked. Thankfully, those angry personalities help with direct care. Y moved to Florida two years ago. She takes Mom two days each week. X visits Y, and together they are a team of infidels, but they do care, for Mom.

Home care has grown exponentially from a bit of companionship and weekly outings to 24-hour support—a luxury of income and preparedness. Mom has remained in familiar surroundings, comfortable as one can be with this awful disease. Her days are monitored and managed, people and schedules keep her safe, clean, secure *and loved* in her own home. I am so grateful for wonderful professional people who truly care about Jean, who work for her, and who recognize what we have accomplished.

Tonight, I ache with the exhaustion, fully aware of existing irony: I am grateful for the gradual slide down to Mom's present, yet exhausted by the duration of it! It is precisely all those years that have enabled the buildup of everything that was needed *over time* to secure Mom's present path.

Mom will finish her days at home. I remain her director, mastering unfolding circumstance while thwarting detractors, my resolve sorely tested and sometimes mucked up by negative forces.

But we are here. Her money has lasted--my father's pension, Mom's Social Security and a bit of carefully managed inheritance. Far from perfect, greatly uneasy and permanently hard. The knot in my gut has hardened, fending off disagreements and vitriol, even as I remain incredulous to the sheer volume of it!

THERE'S A LESSON FOR YOU! I type out loud!

"It's why she chose you," Nurse Debbie says over and over.

"It will get worse and worse, " Debbie adds. And I wonder how?? I cannot imagine *worse*.

"It will get harder to watch and be part of," she repeats. "But about the time you think you can't handle any of it, not one more bit, it will end. Jean took another step today."

That was February. It is not over.

But as road signs go, this points to a final stretch. We have persevered to arrive at the future Mom contemplated way back when. We are at a place where the armor of legal paperwork in Mom's tool box has been used over and over, and no, despite fanciful ruminations, it is definitely not time to loosen my grip on the wheel.

The learning curve hasn't ended. I know Mom, my family and myself at a level I could not otherwise have believed possible, though I wish the education could have been more agreeable. But less fractured is not to be.

Mom's good days are appreciated as they float on that heavy undercurrent. Bad days are a disease of their own. Mom, too, is worn out. We are consumed.

But I think I have really come to understand it all, finally.

Love remains. Love is what matters.

As for the rest? Lean in a little longer, Jan. (Thank you Bob Seeger, *Against the Wind*.)

***

Today is still March 15, and Mom has been admitted to Hospice for the third and final time. I think I am writing the story of us--how we got here, what we are doing and where we go, to write it *out* of me. To preserve myself for meeting the last days…the worse and worst Debbie speaks of.

I counsel myself to hang onto the goal—to be there for her. I have done all I can to respect Mom's wishes, be her advocate, hold her hand and hold ground against anyone who would seek otherwise.

Name an emotion, it is part of the ride. Heartache, hurt, hate, distrust, thankfully countered by joy, acceptance, love, faith, friendship, family.

What do I know right now? I believe the Holy Spirit is with me, along with my own special loved ones who have shared themselves, held me in their arms and lifted me up just so I could keep walking with Mom.

I know what is yet to come. I don't know timing, or how we will tread, except as always, one foot in front of the other, a day at a time. I have no confidence in anything easing up. I hate it. HATE IT! My nerves are shaky.

I'm channeling Ringo Starr, *It Don't Come Easy*. I channel Corinne O'Kelley and Sally Quinn who cared for husbands with terminal illness. Fact is, I channel anybody I can get my hands on to help make sense of our walk to Mom's finish line.

"A certain peace has come over me. Caretaking has become almost sacred…" Sally Quinn. I understand what she's saying.

It sounds crazy saying this out loud, but I am okay with being uncomfortable. Crazy, right?

Did I mention I was shaky? I am amazed by what things I know, what things I can accept. This stream of thought pouring out, this dumping of angst is built upon certitude, moral wellbeing, patience. Inner strength. Faith. God. So much to be grateful for.

Okay, okay, self. Settle down. Leaps in personal awareness. Growth.

I have learned what I can control, which is not much beyond

myself. I do the next right thing. I can choose to respond or not to personal attacks and charged emotions. I simply know that where Mom and I are now, will not go on forever. My friend Ann says so.

It's late. Past my bedtime. My pillow is calling. I am spent, but also just realized that sitting here has been magic. My first "message to self" has lifted me up at a nearly impossible time. Pounding the keyboard has pushed some yuck out and away, enabled me to continue my embrace of Mom's bigger picture.

These last months have been more complicated than imaginable, an arduous journey of love *and* a ravaging disease, intervention *and* interference, supreme joy *and* immeasurable hardship, converging on Mom's earthly dead end.

No one comes out the other side of this life story unscathed. Love remains.

March 16

The mind is a wondrous thing, our unique ability to think and weigh decisions is life in the balance. The impact of choice. Choices. The steady buoyancy of support unconditionally gifted by friends and family, remains a salve for circumstance and not very nice people. Yeah, ok, I still want to banish the detractors. Push them out of my head!

Whether by cancer, Alzheimer's, another or any path, I know the end road needs all the friends and loving family it can get. This one feels like war, all the symptoms, sadness, loss, a road with minefields and enemies. I am humbled by the tenacity of hospice professionals who face this stuff every day.

I have never been this far along anyone's end game until now. I am weary and I feel the road. But talk about continuing education! I am well-seasoned.

The first thing I know, though, is we must, must have that end of life discussion with our parents and our children. Do our best to get everyone on our page. Work diligently and purposefully. Figure out what you want for days ahead when you may not be able to express, explain or advocate for yourself.

ASK everyone, everyone, to honor and respect your choices. Whether they will or not is something for later. But ask. Start asking when you bask in the stronger, better, healthy days of your life continuum.

My mother asked me, she asked her attorney. After all these days and years with her, I don't believe she asked anyone else. But that's just guessing. Maybe she didn't want a battle she knew would be there. Maybe she was confident her attorney and I would/could handle it, and we have. So far.

I think Mom should have shared her decisions, asked for support from the ones who today are enemies of the very life plan that calls for comfort care. But that's just my opinion. Who knows if sharing would have made a difference. Doubtful, based on experience, but wondering doesn't matter anymore.

I do know this: they are against me. They disrespect their mother. When it is my time, about me, I will handle it differently.

I swallow the double-edged sword. I remain grateful for the care, involvement and affection my deceitful sisters and the lying boyfriend have given Mom. Gratitude, however, does not compensate for frustration, consternation or disappointment.

Mom and I continue to share difficult terrain with a trio for whom her directives mean nothing. His staying power in a bad situation contributes to Mom's happiness, but also to the tug of war. My compassion is for my partner on the journey, a very sick old woman with definite plans for herself, and for myself, charged with keeping to the plan. Not for *them*.

Nothing to do but hang on to the rope. As much as possible,

I manage time with Mom outside the hours she has for my sisters or her boyfriend. I am diligent, following instructions and they remain contrary, annoying, angry flies in the ointment.

The doctor will speak with them. Hospice will speak with them. (I've been speaking to them for a decade.) It will go on.

Meanwhile, add more care hours at night, across mealtime, etc. Bed linens and mom are dirty. Lifting, and mobility challenges are increasing. What about assistive medical equipment?

Signs of failure to thrive. She is pocketing food, she tucks it in her clothes, in her cheeks. She has extreme weakness, loss of motor control, no bladder or bowel control.

I am amazed I have been able to keep her home!

March 17

Another Hospice nurse visited yesterday, and Mom showed her reality. We sat by the pool--Mom noticed her pink azalea bushes blooming. So we thought. But looking above the azaleas, she kept asking, "What is that?" We kept trying to see what she saw. Not azaleas. Only a dark shady treetop, branches whispering in the wind.

Later, I move a mermaid plush toy off the mantle because she keeps asking, "Who is that?" She slides back into silence and then to sleep.

March 18

I spend a few hours at Islander Court without home health care support staff, much of it on the phone to fine tune additional care hours, specifics—hygiene, laundry, a daily care focus—all noted, planned for, scheduled.

I observe the boyfriend's ritual departure, out the door about

10 a.m. He was chattering away, telling me she was fine, had eaten a good breakfast, which I took to mean he had put food in her mouth. Mom was silent, swallowed up in an enormous fleece robe that looked like it belonged in Alaska, not Florida. I waited for Hospice, to discuss status and strategy with people who actually know about these things.

A Green Team nurse finds us. Mom is inside herself, immobile, arms locked, vacant, staring, hurting and not hurting. We give a small dose of comfort meds, and she slips into sleep on the sofa. I am given the seminal hospice pamphlet written by Barbara Karnes, an RN, who detailed the dying experience with concrete precision nearly 30 years ago.

While Mom rests, the nurse and I discuss and strategize Suncoast Hospice care. She repeats what I know: each situation is unique. Mom will worsen. Our situation with angry family members and the boyfriend's interference screams for social work intervention, but she is circumspect, freely admitting that nothing really helps those problems.

The nurse says she is witnessing caregiver fatigue. Moi. Says I am doing everything right, but that sometimes, especially after years of managing care for a loved one, some caregivers question themselves, especially when there is dissension.

"Don't do that," she ordered and followed with a pep talk, and the promise I had been dreaming about: "When your mom is worse, she will receive continuous care. When 24-hour support takes over, it will make these people issues go away."

I thanked her for her care of me, for validation of the mess and for all future support efforts. I found myself briefly wondering about other families in this hospice arena, in this city, in this state, in the country? I was feeling bad for them too.

I called Tee about Mom—the physical and mental decline, her

honest desire to be done, how she hurts, how she complains about living this way, how she cannot decipher her life. Mom doesn't "know" anything these days. She doesn't know if she lives there. She doesn't know if the boyfriend still comes over. She doesn't know, she doesn't know.

Later this afternoon I was on the phone when the boyfriend arrived. He immediately pulled Mom up off the sofa, man on a mission, propelling her and the tripod walker to the table. He prepared a plateful of small broccoli bits, dip and chips, sausage slivers, cheese, fish crackers, with tea or juice in blue flamingo cups. Jean has limited finger and hand control these days but picked up a piece and ate at his urging. She sipped her drink through a straw, brightening in his presence.

First, he said something like, "Try some of this." She does but stops. Then he ordered her to eat and she took another bite. Then said she doesn't want it.

He tried again, a second order to eat. I tasked him to remember that Jean has said no. Immediately he defended himself, says he has stopped putting food in her mouth (I knew it!), but that really, really, she has a great appetite. Feeds herself all the time.

She keeps eyeing the sofa. She spatters her minutes at the table with noisy sighs, she hums, she grimaces, asks about her dead sister, looks around, reads the dry erase board. But she does not eat.

trash out please Sunday night
Extending care hours, soft food
"Where is your dad?"

For 15 minutes, his attentions all to her and her eyes following him, a confounding mix of repetitive questions and perfect reading skills. Her eyes returned to the couch.

I asked if she wants to lie down. She nods. I put her hands to the walker grips, used a full lift under both arms and with a slightly forward roll, raised her to standing. She maneuvered while I blocked his view with my body. She walked to the sofa and worked at folding into some position that allows her to sit. I raised the tightly locked limbs, put Aunt Sue's quilt on her legs.

"Where is Susan? Who was I married to? Where is Joan? Is Dad dead?"

I answered slowly.

"Susan died, Mom. You were married to Tom. Dad is dead, too." Answers just beyond reach.

The boyfriend bursts in, a chuckling volley.

"Joan? You know Joan. She lives in Shady Acres. Oh, she's fine, don'cha know? Ha-ha, over there in Shady Acres." There is no such place.

Once again, he tells me things are fine, that he is the best caregiver, that he knows her best, that he just adapts. I tune out. "Just fine" cannot explain poo in the bed, or aides finding Mom in dirty diapers, or poo folded into towels in the linen closet. It must be the aides' doing, he says, he has no problems.

He says he knows how to lift her and move her. He says broccoli is recommended to improve memory by "a TV ALZ doc." Really, he says this stuff. He also says he has tried to instruct aides how to handle Mom in the shower, because he has no problems with her in the shower. (I can't imagine when he last helped Mom into a shower). He says they come late, he says once they didn't come at all. I remind him to call me if an absence occurs. Says he arrives by 6 p.m. and "prefers" no one but himself at night because he does best by himself. They like to sleep together, he says. He changes her diaper before bed, and once in the night. Says she still walks herself to the toilet.

I know he lies. She does not get up on her own. She can't find the bathroom. I know about poo in the bed. I know he layers towels upon soiled sheets. I also know, one night she pooped in the closet.

I kiss her goodbye, tell him I will be in touch. She says goodbye as I leave.

What happens, what is it like when I am not there? A friend says, "get a nanny cam." I don't think I want to see all that. But should I?

I come home and take care of me. Bob gets carryout Chinese, I zone out with two movies on a free HBO weekend. I remember that Churchill quote about hell.

God, help me hold peace and let go the whine I hear in my words.

March 19

I wake up this morning muddled, thinking about honesty between Mom and me. Different from the happy face she wears with her boyfriend. It must be exhausting! Two different faces. Two realities. More fodder for a social worker.

Another Hospice nurse called today to set up a 1 p meet tomorrow to discuss the "plan." We put pain management and comfort care on our agenda. I need to call care management about extending their coverage across 5:30 to 7p. Despite telling me otherwise, I know the boyfriend is late, absent, not completely reliable on these worsening days. The care company prints out a two-week schedule. I tape it up so everyone can see coverage hours, straightforward details, a calendar of who is working when.

March 20

I belong to an email gratitude list, a group of women sharing their lives and moments, reminding each other about mindfulness for all moments in our lives. Gratitude for: the "cool side of the pillow," a hint of Spring in longer hours of sunshine, a gentle breeze, growing forward, and one awesome reminder that we all have permission to step away from an argument.

I used to think about COINCIDENCE when I would find a relevant thought, a call from a friend, a billboard message, or a song lyric that seemed particularly relevant. As I continue to care for Mom, study what to do, process what I know, pray and strive for optimal strength, I believe now there are no coincidences......

I hear Joni Mitchell sing *"Help me"* and I look out my kitchen's east facing window every morning, towards Mom's house, watching the sky change color. What will today bring?

Even when I'm not searching, the perfect phrase or message has been showing up, reminding me who I am, what I'm doing, how to be there for her. Her plan, my mindfulness, unaltering faith.

I subscribe to a daily meditation group about peace, wholeness, self-care and health. Several "signs" appeared in the last 24 hours: "By being honest with others, we set ourselves free." "Accept the act as if you had chosen it."

A bit of 12-step logic means I've given this all over to God--by mindfulness, paying attention. It dawns on me this morning that I have been growing into serenity over Mom for a long time. I have adopted the mantra -- "signs are everywhere."

I believe I am that victim of caregiver fatigue.

March 22

Hospice had delivered comfort care meds. For the third day, I have asked Mom if she is hurting. She says yes. She has taken a minimum dose once each day. About the equivalent of a Vicodin pain pill. Tiny in the scheme of medical possibility. I watched relief flood her face as this sublingual drug took effect. Her eyes soften, the grimace disappears, a deep groove between her brows lessens. She is calm, restful, relaxed. This is what she wants.

I returned this afternoon to ask again: is she hurting? This time, the answer is no. The aide and I are encouraged.

There is a note overnight in the table log. Dual versions of yesterday. The private care aide writes, *Jean is tired but resting comfortably.* Scribbled below is the boyfriend's contrary review claiming Mom is, "*out of this world out of it.*" He blames morphine.

Mom had been in Suncoast care for a week. There is new trouble. The decriers have stepped up their game, questioning doctor's ordered medications. The boyfriend called X, who is not here, but who is determined to insert herself. X had phoned Mom's doctor, asking for different meds and treatment. The doctor's office called me to ask what's going on, complaining that X is off course.

The doctor's office has spent time checking with Hospice. Hospice has spent time on their end, and now they've both called me. It's all fishy. I hear frustration in their voices as they described first-hand experience with my sister's malice. They do not like wasting precious time on days already too full.

It is another day at my ranch: angry boyfriend imagines himself a drug expert, collusion by angry sister (LPN, no less). Both think they know better than Hospice. I fantasize about removing the boyfriend, but short of a restraining order, there is no way to stop the devil twin train. I won't do it.

"Welcome to caring for my mom, " I told both nurses. "This is the stuff I've been telling you about. I've been dealing with them for a long, long time."

I apologized multiple times and sadly point out they've been victims of what I face. Dear Marcella, Dr. A's nurse, said she "tried to educate" my sister about different drug delivery methods and effect--sublingual versus IV drip. She told me that Hospice confirmed sublingual is working, that Mom is resting comfortably, doing well on these tiny under the tongue doses, **as needed. PRN.**

I hate the unfairness, the imposition of extra work for good doctors and nurses. I hate the work required to protect Mom's rights.

"I feel really awful for you," says the hospice nurse. "But we've seen this before. It's too bad. But you were chosen by your mom for a reason, to help with hard episodes like this."

This is a hospice answer. She emphasized what I need to do.

"You need to remind your sister that your mother's doctor and Hospice are working to protect your mom. And, you should tell your sister that her suggesting liquid codeine is totally wrong. It makes us worry about aspiration and choking."

Nearly laughable, but sad. *I need to remind my sister....as if.*

This particular nurse is on vacation soon, but she wants a social worker to speak directly with the sisters and the boyfriend--to help them understand. Have at it! Good luck!

I tried convincing myself their latest wrongs are due to denial. I know they love Mom. Right? Are they rendered incapable by stress? I know each person is entitled to experience Mom's situation in their own way. I am supremely tired of trying to explain what is right.

Messing with doctor's orders is the latest low.

April is around the corner.

April 17

A Hospice physician saw Mom today to "re-certify" her eligibility for services. Standard procedure a few weeks into a Hospice contract. As if documentation today would suddenly find Mom *not* to have Alzheimer's or its accompanying debilitations? Mom's home care nurse caught my eye with a "duh" look about wasting time.

Hospice labels recertification a "procedural safeguard," because Alzheimer's and dementia are tricky. Could be less than 6 months or 2 years longer, with a gradual lessening of abilities. Mom couldn't/didn't/wouldn't respond during most of the interview. When she did, it was with worry about having to leave her house. He seemed kind, compassionate, and told us he will go with eligibility for another couple months. For now.

Sister X called the house moments after the doctor left, keenly disappointed to miss him, utterly dissatisfied to find herself speaking with me. I told her what I've said before—Mom is more confused, weaker, hurting, and continues to qualify for Hospice. That the doctor recommends everyone watch physical cues because Mom is less and less verbal. That comfort care treatment, which Mom wants, is helping. I also told her straight out how I resent her attempt to maneuver around hospice and me to stop the medicine.

X mounted an angry tirade, ranting. Said she knows ONLY ONE person can be in charge and we should agree to disagree. I caught myself, almost responding that this was a wrongful act, not a disagreement. But I kept silent. She doesn't care what I think. She raged on, a tiresome harangue that Mom wasn't thinking about NOW when she wrote advanced directives. She paused finally, maybe, to catch her breath? My turn.

"This is **exactly what** Mom thought about and planned for, and **why** she wrote advanced directives."

Her claims once again that I am mental, probably too worn out. That I would have to answer to God for how I was handling things. I heard words but wasn't really listening. When she paused again, I said something about Mom being in God's hands, good bye.

Hanging up, I began to laugh. I am in good shape with God. In fact, I am in great shape with God. God knows, I am following Mom's plan.

So maybe next time, because I'm sure there will be one, I will ask one of these sisters: "Let me get this straight. If when you were healthy and clear headed, and you wrote down how you wanted to be treated when you are old and sick, you would be OK with someone treating you differently? You would be OK with other people NOT doing what you said you wanted?" Delicious thoughts, but I won't waste my breath.

I write this record instead. Today was more validation of what has been said many times—one person. Tough times. Hard questions. Hard answers. I believe Mom asked me, her "one person," to follow her plan, for good reason.

Oh yeah, I just remembered. Before the hang up, I mentioned that ALL care professionals are telling me to get rid of the boyfriend because he impedes Mom's medical care and her directives. My sister, the nurse, doesn't have much to say about that, likely too caught up in imagining me answering to God.

Mom and I will meet with Dr. A tomorrow, a regular checkup. See what he thinks about ditching the boyfriend. Though I am sure it will come to this, and probably soon, I still witness Mom's enjoyment from his company. I remain unwilling to force this odd person from her side, no matter what he does against me. But I cannot stop imagining what effort might be needed to get him gone when the time is right.

April 18

We have reached the point where I speak to a different kind of attorney, who tells me it will take written documentation from Hospice, the care company and Mom's primary care physician to remove the boyfriend.

"Following my mother's recent admission to Hospice under orders from her primary care physician, we have experienced some "glitches" with the continuum of care delivery due to interference by several people who refuse to honor my mother's advanced directives, choosing instead to attempt their own control of her end of life care.

"Sadly, I am writing to request the additional support you offered me as we move forward. To respect my mom's wishes and directives at this end stage condition, I need written advice, (documented recommendations) from you, to remove anyone who is interfering with Mom's care. Thank you so very much for your support of my mom at this difficult time."

Dr. A writes an amazing letter. He orders the boyfriend to stop interfering with his patient, a woman with "end stage Alzheimer's." I share a copy with the care company. Tell my sisters.

The care company owner puts pen to paper to document what she's been saying for years.

Hospice, however, "doesn't like" to do this kind of thing, conflicts of interest (family issues), and informs me there will be no letter.

Two of three isn't bad. I'll see if it goes anywhere.

April 25

The best sleep I've had in weeks! Waking refreshed with memories of a night time visitor. Aunt Sue woke me up. In my face. I goggled at shiny golden hair, and the glow about her head. Smiling eyes. Her grin. She knew I saw her. The moment is infused, full of happiness, even giggles. Behind her, all white, an undulating ribbon of movement. I think it is a group of friends, crowding closer, and I immediately slip back to sleep as a soft hand cupped my cheek, and that whole moment disappeared.

May 1

I have my wonderful two-year-old grandson staying here for one more night while his mommy and dad take a vacation. The happiness in this kid in the everyday wonder of exploring water, helping stir, playing with toys, using my iPhone, and holding my hand at 'lay me down to sleep' is a great gift of love. A big gratitude. I listen with pure joy to his emerging language skills, words popping out. It is a strong antidote to that ugly other sad part. Having him here has been exhausting in a good way, awesome for self-care.

May 10

Today I caught Mom as she stumbled forward with the walker. Only to her knees and she is still holding on. I was surprised how difficult it was to steady her back to standing. The aide came to help us. I think someone must walk at her side from now on, maybe even hold onto her. She is ok. When asked if she hurts, she shakes her head. No.

May 17

I heard a creepy story today. That the boyfriend is talking to aides about sex, in general, and sex, specifically, with Mom. I also hear he is invading their space, getting "too close" physically, as they do their work. He apparently tried touching one aide's silky black hair.

She stepped away and told him to back off. These young CNAs have been in this house long enough to know him and how to handle weirdo moments. I'm grateful these long-term helpers have grit. There is no recourse, however, it is another he said-she said moment. But what about that nanny-cam?

May 28

I have missed my youngest's birthday. I was here instead, for a Hospice morning progress report. Today Mom's oxygen levels were up. Last time, they were down. She was so sick a week ago with fever and another UTI, that some professionals thought she might be headed out. But Hospice quickly ordered antibiotics and Jean sat here today, able to follow instruction. She took a breath for the nurse, something that doesn't always happen.

Her arm circumference is down two inches from a month ago—confirmation she is losing weight despite how much food Y or the boyfriend put into her. Yes, that still happens. Eyes in the house. Sure, she never wanted to be fed. Short of moving her out, or denying admittance to these loved ones, or being there 24/7 myself, it won't stop.

I cannot imagine being there 24/7, and I will not refuse Mom the "pleasure" of their company. I am unwilling to move against them for the sake of love. I am a broken record. But I don't beat myself up. I've latched onto another saying....*it is what it is.*

The result is that Mom suffers and will be forced to eat when they are around, until she stops eating. Today I saw her turn away from a straw. It is beginning. <u>Progress on her own time line.</u> The nurse and I talk, and Mom has a clear moment. Answers with head shakes yes, no. Y is putting food in her mouth. Head shake, yes. Does she like living this way? Head shake, no. I tell her I have done everything I can, but she is in charge. She can refuse as best as she is able. A nod. A frown. Very sad. I don't want to ask if I should keep them away. Any answer is a no-win. I think about her pocketing food, I think about her drooling chocolate when she arrives at day care. Their attempts are losing ground.

June 5

About day care. I go there every couple weeks to get a feel for how things are going. Neighborly Care is funded partly by private pay for those who can, subsidized for those who cannot. The program has switched locations several times and now is in brand new secure space in north county. There is a transport bus, but locations and timing fit better with Mom's own customized drop off and pick up. The aides do the bulk of it, but I pick Mom up plenty, carting her off to doctor's appointments, or a drive back home via the local pier. It is my chance to check with the lovely Mari, program administrator, on how it goes.

Mari says she has a quiet group, permanently on recess, old people hanging out in a supervised safe place until it is time to load the buses, or until they don't come anymore.

Mom has been coming for almost two years. Can that be? Yes. She doesn't eat much except that occasional afternoon ice cream. Scheduled toileting has worked 99% of the time. Mom is compliant. She hasn't signed her name at morning check-in for the last year. A mark on the page works. Mari says Mom sits with a group of admirers. Mari describes the pleasure all her quiet charges take from one another's company, the attraction between sexes not lost even when so much else is gone. Mom is passive, they all are. She listens to the weather, they have music, they clap. A lot of time is spent at round tables, for breakfast, for lunch, for sitting with friends. Watching. Waiting. I've heard Mom has one particular favorite friend. I want to see who.

Tony. The program manager points him out, sitting next to Mom during an afternoon video. A slightly built man in a plaid shirt. Wavy salt and pepper hair, glasses. I move into the row and sit down next to Mom, who appears confused to see me sitting here. I take her hand, smile, say I'm here for a visit.

I look past her to greet Tony. Olive skin. Roman nose. Crooked smile. My heart tumbles. I am teary. Thunderstruck. I am looking at a shrunken version of my dad.

Perhaps the best news today was from Tess. She tells me that sister X, who is visiting, called her into the garage to demonstrate how to put my mother into a car. Tess is chuckling with the tale. By pulling on a towel placed underneath the nearly dead weight of a client, the towel becomes an assistive people mover.[*] Tess responded to the *lesson,* informing X that this is HOW she has been moving Mom for more than a year.

The other sister was also there and admitted, (again to Tess), that it appears Jean is declining.

I call that progress and continue my prayers to God for Mom's release from disease, sooner rather than later.

June 10

Almost 6 years of personal in-home care. Six years down a slippery slope. Both of us bruised by the journey. Time and disease taking a toll.

By all appearances, Mom is vanishing. Vegetating. We both seem stressed by the wait. Hospice comes again tomorrow.

---

1   If you are wondering, one of the best ways to assist people with challenged mobility into a car is to use a chuck, a plastic-sided hygienic bed or chair pad. On cloth seats, place the plastic side down--the slippery surface allows it to move more easily than a towel. Pull from the driver's side to move the patient securely into the passenger seat. Reverse for exiting.

Cannot forget the nastiness of sisters. Can I be any more tired?

June 11

Mom has a decent O2 level today for someone in end stage ALZ. 94%. It has been as low as 82% but hasn't gone beyond 95 since the very beginning of Hospice's third round.

Today's aide reports my sisters say they found Mom mouthing a peanut—*pocketing food.* What about a peanut qualifies as soft food? But apparently, they don't hear her moans or gasps for air, don't see her inability to move, don't notice fingers curled tightly into her palms, don't watch grimaces of pain and confusion, don't see darkening eyes or agitation on her face. Tess and I eased these symptoms with comfort meds to provide a restful afternoon. Tess has painted Mom's toes and fingernails a happy pink.

I believe Tess is an angel.

Hospice nurse and social worker/counselor have their visit and we talk about music, about how they joke around, how sometimes they even laugh at funerals. Not that this business is funny, but why laughter is a "life skill," a useful, necessary diversion from the difficult and darker realities they face daily. Laughing is self-care.

"Otherwise we would go nuts," one chuckled.

We are two weeks from Mom's 85th birthday and Hospice is wondering about a big party? Bringing volunteers, strangers into the house to make a fuss. I say no. The social workers calls HQ and asks that teen volunteers DO NOT plan a birthday celebration for July 4. The social worker gives an earful to the nurse in charge of the well-meaning teens. Says this suggestion is "upsetting" the caregiver. I am put on the phone to end the prank. This is just a bit of weird Hospice humor, a tension releasing tease among professionals. It happens only because I am personally acquainted with the nurse in charge of teen volunteers. I identify myself, and we chuckled about who set her up, the social worker with oddball stress reduction humor. Mom lies clueless in a torpor of end stage, but I think she likes hearing the laughter. We are chuckling about nothing but life.

It is a reminder to keep humor as medicine in the midst of tough business. The social worker says every day is about dying, death, pain, confusion, hurt, grief, you name your end of life issue. So much sadness that she works hard to bring in a laugh, a bit of the normal *other side* of the emotional spectrum. That is what was happening with this quirky joke on the teen coordinator.

Permission to have fun. It is okay to joke. She tells a story about how she once put a phone on speaker at the home of a young client dying of ALS and proceeded to ask the other Hospice staffer to describe herself, so everyone could envision who would be coming into the house later.

About halfway through proper and polite responses--"I'm kinda short, with curly brown hair…" the social worker reveals the prank, and everyone, including the patient laughed.

I learned more about the compassionate people in this dying business today. Professionals do what they can, with every client/family situation to lighten the load, even if it is a practical joke on one another. They gauge whether or not the family is healthy enough to laugh. Sometimes they are not. But we are.

I played along. We remember to think and talk about other things when Hospice visits, and there was a tic of cognition from Mom, who suddenly announced that she likes the nurse's aquamarine nail polish, before dropping back out of the moment. Social worker said Mom was there, in tune. Enjoy that.

I found it amazing. I am thrilled she still is in there, still showing up. Grateful I was there to see it.

When not visiting, these same folks call for status checks.

They nearly always block their phone numbers, completely understandable because otherwise their phones would be blowing up--client families calling at all hours, interrupting visits with other clients, invading personal time, etc. Protocol is to call the office and leave a message and expect a return call.

Today, as the Hospice women leave, I give them a good giggle. A quick check-in call from hospice is a Friday requisite prior to on-call teams taking over weekend coverage. So far, these Friday calls have been uneventful, nothing to report. We decided earlier that I would not answer unless I had a question or something to report. For efficiency, I also had given my okay for a nurse to leave voicemail.

As I walk them to the front door, I say, "Do you get it? *I* will be BLOCKING *your* calls." Perhaps only a 5 on the humor meter, but gotcha! They get it.

***

My dear friend Ann called today to check in. Friends for nearly 30 years, we have shared a lot, including the Alzheimer's highway, staying beside our mothers through the journey. Her mother had about 12 years on the road, 8 or 9 years in a care facility. We have that "mutual admiration" thing going on. We know we have helped each other through, that our mutual experiences have eased each other. We've spent enough time at this — we share the bits to look for, signals toward death and the beyond. People are saying goodbye, asking for help with their belongings. Sometimes they want a favorite food.

For years, we've wondered out loud if our voices could, would help ease anyone else along the path. We speculate that the answer is yes, but we both recognize *how hard* sharing pain might be.

We know about this journey, this awful complicated, seriously convoluted meandering trail. We chuckle that *ease* is not a word we associate with what we know. We toss it back and forth. Do we know enough? Do we have anything at all to "ease" someone's way? Can common experience lighten a load? Would our message simply be cheerleading the cause of love and perseverance? A flag bearer pronouncement for the one left behind? You can live through it?

Fortitude is one message. Compassion should count too. We know in our hearts how much we have appreciated each other support, because we *feel* it. But Ann's story is too fresh and painful for reliving and caught as I am in the throes of Mom's big picture RIGHT NOW, helping anyone else is a decision for another day. But we speculate. We both *know* what it has been like and we think this fact alone could help a few people.

We also know that we are forever changed. We wonder if Hospice people feel that shift with each family. We could never, ever work for Hospice! In fact, both of us feel completely undone to even consider doing this more than once. What on earth can those Hospice people be getting from all this end of life living and dying?

Ann's mom left the world the day my grandson was born. One soul departing, another arriving. She tells me today that even though two years have passed, she still is working out who and where she is on the journey of her life. This makes perfect sense to me. I tell her I've begun journaling. So I can remember. So I won't forget.

We have mutual blessings for each other in our prayers. We love each other. I always thank her for her road wisdom. I have learned to do a lot, do what I can, and put down the rest, but Ann has helped me navigate. I have gratitude for her care of me.

I hang onto many things she has shared over the years, but at least once every day, there is a thread from our conversations that flits thru my solace seeking, high-wired consciousness: this cannot last forever.

Someone told Ann this, and she has told me.

June 14

I am headed over to see the hospice client--her breathing changed yesterday, and aides report mobility is further down, noticeably more difficult... we discuss getting a wheel chair or a seated walker for home. The future at Islander Court will mean installing a hospital bed soon. Positioning, bathing, sitting are all more labor intensive for Mom, for the aides, for me. I know lifting Mom is nearly impossible from my own experience. It will become more and more difficult.

Only a few short days between delight at turquoise nail polish and breathing problems. Observable. We dosed her with comfort meds, her breathing smoothed out. She rests.

Later today, she was asking repeatedly, "Jan, what is wrong with me?" Nurse Debbie was there listening, and so we tried to tell her. Truthfully. Gently.

She is old, she is sick, she has had a good life, to not be afraid, that she is dying, and it is ok, etc. She leans into my hand when I tenderly stroke her cheek, we hang on to one another.

Later, she pushes a drink away.

We are three months into the current Hospice contract.

Tess, who has been with her the longest, says Mom told her she is mad today because no one likes her boyfriend--what a hoot. We laugh together. She shares another funny story. The boyfriend's latest tall tale is claiming to be a CNA. (Nurse Debbie got a roaring chortle out of that). He has informed Tess that he has all the credentials, better in fact, than any aide who has been friend, companion, driver, carer, lady-in-waiting, attendant since the beginning of Mom's care dates. Of course, he is not a CNA. But chuckling helps us all.

Mom interrupts Tess's story.

"Do I still have my place in the mobile home park?" (Maybe the 1,000th time she has asked this, but who's counting?) Mom's alertness travels backwards, picking a fact or idea from years ago, out of all context except her own. The answer I give always is the same. *You sold it, you don't own it anymore.* Sometimes I give a bit more information: *We sold it, Mom, so you have money to live here.*

The repetitious questions are dangling and diverging conversations. Dementia does not mean crazed but rather, a befuddled old brain trying to make sense of all the data in storage. Things Mom once knew. Things she cared about and wants to know again, wants to hang onto.

But information and answers just will not stick. We are too far on this journey, and only a fragment, a scrambled memory about that mobile home, has surfaced. Mom knows she once owned a mobile home and for some reason, remembers about it, right now.

You sold it. The money helps you live here.

Tess helped take one of the big gold cocktail rings off her swollen finger on Thursday after watching her hand swell for three days. (Another sign I am told.) It came off with twisting, kitchen dishwashing liquid and elbow grease. The deep groove below her knuckle where the band had been squeezing the skin began to smooth out once Tess wriggled it free. I took the ring home for safe keeping. It is for Tee.

Touching her skin today has made Mom cry out, even though she says she doesn't hurt. Movement is too much exertion for her tired body. She winces with effort. We can move her, or help her, but Mom is permanently showing visual discomfort. Lately there has been additional audio--more frequent sighs and moans.

She says she isn't hurting but it does not compute. Anything but lying there is gargantuan effort. The aide and I offer a PRN dose. As needed. Comfort care. We cuddle Mom into the sheets for another rest.

Am beginning to think it might be time for Tee to make a final visit, to leave the coyotes for a day and fly down here if she wants to visit Mom before she dies. There is no way to predict anything. But I know we are closer.

So many months and years. All that growing confusion, a loss of appetite, a lessening of speech. But she is still smiling, she can laugh. She can help us--help get herself to a car, help herself sit down to the toilet, sit in a shower.

Seeing smiles, hearing her laugh, are rewards for my vigilance while I acknowledge the emptying of a vessel. If the slow saunter of final years has been a trial of patience and illness, these last months and days, her final plummet, is special with any moment we enjoy together.

But *I see less of her.* It remains an unsettling reality, watching her essence disappear. The quiet blankness grows. Vibrancy fades like muted colors after sunset. Awake hours shrink further. I calculate 17-18 hours of sleep each day, maybe more. I watched her sleep somedays, never waking while I'm there. I wondered does she sleeps at day care too?

Would it be tomorrow, the day after? How do I help her anymore? When will she disappear? How can I know?

After Nurse Debbie explained about dying, I watched Mom thinking it through for herself: a gentle message on a sweet summer day, about nearing the end. Then we saw her eyes roll backward, and she slept. It is poignant, real.

When she woke in the afternoon, pain was back. Deep grooves, scrunching eyes, more wincing as we helped her sit up. Dosed with a minimum comfort/anxiety med to ease whatever hurt. Another day down and downward. Poor Mom. So hard to watch. I was simply present, bearing witness. There was no escaping the countdown. I knew Hospice would not be leaving this time, before she did.

I ate ice cream for dinner tonight.

June 15

The morning aide tells me the boyfriend has decided Mom is "on her way out." Incredible news from someone who's been in permanent denial. I have a hunch something must have happened overnight, in his time with her, and I'm back to thinking about nanny cams.

But mostly, I really don't need to know what causes his declaration. I don't want to know.

June 16

Today is June 16 and Mom has taken to bed. Well, more correctly, the aide, Sandy, has assisted getting her back into bed, under the covers. She is sleeping deeply, soundly, victim of an extra tiring morning regimen of cleanliness and personal care that sapped her strength, kept her moving and literally wiped her out. Instead of lying back on the couch staring blankly at a television which prompts inconsequential comments and remarks about the jumbles of colors and sounds, Mom had asked to go back to bed.

It is a first. It is about 12:30 and Mom was exhausted after being assisted into the shower-- four showers in two hours after pooing herself unknowingly and repeatedly on each trip out of the bath as Sandy and Mom struggled to get her ready for the day.

"What's that?" she kept saying, looking at the shit which seemed to appear out of nowhere, on the floor at her feet, in her makeup chair, in the shower, on the rug.

"What's that?"

"Jean," says Sandy. "Do you think you should sit on the toilet?" She obliges and with a great assist from Sandy settling her down, continues to drop anchor, finally in an appropriate and flushable location.*

Everything is darkness. Everything is taking longer and longer. The washer is humming in the background. I wonder for the umpteenth time, but only briefly, why my sisters don't acknowledge the debilitation or the unhappiness. Sandy is sweeping crumbs in the kitchen. Mom sleeps like a log. What used to be accomplished in two hours, now takes nearly four.

How does anyone suggest that this is quality of life, "just fine, we adapt" or any number of other rejections about how her life is *not that bad.* Beyond comprehension. This is bad, this is sad, and how Nurse Debbie described it, echoes.

"The time will come when it will be so bad you think YOU hardly can stand it anymore yourself….and then it will be almost over."

I find myself hanging on to that conversation. She's right. Already I can hardly stand it. It is too much. Too long. Mom is headed toward the release she scripted. The release I have prayed for and wished for her. I pray for soon because finally, finally, I think I too, need to be free.

---

* A year later, I read an essay in the Wall Street Journal weekend edition. A son, remembering his father's last days, has penned a memoir of an old man coming to live with him for what time is left, the effect on his family, and the reality of poo. Every carer gets there, he says. It is not unlike taking care of babies but features the additional problems of proportion and embarrassment. Babies get themselves toilet trained, while the elderly and infirm move in the opposite direction. We all deal. Experienced travelers recognize the scenery.

June 17

Mom is nonverbal, swollen, immobile. Her face is drawn, deep grooves at the corners of her mouth, a furrowed brow. We're talking anxiety, discomfort with plenty of revealing body language and alarmed eyes. Hospice has said that expecting words to express herself is akin to expecting her to know she is pooing, which clearly, she does not. Her left hand is still puffy and upon examination, the underside is mottled. She winces as I pick it up. The aide noticed increased tactile sensitivity. This aide is not a regular, but an irregular, a temp, an as-needed vacation replacement who knows Mom but has not seen her for a while. She doesn't know the medical directives about comfort care meds. We go over it together, dose Mom and watch, hoping to get relief flowing into the aching body that is what is left of Jean.

June 18

I have brought fresh flowers in pinks and fuchsia. They match the top Mom is wearing. We toss out roses which have fallen over. In and out of Florida's summer heat and air conditioning is too much. Blossoms don't last. The aide has something to do-- flower arranging.

Mom is stretched out as usual on her couch. She has fallen asleep as the Hospice nurse arrives. The nurse is slightly late, remarkable given that she explained two earlier house visits required extra time. It is the dynamics of hospice business. I'm good with however the schedule works.

We sit down to go over what we know, the weekly observation and measure. We note that neither of us are seeing the relief we had witnessed earlier from the comfort medicine. Irregular delivery (more correctly, the lack so far of anyone but me or Nurse Debbie delivering comfort meds), can make overall pain management more difficult, she explains, as would Mom's anxiety or deterioration. "As needed" delivery also can make meds less effective, but Hospice maintains that medicine should still take effect within 5-10 minutes.

Something is not working.

Into her mouth, under her tongue and relief should be happening. I shared what transpired last Friday, when Mom's observable distress signals—confusion, discomfort, grimacing, stiffness, contracture of the hands, nonverbal, lack of responsiveness, were so pronounced that Nurse Debbie, as case manager, authorized a second .25ml dose, a "push" as it is called, to help soothe Mom. There was such limited visible relief, we had wondered aloud if someone had tampered with Mom's prescription. My stomach flipped over.

Today, I shared our suspicions with the hospice nurse, who admitted she also noticed Mom's rising discomfort, but says only that it might be time to up the dosage. She discusses this with her supervisor, who agrees to a rush refill for later this day. I leave a note on the dry erase board about expecting the delivery.

We talk about birthdays a bit and I mention that Mom was born on the 4th of July.

"Really?" she says. "I have another patient who is a New Year's Day birthday." And suddenly, Mom jumps into this conversation.

"Yes, everybody celebrates my birthday." She smiles. A bit of her old self has breezed in. A gift. I mouth a surprised O to the aide who says everyone celebrates because she is so beautiful.

"Where is Susan?" she asks next. Had she been dreaming of Susan? Susan always attended the Fourth of July birthday parties I remember as a kid. But Susan has been dead 4 years.

I try something else:

"Tomorrow is my mom's and dad's wedding anniversary, " I say. My parents would have been married 65 years.

"Mom, tomorrow is June 19. Do you know that day?"

"It was my wedding," she says softly. The window is open again. Amazing. But just for a moment. Her eyes roll up and inward. I wish her happy memory dreams as silence returns.

Hospice performs their measures. Pulse is ok, blood oxygen is ok, though this doesn't say much about the exercise of breathing. Even with swelling, Mom has lost another 2.5cm in arm width, blood pressure is up, as is vacancy in her eyes.

Hospice's traveling physician assistant will make a house visit next week, another three-month recertifying evaluation. This is more Medicare documentation to qualify Mom for continued care. Nurse Debbie and I will be there to share our observations and discuss these last three months.

I asked about a motorized hospital bed because of increasing difficulty aides have moving, manipulating and lifting. I remembered my own experience with a motorized bed. A Godsend after knee surgery. It sat me up and laid me down. Mom could not operate the controls, but aides and loved ones could.

One of the Hospice bathing assistants has already called in twice to report difficulty, additional confirmation that assistive equipment would be welcome. The bed will eventually be Mom's home and the hospice nurse is ready to order it now, advising that Mom will rest easier because the bed can make almost everything easier. But she counsels that the "visual," the actual bed in the house, will be another gotcha for anyone in denial.

I digest this, I know what she means. I can do this for Mom. I appreciate the heads up. Go buy extra-long twin sheets, make space in the house. Out in the open, the nurse recommends, not in the bedroom, too depressing.

"They'll bring it in, but they won't move your furniture. You need to pick a place." We scan possible locations. I have ruminated myself and it is the family room sofa that will move to the garage. Excited to use equipment to help us be there for Mom. Dreadful task, informing others.

We are almost finished so I checked our inventory of bed pads, diapers, lotions, gentle wash soaps, things offered for Hospice clients. We have plenty of pull-up adult diapers, a substitute for the hospice wrap and tape for bed-bound. We don't need wrap & tape—yet.

I find a note heavily taped to the closet rack in Mom's bedroom from the sisters demanding that Mom be dressed in long pants and tube socks to combat coolness in hands and feet.

I tell this nurse and she responded: "It would be one thing if they were just doing this to bother you, but it is your Mom who suffers. Why wouldn't you dress appropriate **to the weather?**"

What exactly does she mean, if only they were doing this to bug me? Ugh.

It is June in Pinellas County, Florida, and by crackee, it is HOT and humid. Pants and athletic tube sox don't match the climate.

I pen an unemotional response at the bottom of their note: *Temperature fluctuations are symptomatic. Hospice says to dress appropriate to weather.* I'm wondering when their note went up and what has happened to all of Mom's shorts and capris. I also wonder what they have done with her shoes. All but one pair have disappeared. What is the matter with these people?

I came home and began to record today's lengthy details as body tremors alerted me to "caregiver fatigue" and my high outrage and sadness for Mom's sake over what I believe has happened. Medicine tampering. But Hospice won't commit.

I tried taking big, deep slow breaths, and long slow exhalations while gripping my hands together, willing myself toward calm. In the quiet, I feel a very soft brush on my upper arm. A gentle stroke.

I feel it again, on the left now. No breeze, the AC is on. It feels delicate, silky, a caress, when no one is here.

I think it is angel wings, folding me in comfort. Peace descends on my tired heart like a soft blanket.

June 19

I scooted into the edge of the couch by Mom's head for a semi-snuggle. We don't discuss this day as her 65th wedding anniversary. She leans into me, relaxing, I rub her hand softly. She is home from day care, and resting as near always, a small immobile lady on the sofa in front of cable weather TV. The aide is on her phone working out her own medical coverage for a diabetic scare. The aide is a spry 69-year-old Filipina who has been a rock. She has arms of iron, able to help Mom into a chair and into the shower.

We are comforted by the calm which has come over Mom. Yes, Mom had a dose of the newly supplied comfort medicine and she has responded nicely.

The shutters open. Mom looks up at me.

Am I dying?

Yes.

What about my body?

Cremated and ashes spread, I say. What you planned. I am paying close attention and see her near imperceptible nod. Troubled eyes lock onto mine. I'm reading it loud and clear. The silent language of terminal illness. Unspoken is her "why am I here, this sucks" impatience. I gently take her hand, the reassuring language of touch a replacement for words.

I know this is hard and you don't like it. I am doing everything, so you are comfortable. Home. Safe.

The tiniest dip of her chin. She knows. Her eyes close.

Am I dying? She asks again a minute later.

My answer is the same.

Yes. You have had a wonderful long life. It is okay.

Again, her eyes lock on mine.

Does he know?

The boyfriend. What do I say about him, the irascible man in near-permanent denial, the lover putting food in her mouth, the guy who insists that everything is fine, even though he has verbally slipped, that "Jean is on her way out."

She asks again. I offer what I know.

"I think he knows, but he lies to you, Mom. Lies that everything is alright. I'll talk to him again. You know I am always honest."

Who is my husband?

Where is he?

Do I still have my house? Are you down here now?

The window has closed.

June 25

It is Tuesday, the weekday to monitor Mom's decline. The Hospice physician assistant will evaluate Jean's condition to recertify coverage.

I'm here with lovely Nurse Debbie, who still manages Mom's private care. An aide is here. A social worker and another hospice nurse are here. A regular crowd.

Mom takes one look at all of us and asks if she is going to the hospital.

No, I tell her. Debbie smiles. This is a meeting to keep you home.

The professionals sit around Mom's kitchen table while I lean along the counter, looking at Mom on her sofa, watching us.

Tess reports another terrible morning with bathing and hygiene…. Jean pooping her way from kitchen through family room, dining room, living room, bedroom, and bathroom, unaware. In and out of the shower several times. All cleaned up and hair done. And then one more time. The washer has been running full tilt.

The Hospice evaluator says this is about Jean's body no longer processing food— "in one end, out the other." I share the food list my sister has yelled into the log book. A Greek Salad for dinner.

"I'd have diarrhea too, if I ate that," says the PA. "I know salad is soft, but can you suggest that they feed her SOFT and mild foods?"

Debbie looks from me to the Hospice PA, and I start laughing.

"Sure," I shake my head, "except they are feeding her nuts and apples and broccoli, too. There is a bit of disconnect with these people."

I watch this register. The PA remembered meeting Mom's boyfriend, and contends he also has dementia. She reiterates what others have said: that people in denial don't change.

"It's only as good as it is," she added. "But maybe it will help if you remember 'he' is sick too. Keep instructions short. Write things down." All good ideas, already in place. I'm sure she means well, but hey, I'm a veteran. What the Hospice people don't want to understand is my reality. The reality that instruction and guidance are willfully, purposely ignored. Detractors do whatever they want.

I made introductions after discovering that not everyone knows everyone else. When Mom's assigned social worker showed up later, I made sure to introduce her too.

"Oh, I know Debbie," she says. "She is pretty famous. Quite the reputation."

Huh. Maybe Debbie is really well connected in end of life care and home health supports. More than I realized.

"Yeah, I remember Debbie," the social worker continues, droll. "From the county lock up."

There is a bit of laughter and Debbie doesn't miss a beat.

"Yeah, I know you too," she answers, equally dry. "You were in the next cell." It is how we laugh today.

June 27

There is hate mail from sister Y about the hospital bed. It had been expected. Everyone also expected it would be aimed at me. I do feel bad that Y is having such a difficult time dealing with the gravity of end stage Alzheimer's. She attacks my education. She calls me an idiot. She remains angry with what she calls "my decisions." She says I am "trying to put our mother in her grave." She says Mom is questioning why she is in bed. The private duty aide tells me she watched Y read the dry erase board note explaining about the hospice recommendation of the hospital bed for safety, to protect their physical efforts and ease the strain necessary to move Mom, to position her, to help her sit or lie down. Getting her up from the sofa, pulling her into a sit and helping her stand had become a risk to both Mom and to aides who cannot handle the weight. The aide watched Y quickly erase the message, apparently before it has time to sink into her conscious.

I put up a short magic marker response about safety and comfort. State I will share her complaint with Hospice and doctor. I make a copy for the evidence file. So it goes. Mom looks beautiful against the soft pink sheets, propped up with multiple pillows. The aide and I love the electronic controls.

June 30

I took respite in a trip to Michigan. There was an angel on the plane today. I had found myself listening to the hum of jet engines, eyes closed, and wondering how it happens that God places an angel in the seat next to me. She had a head full of ethereal red curls and for the next two hours, we talked about God, spirituality, what we are supposed to know and what remains mysterious; we speak of blessings, life and acceptance, awareness and more, in simplicity and depth. It is like we have known one another for years.

I feel myself tingling. Marveling at the revealed soul of a stranger, sharing thoughts that mirror my own. She speaks about *what is right* and how we must only be in charge of ourselves for listening and growing along the road.

Suddenly George Harrison is in my head. My buddy George. The Beatle died more than a decade ago (2001), and like lightning crackling in a darkening sky, the soundtrack of Harrison's final album, literally bursts brilliantly into my conscious. It's a live performance in sync with this strange yet marvelous conversation. I tell Buzz, because of course, Buzz is the name of the woman beside me, whose hair fits the name, that Harrison's music has arrived. Does she know George, the Beatle?

"He was dying of cancer when he wrote and sang this last album," I added. "His son helped him finish." What I've just said out loud hits me deep in my chest… *his son helped him finish…*

For Pete's sake, I am on an airplane, talking to a stranger. Who indeed has chosen the music? Had Buzz brought George along??

Harrison's last CD is called <u>Brainwashed</u>, and now both music *and* lyrics have been racing through my head, song after song, a mastery of sentiment in melody and words, surging into a personal playlist about living and dying.

The Universe is multi-tasking. Saying pay attention. Music in my head, meaningful conversations in my ear, every cell firing alert. I had loved these songs, the whole album way back when. Realizing anew, the deep message Harrison final songs held.

Had left for me.

And I was flying through the air, talking to an angel, with this halo shock of ridiculously red tendrils, who happened to end up sitting in my row. Coincidence? I think not.

Harrison's songs are celebration and epitaph, fun, sentimental, joyous, introspective, emotional, grand. The lyrics that leapt into my conscious, are all about his journey. A beautiful flow of belief, circumstance and self-awareness. Pure music of who he was, what he knew and how he believed in the journey of his last months and days.

"Going down to the river, gonna take me my rocking chair," and *"Any road will take you there."* I tell Buzz. Down the river of life, any road gets you there. Again, I nearly choke at the lyric…any road.

I had visualized Harrison rocking comfortably at the water's edge, best as able, I heard the airy tinkle of homage to his Hindu-inspired spiritualism, I embraced his fondness for Father Murray, living, while dying of cancer.

Long before today I had wondered about George creating these lyrics of passage, his son Dhani doing the recording. Music and life, father and son, artistry and effort, love and disease journeying together. It would be another year before Dhani and fellow musician Jeff Lynne released the finished album.

Peace and harmony. An amazing start to my northern reprieve. A few days to recharge. Buzz disappears as we deplane. Maybe into thin air.

July 16

It has been quite a ride between the angel visit on that Delta flight and today. I am back in Florida since late Tuesday afternoon. I am refreshed, meeting up with Debbie, who has been on alert while I was away. There was another minor difficulty a week ago. Not enough to call me, she says. She handled it.

One of Mom's lower front teeth had cracked off, and Y had entreated an aide to accompany them to the dentist. Mom hadn't complained of pain or discomfort. The managed care folks and I had been aware of the tooth, already knew this was just one of the things that happen to the human form as bodies descend toward an earthly end. But Y and the boyfriend had decided for themselves, that she needed a new front tooth. The aide was carried along, to a point when, clearly uncomfortable, she called Nurse Debbie. Debbie had stepped in immediately to halt any dental procedures.

Her action had proved unnecessary because simultaneously, Mom's compassionate, long time dentist was already in the process of sending them home, with no more than an acknowledgement that tooth breakage happens at this time in life. This dentist is a kind man who had always been on Mom's page. On our last routine checkup visit more than a year prior, he had said goodbye and wished us Godspeed. He knew Mom needed no more dental care.

Debbie and I used this "teaching moment" to remind the aides of Mom's plan and procedures--that neither boyfriend nor my sisters could take steps without contacting the supervisor or me. I am grateful the aide had known enough to call Debbie. Grateful it has been handled. Shrugged off my usual consternation and then half-listened to the boyfriend's dinner time drivel (blah blah). He claims the same thing happened to his own mother, but *he* had that tooth fixed (of course), and his mother lived another 15 years.

Fifteen more years. Nope. Hospice was in the house. These people might never see the truth, but Debbie's prediction about ramping up was true. It was getting crazier awful.

July 17

Wednesday, Mom's facial expressions shows signs of distress, and when we pull the comfort medicine out of the cabinet, suspicions are confirmed. I test it on my tongue. Someone had again tampered with Class Two narcotics—heavily diluting both lorazepam and roxanol with water. I was angry.

Who would do this? I doubted there was a drug addict among Mom's caregivers. But I wouldn't put this abominable act beyond anyone who disagreed with Mom receiving comfort care.

Debbie and I had already wondered why this latest refill lost its effectiveness as the first one had. We speculated. The boyfriend had been sternly warned to keep away from her medicines after the faulty cold medicine fiasco, and maybe he just wasn't smart enough to try this (small laugh, Debbie). The twins?

Daughters of the same mother. Misguided enough to think that refusing Mom comfort care is okay?

I call Hospice to re-order. Another day on Mom's road.

July 18

In the way the Universe works, I saw one of those sisters at a lunch today.

"I don't want to speak to you." She bites off.

"Well, it's important. Someone has tampered with mom's medicine. It's serious."

"I don't know what you're talking about," she spits out. There is blackness in her blue eyes, a look on her face I only describe as poisonous. But she's the one stepping back.

"Mom's medicine for comfort care has been replaced with water. It's awful and Hospice and private duty are aware that this has happened. Twice. It's illegal." I have spoken low and slow. Calmly. I have her attention.

She glares, lips compressed, arms crossed, defensive posturing. No look of concern, no surprise. She doesn't ask if Mom is okay.

I'm looking deep into angry eyes, wishing I was elsewhere, yet knowing I was exactly where I was supposed to be.

"It could be any one of the 500 people you have coming in and out of the house," she finally barks. I'm thinking, *how bizarre to be having this conversation.*

I hold her with my eyes. I know there is no proof. No nanny-cam. There are not 500 but maybe a dozen people who come into Mom's home--nurses and aides, Hospice personnel, three daughters and a boyfriend. Employees are screened and known. Not druggies. Not someone from Hospice.

The short list of whodunits is three. Her response is telltale. They previously tried to disrupt comfort care by lying to the doctor. They leave nasty messages everywhere, send mean letters through the mail (I really should call the post office complaint desk). They've claimed my advocacy for Mom's comfort care makes me a contemporary Lizzy Borden. You know what they mean? Not an axe, but a prescription? Give me a break.

I have done the math. Two daughters and the boyfriend disrespect Mom's directives, disagree with me, and yes, disagree with the delivery of comfort medicine.

It is the middle of Summer in Florida. Abundant sunshine and blue skies and people keep trying to suck me into a dark hole. My mom, our mom, under Hospice care. My stomach had been flipping like some big snook when I first saw her, but there was this outward iron calm. I won't back down. (Thank you, Tom Petty).

"Oh, who knows who all those people are," she adds, trying to brush me off. "Any one of them could have done it."

It is surely not her intention, but I am aware she is acknowledging the TRUTH, somebody has "done it." She knows there has been drug tampering. So much malice, so much hate for Mom's plan, for me. Where is their compassion?

"Hospice is working to fix this. Mom wants comfort care. Her doctor wants it." I should have quit right there, but I just couldn't. There was this one more thing.

"I know about the dentist visit, too. Not appropriate. There was nothing to be done about Mom's tooth."

"You went out of town and didn't even tell us," she yells back, bitter.

Angry when I don't share information? Angry when I do? Which is it? Share or don't share? How does that work?

Oh, that's right. It doesn't.

"The care company is always in charge in my absence, and Mom's care team always knows my schedule." She is right, I didn't tell her. Sure, she is my sister, but sadly, she is presently an enemy to Mom's plan.

"You just want control." She practically spits each word.

I don't argue. My management of these hard days is exactly what she was now complaining about. It is control that our mother established, all those years ago when she thought through her end of life care. The devil twins had been excluded from control. It rubs forever raw.

Does medicine tampering qualify as revenge? Could they be really that mad at our mom? A festering seething wound of exclusion, a deepening blackness of hatred toward me, with control, ending up as medicine tampering? I reach out my hand to her arm in compassion. She snaps her arm away. I step in closer.

"Listen," I begin. "Please, stop. Please do this right," I plead with her, softly serious. "Or you won't be able to see her. I could do that. I don't want to…but you know I could."

There. My ultimate ammunition is out there. I am done doing this.

"Oh, fuck you," she says, and in a spin that is all scowl and glaring thunder, she stomps away, throwing her hand up in a crossing guard gesture to keep me from following or speaking further. A whoosh of negative energy trailing behind her.

My sister? My mom is her mom? I feel a passing moment of nausea. Probably exactly why Hospice avoids choosing sides.

What about Mom's side?

This sister is on notice. I caught sight of her driving away, phone to her ear, Cruella over a steering wheel. Sad for her. I head to the podium to welcome guests.

As I reflect tonight, I find disbelief, a sickly humor from my absurdly wishful thinking of a dozen years. Trying to fix the unfixable over and over. Mostly because these are her daughters, because I know they have always been difficult, I have let a lot of bad behavior go. Been able to stop none of it anyway, in exchange for their care of Mom.

A friend says with all certainty, that this is my sister's essence, that she can't do any better. This is who she is, messed up into believing that bad behavior and negativity is how she helps Mom. Yikes, that makes no sense. I will never understand, but I don't have to.

Flashback to that first Hospice social worker years ago. "Difficult people don't get easier in difficult times." Okay, Nancy. Point taken.

Good night.

July 21

This is weird! I am sitting inside a gleaming mirror ball. Shimmery inside and out. I feel safe, protected, serene. The glow of the ball completely surrounds me. It feels so peaceful.

Just outside all the sparkle are shadows, what looks like a swirling dust storm, and just beyond the dust looks dark and gloomy.

None of it gets to me. The shiny surface deflects all of it. I'm busy working, putting one foot in front of the other, doing whatever needs doing.

I like being in the ball! After too many years of discord, too many days deflecting bad vibes that threaten my resolve or have me questioning my actions, today, I have armor. The nightmare is firmly outside my shiny bright ball. I am in a good place.

I realize I'm dreaming, but I wake up and here is the kicker.

I walk around all day, inside that ball.

July 23

Two days later I'm back at the keyboard. I feel my dad hanging with me today, his strength running through me, electric. I am my own kind of hero--mother, wife, daughter, student, citizen of the Universe, imperfect human, but alive with purpose. I've been boosted into the air for a 360-degree view of what I have been taught: some things cannot be fixed, and other things are not supposed to be fixed. But I am okay. Standing at Mom's side.

My closest friends and family listen, lightening my load, allowing me to share. One friend recently described me as one-half of a long-established partnership, a pact that created a two-person circle of trust. She refers to me as Mom's guardian angel, in a deal struck by Spirit. Timeless, holding Mom and me together in shared Mother/Daughter love to stand invincible across time.

It is a powerful notion even though I have never thought of myself as a guardian angel. Daughter, yes. Advocate, yes. Support, of course. A protector of rights, yes. An educated guide for procedure, maybe. Someone willing to learn how to do it? Yes, that too.

I have held onto the strangest peaceful feeling. For a while now. The pressure is seriously off! I don't have to understand any of it. I have remained inside the silver mirror ball and I am free.

Psychotherapists tell you that sometimes our brains can get stuck in a stream of negative thoughts. I've been there. Psychotherapists also tell you that we can change our thoughts. I'm there.

I don't have all the answers, but I've had an overwhelming new realization that our paired route was a journey to discover, Let It Be. (Thank you, Beatles.)

Inside that mirror ball I understand, perhaps for the first time, that it has taken years, all these years, for me to learn my way through the pain and come out the other side.

Sometimes the *action* required by me is nothing. And sometimes the action is only observation because some moments have no choices. Sometimes, choices abound. It is all OK.

I can continue to do the next right thing. To channel Frank Sinatra. Do. Be. Do.

I am up late tonight, more reflecting, thinking this through. Peaceful, amazingly so, still smarting from this last confrontation with medicine destroyers. But I am the carer, a seeker, a thinker. A believer in the God of my understanding, who put me on this path.

The solution is to just be. Accept what is.

I find myself remembering a conversation with my pastor about decisions and journeys. Neal told me two things.

"Nothing worth doing is ever easy" he began, "and things that are important feel uncomfortable. This is your signal that those things are important."

These years walking alongside Mom have been uncomfortable much of the time. But today, for so many wonderful reasons, I somehow know that even the worst has been bearable. I have lived it.

There is stuff I am not supposed to understand. Mom's journey was supposed to unfold across these years, in this way, *just for us.*

Just be.

Those are the shimmery words floating inside my mirror ball. Not fairy dust, diamond points of truth. Just be.

Mom and I will continue to wander a bit, finishing up. But the mirror ball is a sign. I think I finally see this journey in its purest form—this caring, connected loving partnership with my beautiful mother. Frustrating, intense, exhausting, at times brutal. But also, beautiful. I can accept what is unacceptable in order to endure.

We are near my final footsteps with the lady who brought me into the world. The symbiosis of her bringing me in, and me walking her out is not lost on me. Our map was pretty good, and there have been road hazards, but George Harrison had already informed me, "…any road will get you there."

Yesterday was a very hard day, but a gratitude day. It is just how it is. I am safe inside the ball. Do. Be. Do.

By the way, Hospice has brought a coded locking box. Only one aide and I have the combination. We secure Mom's comfort care medicines. It is how it will be. The care company knows, and the schedule is set. I tell Mom I'll be back next week. I fly out to an annual family and friends reunion.

I am already wondering if there will be another angel on the plane.

July 29

Time away had put physical distance between me and Mom, but not mental. She is constantly in my thoughts and I feel her grow weaker each day, each hour. If I have the silver ball, she has a huge shining light at the end of her tunnel. There is a hint of daylight at my end of the tunnel too.

I'm looking at the lake today, and the revelations don't quit. I find it curious yet comforting to realize I've been learning my entire life for just these moments. Moral ground, ample space for love and peace, acceptance.

It just took a while to get here.

It might be one of life's profound mysteries, that there is space for great joy and great sadness simultaneously. My growing awareness of a realm of total simultaneous existence of good and bad. My continuing education. My discovery lesson on the shared path.

The mirror ball was filled with white light and in ways I cannot explain, my head has room for more hope of the best things. Being there for my mom, will outweigh whatever the worst can be. I understand that best things may not happen my way or even in a way I might imagine or understand, but I am OK with that.

I know that when my mom is gone, when our partnership is done, there will still be people who don't like it, don't accept it, don't understand it. I am anxious to be done dealing with all that negative energy. I know that my responsibility for Mom has been hard on my husband and my kids, and even upon the detractors.

I have compassion for us all.

Deb, the nurse, says that what has finally happened to me, is that after all these years, I have become numb to the emotions and anger I should feel over the atrociousness of my sisters. I think it something else.

I have plenty of emotions, but I reside inside the mirror ball. I have put myself on bypass to their darkness. Whatever they do can't hurt me anymore. I am above and beyond. I can wait.

Wednesday, July 31

There is a large note in capital block letters taped to the stainless fridge from one of the sisters asking Hospice for the lock box code. I am amused. She wants access to comfort care medicine which is now locked safely away. In part, her note reads, "IN CASE THE PATIENT NEEDS IT." (Oddly funny.) Really? Desiring access for medicine you don't want her to have. Somehow, she must have not noticed the two ready-to-go doses *outside* the lockbox.

I have posted Mom's directives on the cabinet, near the calendar. Also, emergency phone numbers. There are procedural instructions: administer medicine, then call Hospice, me, or the private care company nurse to reset the dose. Not good enough, I guess.

Mom is sleeping. Nurse Deb and I had a few moments to chat about the latest hate mail, a large packet of diatribes and vitriol the sisters have assembled and mailed to all parties. Their latest accusations claim elder abuse and negligence by the care team, by Hospice, by me, together and/or separately. I hadn't even bothered opening my packet.

But this poison has taken a toe-hold. Hospice and private duty are downright angry. The claims are deliberate misinformation, allegations of illegal acts. The care company dismissed their wickedness in favor of supporting Mom, but Hospice wants to respond. Whatever. I figure Hospice can go to the battlefield.

I find myself mostly unaffected. Numb? Distastefully resigned? No matter. Time is running out. I concentrate on Mom.

Spoke with the boyfriend tonight for about an hour. Mom is motionless in the hospital bed, awake but glassy eyed. I don't know how much she hears. I wanted to review the details of Mom's living will that I've taped up again. (Copies keep getting torn down.) Wanted to be clear that the situation is grave.

"Well, it depends on how you see things," he says. "I'm a positive guy and we don't have any trouble, never any bad words," deliberately missing my point. I am stone-faced, internally groaning, stuck in a perpetual Groundhog Day rerun, tolerating his umpteenth tiresome response for the sake of my mom.

Right this moment, she is focused on sunset light coming through the sliding doors. She has mentioned spiritual visitors in her family room. She stares into the high corners and tells the aides and me her sister is there. Sometimes her mom. My dad.

The here and hereafter watching and waiting. I watch her drifting in and out, caught in a ray of sunlight. Yet the boyfriend still holds to denial, refusing Mom's waning light. Remarkably, I have watched her conceal that imminent departure in a smile for him. It happened again tonight. Her life force, holding on for a few more precious moments with him.

"Well, I'm redoing all my papers now because of this," he says, "and my son is ready to step in and take care of me for the rest of his life when I need it." My internal groan now an amused chuckle: He rejects her reality, refuses her directives, but plans his own?

I recall what professionals have already suggested. He is not right in the head. I've said enough, have given him more detail of Mom's intentions, trying to help him understand difficulties we all face.

"You're telling me I just have to let her go, right?" His eyes are red. Our conversation has hit a nerve. Not happy looking at the truth, he suggests we are arguing. I shake my head.

"I'm not arguing. I'm trying to have enough exchange of information for a reality view here." I use his name, "I think you know this." And I am calm, quiet.

"Maybe I'm saying she needs to let you go too?" I offer. There is no happy ending. But sometimes even that kind of clarity is not enough. I see consternation, anger looking back at me. The air looks gray, and he is fanning a coal of indignation.

Mom has come back, a brightening of her eyes. She's watching. She has told me she wants to die. I share this and see him wince. I know she says other things to him. He chooses this moment to stop talking with me.

"Don't you like it this way, Jean?" he asks.

Yes, she nods, yes, she likes it this way, and she gives him a tiny grin. His girlfriend.

We are at a truth point. She wants him *and she wants to die.* Disease has her wanting it both ways.

I am exhausted. He jabbers on, a broken record about a great time all these years, and every night. He continues, saying he would do diapers, bathing and bathroom runs 24/7 if that would keep this great time going.

We acknowledge different viewpoints, but from necessity I tell him our viewpoints are empty air. Only my mother's views matter at this moment. Despite their feelings for one another, I knew this hard conversation tonight had exposed the final jeopardy of their togetherness, their routine, his dinner hour. It has raised that undeniable brush with mortality.

In all that cloudy air, I remain determined to fulfill Mom's life choices. Today her choices still include this man. His contrary attacks on me and her plan are part of the package. That won't change. I use her answers, while the Universe takes its time moving her down the road.

"You know she asked me to manage this all," I say, my own broken record. "Her way. As best as I can."

I added this caveat because of what I've learned: the journey, the delivery of Mom's plan is perfectly imperfect. Flawed by conflicting choices, by people, perhaps also by Mom's steadfast refusal to ever share her choices with anyone but the attorney and me.

How many times have I wondered if she knew what the lawyer and I would face? In my eyes, her refusal to share was still a miss, but it didn't matter. She was living according to her choices. In a rock and hard place, I just had to keep holding them up.

He sees an opening for a snide rejoinder.

"Well, I guess you could say you haven't been able to completely do your job, huh?" He finished with a satisfied sneer, so very typical of his passive/aggressive behavior that insults my abilities and care of Mom. He is gratified by my difficulties. I feel my own internal chuckle again, though he is mocking and serious. He will continue to disrespect me for as long as he can.

With renewed energy, he boldly moved on to another sticking point, suggesting that the food question was another grand failure for me, that I have been unable to succeed with Mom's feeding directives. I hadn't been able to stop them, no matter about dribbling chocolate, choking hazards or pocketing food. He switched from irony to aggression.

"If I stop feeding her, she will be dead in a week and you can be planning a funeral." He is in my face, scare tactics and drama. To suggest what? That without his intervention, I might have starved Mom to death?

I find however, that I have stayed cool, detached. I note the unpleasantness, but he cannot provoke me. Sticking to Mom's guns means bearing his contempt, from within the crystal ball.

"Don't for one minute disrespect me by suggesting my grief will be less than yours," I respond. "But this isn't about you. Or me. It is about what she wants, what she planned for herself when these days arrived. These days are here."

"Well, well…maybe she doesn't want now what she wanted when she wrote all that," he bites off each word. Scripted by one of the sisters? I know we are in the toughest days yet.

There is her voice now, gravelly, terse, coming up from the cloud of pink sheets, up from the depths of disease. Mom has once again returned, sadly to this moment, speaking from the hospital bed across the room.

"I'm lying here," she said abruptly, "listening to you two argue." Her lips are set, face grim, rheumy eyes dark. This is NOT how I ever wanted her days to be, a sick lady witness to a chronic verbal standoff. I tell myself, *stop having this conversation.*

But I can also accept this circumstance. Part of her own doing. She has me as final road traveler while wanting this man in her life. I respect that choice. An impasse of years.

"Oh, Mom, I am not arguing. We just have different opinions," I said, the endless tug of war across a line he doesn't want to see. Frustration bubbles up each time we are in the same room.

It is my time to leave the house.

I'm home again, pounding out unwavering loyalty on a keyboard. I am bonded forever to Mom and what she wants.

There is an aha moment here. Here, in the steamy heat that would soon be August, there was no ambiguity. Once more I revisited all my attempts to convince any of them about what Mom wanted for herself. A road paved with good intentions but destined for failure. They were incapable, and it wasn't just me they were angry about. They were incredibly mad at circumstance and Mom.

The situation had evolved yet parts remained exactly the same. I am keeper of Mom and her plan. Mom is dying. Two sisters and boyfriend paint me enemy and executioner. I am my own worst kind of idiot, repeatedly sought ill-fated attempts to change the unchangeable. Worse yet, I was able to see that my dogged best intentions added to my own misery!

Strained before we began, relationships had crumbled. I had made myself vulnerable, again and again. That was the lesson, but I regretted none of my efforts. I wasn't wired to do this any other way. I didn't cause it, I couldn't cure it, and I certainly couldn't control any of them. Throw that one off, no beating myself up, no uncertainty--I had learned too much enroute.

Like the TV show Survivor, I would out last them.

I was exactly where I was supposed to be, coolly digging in my nearly worn out heels to keep Mom's end game as her own, best as it could be kept. I was not getting off the road. If I was driving, Mom's head and heart had plotted the route. Other drivers were beyond my control, and the burble of road rage was permanently outside the silver ball.

Escalated difficulties, years gone by, and I had this bizarre vision of Mom's final walk being accomplished in a mine field. Mines blew up. As her soldier, I was wounded, bruised and uncomfortable. I resented them all for each added injustice. But inner strength was burbling up too.

I had done everything possible to maintain as Mom had intended. I was doing what I could to fortify myself. I was not beating myself up. I was stronger and more peaceful than I had been in years.

I could accept imperfection. Know it would never be fixed. Endure. Hang on just a bit longer. I was okay with a losing battle and it had taken a dozen years to get here.

Pounding these affirmations out, got me revved up. I could do this for as long as needed! I prayed and prayed for her release, for ultimate peace sooner than later. I would sleep and get up and do it again the next day, and the next because I knew, I knew, the days would come when I would not have her anymore. I could stick with truth and hold tightly to my calm. They would lose her too.

The haters will see me take it to the end. Tonight, I heard her gulp and struggle for a breath as I left the love birds to their evening. At the end of the day they might really be in love, the dying lady in a pretty pink cloud of sheets on the hospital bed, whose eyes roll back into her head, and this odd man who doesn't see what it is in his face.

Mom kisses me noisily, deeply as I say goodbye. I want to believe the noise is to let him know how much she loves me too

Tomorrow is August. I'm closing this file and going to bed.

August

I am usually in Michigan during these dog days, but this year is different. Mom is dying and I know it. Not today. But soon.

That toehold of hate mail had made waves. Hospice is feeling pressured. I still hadn't othered reading their latest lies, but care professionals had supplied detail enough from their copies of my sisters' spiteful contentions of neglect, overdose and abuse. The Hospice nurse assured me she has dismissed their allegations and described all our efforts on Mom's behalf, but the higher ups are calling for action. Official face time, a family meeting. An attempt at amelioration. She says these meetings are typical for families rife with dissension. UGH.

Though a face-to-face can demonstrate professionalism and share the realities of dying people, I highly doubted it would eliminate the ick. My head and heart knew Hospice would not be able to cure what ailed my sisters. Procedural protocol, a willingness to hear those unhappy girls out was a Hospice CYA--covering one's own ass. It wasn't lost on me that the powwow would be documented—another safeguard in case the sisters went further. And meanwhile, my mother was dying.

I would be at this meeting but knew I would not have much to say.

August 13, 10 a.m

I was inside with Mom and Nurse Debbie, waiting, shrugging our shoulders. Mom and her favorite aide were handling morning hygiene. The boyfriend was in the garage dusting his Buick, awaiting my sister and Hospice. On arrival, they trooped through the back door, headed for the kitchen table. The doctor began immediately. My sister put a tape recorder on the table.

The first thing to happen was the doctor handing back the tape recorder, softly saying this was a family meeting and Hospice didn't do recordings. My sister next tossed a photo stack onto the table showing Mom's broken tooth, vacant eyes and facial bruising. The doctor glanced briefly, then pushed them aside. Debbie and I were silent. Old news. We let the doctor explain.

Old people fall down. Everyone tries to prevent it. Imbalance, weakness and falls are normal old age hazards of existence.

Bones and teeth break in old age.

Mom's care team had previously documented the incident, the exact day and time frame. An aide and I had left the house at 7 p.m. on a Friday as the boyfriend arrived. Mom was bruise free at our departure, but she was bruised the next morning when both of us returned. We already knew that whatever had happened, Mom had been with the boyfriend when she got banged up and broke a tooth.

Have you heard the term *playing dumb?* He already denied knowing anything. I don't think he abused Mom, but maybe he had *neglected* to support a stroll through the house. Accident or not, he would never take responsibility. But see #1.

So? Two nurses, the doctor and I are quiet. Body language of boyfriend and sister indicated they are puffed up with their spotlight moment. When a freshly showered Jean and her aide join the group, the doctor speaks gently, directly to her, several times. No response. Her eyes are very blue this morning, very vacant. She is tiny, beautiful, fragile.

Not sure what anyone thought could happen today, Mom's appearance basically ended the meeting. The doctor summing it up: elderly people fall, medications can and do need adjustments, professional monitoring is standard.

"Your mother is well cared for, absolutely no evidence of

neglect, overdose or abuse."

And, by the way, he says, these are difficult days. Family should try to get along. (Nice try, I think, and appreciated, but I refrained from saying, "Duh.") As expected, Hospice's only purpose is acknowledgement of differing viewpoints. Feels like another wasted hour with unpleasant people working against our best, loving efforts to care for Mom as she wanted.

The doctor, sister and boyfriend file out. Hospice support will return on Friday.

Nurse Debbie and I discussed our calendar. We make sure Mom is covered with back to back shifts of hired home staff. Hospice staffers will be in and out, visiting on their own time frame. Mom's other devil twin is coming back to town to share night duties while the boyfriend is away. Mom and I will meet her primary care physician, Dr. A, tomorrow.

August 14

This was a terrible hard day. Well, not all of it. The effort to get Mom in the car from daycare, out at the doctor's, inside the office, then back out and finally back into the car has drained me. Has drained us.

She cannot hardly move and I could barely help her. We huffed with exertion. I hurt bad. My hip was zinging and before I drive away, I sat for a moment finally free from effort wondering how this tiny lady could be so heavy, while thinking about what I had just heard.

While waiting for Dr. A to come into the exam room, Mom looked over at me and said,

"When it is my time, Jan, I want you to pull the plug."

I look her up and down, a wistful smile playing at my mouth. Helper to the end.

"Okay, Mom," I say, "but you won't ever be plugged in. You've already told me not to." She gives me a big nod then, silently affirming what she sees ahead.

Dr. A comes in then, charming as always. Kind. His eyes tell me he knows what I think I know. He kisses her papery cheek. She smiles in appreciation. Then he hugs me hard. Says goodbye. He does not expect to see Mom again. The office nurse and physician assistant tell me how much they have enjoyed having her as a patient, how sorry they are.

I am not numb. Tears burn behind my eyes. Doors are beginning to close.

I started the car.

We did our usual drive home along the water to a favorite bench and the neighborhood pier hoping this familiar and favorite spot eases ache and circumstance. But Mom is too unsettled. She asks to go home. Even viewing her beloved Gulf has become too much. She is exhausted by the sheer rigor of staying alive.

We struggle into the house. I gently lift her sunglasses off. The afternoon aide guides her into the hospital bed. We tuck her in. She rolls her eyes up, immediately falling asleep. Home is her place of ease, the haven of last resort.

August 21

There is a miracle this afternoon. Mom stirs, opening her eyes as I arrived. Her cheeks are rosy. She is bright eyed, smiling.

"Hi," a smile in her voice. Clear and strong, "You're here!"

I smile back. A wonderful gift, I snuggle up next to her. We both laugh. Tess watches us.

"How are you?"

"Pretty good," she says. I laugh again. A wonderful day. A gift. Mom IS here, aware, in the moment, more than in ages. We don't know what to do with ourselves, how long this will last. She calls me her brown-eyed beauty. We continue to touch, to hug, to laugh. I say how good it is to see you!

"I know!" she smiled, giddy. "Are you getting ready to leave?"

"No, I just got here. I'm glad to be here with you!" More hugging and cheek kissing. We are tickled pink.

I feel another round of tears spark behind my eyes. Are we having one of those last days I've read about? A burst of energy? Alert in the here and now after days of disorientation? Is all her withdrawing and internal sorting giving way to a finale of clearheaded recognition?

We hold one another, I stroke her soft cheek, her arms. We hug some more. Smile. Have a moment. It is totally ours. Tremendous good day.

August 23

We are in Month 6 with Hospice. Eligibility criteria echo in my head—"six months or less." The palliative care drugs locked up, medicine log on the counter. Mom still goes to day care. I still say prayers. I come in and out of Mom's house when I know the haters are not there. I have taken a few phone photos, memories for myself. Today, Mom looked distressed, hurting. We offer drinks with a straw. We dose here and there. I notice my sisters have purchased liquid Tylenol. Progress? Not if she aspirates and chokes to death. But apparently, they at least have noticed her discomfort.

I am going North for a week; the care company holds leadership in my absence. I'll swing past their office as I depart, to drop off their check. Mom's costs have risen exponentially these last months, but this is what her money is for. More than ever, I'm grateful for Dad's pension, Mom's inheritance, the sale of her mobile home. I believe in spending every dime for her care if it comes to that. I am proud of my careful, successful management of her assets. But in

Month Six, I am certain the payout will not last so much longer.

I want to stay with Mom. I want to go to my family. I need to stay. I need to go.

We are both used to my comings and goings. We have that history, and Mom's private care supporters and Hospice workers have good hands and capable heads. Mom is home, where she wants to be. I am happy she can be here.

Lately, Mom has been asking me if she's going to take a trip, so we kiss and say goodbye and I tell her she can take her trip whenever she's ready. Leave while I'm away, if she needs to go. I say I would miss her, and I'll always love her, but it is okay, if she has to go.

Do you know when you will go?

She says she is planning to go on Thursday.

I call Tee to tonight. She is looking at dates and finding a coyote sitter so she can come see Mom. We discuss Mom's status, voicing our acceptance that God has all the cards; Mom's course is written as it is supposed to be. We tell each other we can accept, can endure whatever the twins manage in my absence, discussing very real possibilities of Mom choking to death on forced food, or drowning from their idea of medicine or hydration.

Awful thoughts. We pray and hope to God this won't happen, but we bear the possibility. We are willing to *let it happen.* We are not in control.

I'll return after Labor Day, unless called back sooner. The twins should be delighted to have Mom and the boyfriend all to themselves for ten days.

September

"...a time of withdrawing from everything outside of one's self and going inside. Inside where there is sorting out,

evaluating one's self and one's life... there is only room for one."

"...the processing of one's life.... spending more time asleep than awake becomes the norm....This appears to be just sleep, but know that important work is going on inside..." - Barbara Karnes, hospice nurse, author. <u>Gone from my sight: The Dying Experience</u>

September 4

I have returned and the first thing I notice is *further* decline. She is so still. She is deep, deep in sleep in that hospital bed, turned away from the room. My hand to her shoulder does not rouse her. I let her sleep. When she does wake, I watched her eyes move and fix to an upper corner. I wonder who is floating there, watching her get ready.

September 7

The same deep, deep sleep thing is happening. Mom cannot be roused. Only when she brings herself back. Then she is up briefly, before her eyes roll back. Today, she is staring up and off at the corner across the room. I came over to the bed to see from her angle. Who or what does she see?

Are people here, Mom? She nods, looking to me for a moment.
Who is it? She doesn't say.
I put a few names out there. I am interested in her visitors.
My dad? Nod.
Sue? Nod.
Gramma Roberts? Nod.
There are others, too. A veritable party of relatives hanging in the family room on this light-filled afternoon.

September 9

A Friday visit with the Hospice nurse, who sees what I see, noting the significance of deep sleep. A major visual cue of Mom's engagement "somewhere else." Something is going on, some interaction, movement "in the beyond." We are not privy to it, we only watch from our side of the hospital bed.

Mom is getting ready.

The nurse increased Mom's Hospice care coverage, effective immediately. When Mom awoke, the nurse talked to her about what is happening. The three of us hold hands. We have more real conversation about dying. About fear. Slowly, gently, calmly, the nurse talked Mom through what will happen, a peaceful finish after a long good life. When the nurse is done, Mom looks directly at me. Locks eyes.

"You need to tell ___. Tell him." The order from my captain. She absolutely knows what she's asking from me.

I said OK, that I could do it tonight, but I don't know how it will go. I looked at the Hospice nurse. She cannot schedule the necessary increased care Mom now requires until Monday.

I called the private care company. Thankfully, they assign one of their special night staffers without delay. A woman experienced with end of life care. Overnight. She's very qualified I'm told, but we will see whether she can handle this charged situation. The care company owner calls to repeat that removing the boyfriend is overdue. I let Ruth know that Mom has asked me to speak to him. I think it is time to ask an attorney how to make that happen.

I'll meet the new overnight nurse about 5 o'clock but have come home this afternoon to draft a one-page note to leave with the boyfriend tonight. Written reinforcement for what I will say in person.

"*Hospice nurse was here today. Nurse observed physical changes. Based on changes in Mom's condition, Hospice has determined it is time to increase the continuity of home medical care to support my mom's wish to be home until she dies.*

"<u>*What this means: 24-hour care support is appropriate NOW*</u> *for my mom, to determine when there becomes a need for "continuing care" which is 24-hour nursing.*

"<u>*This means a private duty CNA aide will be in the house during the night time.*</u> *A professional medical person who can assess and observe changes AND help determine what might be needed for Mom's care going forward.*

"*Starting tonight.*

"*This should help Mom rest easier and be more efficient for reporting any changes that occur. Hospice can be called immediately.*

"**You are welcome to stay or go**, *but be Mom's boyfriend, which is what she likes about you. Nursing support will be here for her care.*

"*This is new. Until Hospice and private duty can compare notes about what is needed at night,* <u>*this night plan will be in place*</u>*. The aide will help with night needs as they arise. This might mean staying awake all night, or not—nobody knows, but this is a Hospice order. How it starts. Hospice assesses again next Friday.*

"*Also, because Mom is sleeping more and more, and is very weak but comfortable here, day care is being suspended.*

"*Hospice recommends using the wheelchair as needed and using the fixed position walker IF she is able to walk. Mom's weakness increases her fall risk, and the fixed seat walker has more stability.*

"*Hospice is ordering delivery of a portable commode for bedside use.*

"*A chaplain is coming to visit.*"

I meet a very slight Asian woman who will be night nurse. She is uber calm, an air of quiet. She does this work, she says, when the end is close. I am holding Mom's hand and we were just hanging in the late afternoon waiting for the boyfriend.

He arrives and I start to tell him that Mom has no energy, that she wants me to talk to him. But he strides over, all bossy, attempting to push past me. He wants her out of the hospital bed. He wants to take her to the table. She and I both say, "No."

Already, this was not going well.

I block his path because I'm sitting in front of the bed. He gets more worked up, standing over me as I continue sitting quietly, holding Mom's hand. I look over at her and stand up, head and shoulders below his lanky frame, but still in his way. I am holding her hand.

The quiet little nurse is watching everything. He has loomed in, aggressive now, ordering me to move, trying to use size and bluster to back me away, to get to Mom. I have that icy calm thing going on. I repeat that Mom wanted me to tell him today's news.

He won't listen. He is raging now, thrusting out his chest. He steps within inches of my face. He gets louder, leans in threatening. Yelling at me to move. I find myself thinking that the men in my family would already have put him on the ground. The nurse's eyes are widened with alarm. Somehow, I haven't flinched, steely sure in the face of a growing red storm.

I wonder about my poor mother. Today she felt her mortality. Asked for help for where she is. Where we are. I turn to glance at her face. How much of this is touching her? Her eyes are closed. She's gone somewhere else, leaving this to me.

I turn back slowly, to face what is next. I use his name, ask once more to let me speak. In slow motion, I put up my arms, a physical cue to keep his distance. I surprise myself, putting flat palms gently to his shoulders.

Suddenly his mouth makes a giant "O" of surprise and he performs an exaggerated cartoon tumble backwards into the sofa, nearly landing atop the tiny nurse, who jumps up, eyes wider. I would have burst out laughing if only the situation weren't so serious.

"She pushed me, she pushed me, she pushed me!" He is shouting. Quite the performance.

"I'm calling Hospice right now," I say, sitting down and calmly pulling out my phone. I need advice. He retreats to pace the kitchen, angry, complaining loudly about my interference, the disruption of his night.

The night nurse also has reseated herself while I speak with Hospice, who can hear the yelling. I explain the outburst is because Hospice changed Mom's care schedule to include night care, which has upset my mother's special friend.

The on-call contact tells me to call police if I feel danger. The boyfriend hears me ask to document this call, to make sure information reaches the Green Team. Finally, he retreats to the garage.

I hang up and look at this tiny Asian nurse. She nods, a slight distasteful pursing of her lips. She says she will be all right. I shake her hand, with gratitude. I leave, walking out minutes later through the garage where he angrily dusts a dustless car. I watch for a minute and tell him the night nurse is staying. He can stay or go. I ask that he please allow this care person to help Mom.

He won't speak to me. I have left my note on the counter.

So, I'm home and have called Tee. We talked over this latest uproar. We talk about her travel plan to come see Mom soon. She is planning a nonstop flight, one day, in and out. I say I've decided to see the Sheriff tomorrow about what can be done.

September 10

Up early with a full day.

There is an early call from care company management, letting me know that last night at Islander Court was difficult. The boyfriend was in the way, the nurse's ability to care impeded. The company will staff again tonight but will terminate their entire contract if this continues. I will receive a formal letter stating their position.

It has come to this. Dear God, I cannot allow the care company to terminate.

I fired off an email to family about Hospice switching Mom to Continuing Care designation, the Hospice guess that Mom has three more weeks. I sign off with appreciation for support and prayers.

I head out to find a Sheriff.

Not good. I learn that in Florida, the boyfriend has squatter rights--he has slept at Mom's house. Police have no jurisdiction without court orders. From the Sheriff office, I drive to consult a family rights attorney. I've had his name for a while. I spend a couple hour consult learning what is required to get the boyfriend out of Mom's house. Legal action, an ediction notice signed by a judge.

The lawyer says he's in tight with a judge who gets a lot of domestic cases like this, and we could get the Order to Vacate within five days. It would not drag out, and it will cost around $2K.

I will let him know my decision.

9-11

I admire the sad sorry irony of this date. I get a second morning call from the care company in as many days. Another bad night at Islander Court.

The company owner emails The Letter.

It reads in part *"I am requesting that your mother's male companion no longer stay at her house at night effective immediately. In my professional and clinical opinion it is unnecessary and inappropriate.... out of respect....aides needs to go in and out of the bedroom at night without having to worry about the boyfriend's state of dress....notified that he is always welcome to visit during the day."*

I print copies, tape one to Mom's back door. I tell aides to lock the doors. I call the cell number I have for the boyfriend, and his land line, leaving detailed messages both places, suggesting he call me or the care company to discuss. Nurse Debbie does the same.

We wait. He never calls.

But he does not show up either. Day three is quiet and compassionate at Islander Court. Mom has rested comfortably through the night, and there is no drama. Finally.

The sisters may be another story. But one is in Scotland and the other not here. The care team can do its job without interference, a reprieve and relief for us all, at least for another week.

September 23

Tess has told me today that Mom woke up telling her that, "my baby girl has been here." Tess thinks Mom is imagining it, but I confirm what Mom has told her. The "baby girl" was here. Not some spirit walker. She had flown in and out in the space of one special day.

Yesterday. I had seen the joy, had loved watching the smile of recognition reach Mom's eyes as Tee came to her. Lovely. Special. She called her name. I watched the gentle hugs, the soft rub of shoulders, the holding hands, the stroke of cheeks. All of it was helping the house karma. My kid sister finally here in Mom's house! A couple hours together, then a rest.

I took Tee to see my daughter and grandson. I took her to Mom's beach to feel the waves, to share the Gulf's respite from heartache. Then back to Mom's until it was time for the second airport run that day.

And Mom had wakened with the memory of the visit. A lovely gift.

I left Mom when the night duty person arrived. As always, kissing her goodbye, telling her I loved her. Said it was OK if it was time to leave on her trip.

September 25

A busy two days! The attorney, banking, hospice meetings with nurses and the chaplain, who has a beautiful soothing presence. It strikes me that she is a different kind of Hospice connection. I contacted Mom's pre-planned funeral contract service. I had found a pre-payment receipt for cremation among the papers in Great Grampa's desk, something Mom had done for herself years back after Dad died. I wanted to know how this procedure worked, when it was her time.

There were two more Hospice meetings. Y had returned from Scotland. She spits out sparse details of her trip, "it's like Wisconsin" while Debbie's counterpart, another private duty nurse manager, apprises her of Mom's situation. I say I am glad to see her. She snorts.

Other than this, she is polite in front of the nurse. She does not rail against continuous care, Mom's descent, or me. She accepts that Mom is now sleeping alone at night under the eye of 24-hour care, but she reported the boyfriend called X crying about it.

The nurse tries to help Y understand that Mom's own needs at night are greater than those of a boyfriend. I say we are offering food and drink, not forcing her to eat and Y breaks her facade, shouting at me.

"Don't ever disrespect him to me, Jan. He really cares for her."

"Of course, he cares about her," I replied. "But this is her time now, not his anymore. That's all I meant."

She says X is coming back and will help with Mom next week. I will retreat to Michigan for part of that.

Mom is not following any of this. She is asleep, or working elsewhere, both feet partially planted on the other side.

September 26

Today was just another day, except that it was Thursday. In the few afternoon awake moments, when Mom had a sip of water with the bed cranked so she could simultaneously lie back but sit up, she listens to Tess and I talking about the schedule.

"Hey Mom. It is Thursday," I say. "Are you taking a trip today?"

She shuts her eyes to us but shakes her head back and forth. No, not today.

Tess and I look at each other. I kiss Mom goodbye, use the control to lower the bed. Mom rolls her eyes and goes wherever it is she's been going on these long sleep-filled days.

October 3

I am leaving tomorrow on a midday flight for about 10 days. I needed to have my annual artificial knee checkup and see my husband and youngest. I stopped at the care company offices for a departure sit down with Debbie. We talked it through. She would reach me if something happened. She knew how to work around the twins' care time plans. Everyone knew I would come back.

I told her I continued to say goodbye, goodnight to Mom each day I was with her. I knew the care company supported me, had Mom's best interests to heart. I knew Hospice would be in and out, would oversee. I was grateful for their care of Mom. I was grateful for their care of me.

And then I went to Mom's. She was sleeping. All day. I kissed her cheek and went home to pack.

October 4

I dreaded spending any time with the twins, but there was a scheduled Hospice check-in with family and private care just before my flight. I had arrived early because at the last meeting, I walked in to find Mom sitting in a chair two feet from the television, looking distressed, worried eyes transfixed on some grisly movie. Did I mention Y's penchant for horror films? I had immediately flipped to a music channel. No bad television for today.

The sisters walked in laughing with the hospice nurse. Like old buddies. I think Hospice is chummying up, a false camaraderie masking this circumstance. Whatever. X would leave shortly, I had my northern respite plan, and Mom's suffering could not last much longer. She already had twice passed hospice predictions.

But the first announcement is a downer. Sister X has made plans to stay on. Sorely disappointed about her continued presence, even though she and Y would be helping Mom, she wasn't finished.

In place of paying for care company support, she wanted me to pay her instead. That payment request hung in the air.

Silence. I was sitting on the couch, looking across Mom, in her pink-sheeted hospital bed, watching the rest of these people, everyone waiting for me to say something. I had a bitter taste in my mouth.

"Let me get this straight, okay. I'm trying to understand." I began, voice deliberately flat. "Are you asking, do you mean that you want me, want Mom, to pay you, to help take care of her? Is that it? You want Mom to pay you for taking care of her?"

"Yeah, well, if I was home, I'd be looking for a job," she replied. "But I decided to stay. You would be paying somebody, right? Why shouldn't it be me? I'm a nurse. Yeah, you should pay me."

I let the silence hang there a bit, the lazy blades of a ceiling fan roaring in my ears.

"You *really* are asking *me* to pay *you* to take care of *our mother?*" I say it again just to be certain, incredulous of her suggestion.

"Yeah, why not?"

I let the silence hang longer this time before I reply, while I felt my brain visualize catfish, bottom-feeders.

"Pardon me, if I sound surprised. No. The answer is no. No. I'm not going to pay you to take care of Mom. I would think you'd want to help because she's your Mom, not because you need a job. Sorry. Not happening." (I silently wondered if I had time for another shower before I left for the airport.)

Moving on, I asked the Hospice nurse about additional care activities. The meeting ended and the sisters leave. Hospice leaves. I am left with Mom, today's caregiver aide, and the company nurse, who hasn't been a regular here.

The nurse admitted she can't believe what she had just heard.

"Really?" I said, matter of fact. "Stick around a while. Or just ask Debbie. I'm not surprised by anything, anymore."

I get up and come around the electric bed to hug and kiss Mom goodbye. Tell her I am going to Michigan for a few days to be with my family.

"I'll miss you, Mom," I added. "But if you have to leave on your trip before I get back, that's okay. I understand. Bye for now. I love you."

Her eyes are green this morning, wide open, holding my face. She nods. Firmly. She knows.

October 17

It has been a long day. It is the dark of a perfect, soft night on the bayou. There is a full moon, my electric fans are whirring, and the windows are open. It is gentle weather, a seaside air wrapping itself around me.

I'm tingling and exhausted, but I am posting for myself, committing the last 36 hours to written form, too afraid that any delay and I will begin to lose it. I want to safeguard a perfect gift.

I need to journal about yesterday, meaning October 16, but even that really started another 24 hours ago, October 15, when I left Michigan headed back to Mom's side.

The plane had been late, flights delayed by weather, and it was near midnight Tuesday (**October 15**) when I fell into bed. I had returned from a glorious 10-day break with perfect Indian Summer weather. My knee had checked out. There had been no news from Florida. No phone calls. Wonderful family time, prayers of gratitude already thanking God for my breather.

But I was anxious to get back. I woke up early Wednesday (**October 16**) with a standing appointment to meet Chaplain Donna around 2. Paperwork, paying bills, and a few phone calls filled a quiet morning at my desk. I hadn't heard from Hospice or the care company, leaving me with an overall impression that Mom was hanging in there under their care. Pretty good for a lady who was dying.

I headed over to Islander Court.

She was in a cloud of pink lying in the hospital bed, eyes closed, head turned, white hair soft against a pink pillow, pink house dress, with small pillows propped here and there to ease her rest, save wear on tired joints and pressure points. But the soft drone of television weather was being overtaken by noisy breathing--a rough sound, hurting my ears.

Mom was closer than ever to the other side.

Tess was there and the hospice chaplain was due momentarily. Within minutes of my arrival, my phone buzzed, Chaplain Donna asking where I was. Was I coming in? She had expected me, I had expected her, anticipating her visit with Mom, not just me. She came over a short while later, immediately walking back outside to make a phone call.

Later, when Y asked who alerted Hospice, I told her that actually, Hospice called Hospice.

Mom was within final days if not hours.

While I had waited for Chaplain Donna, I had been using the timer on my phone. Mom's breathing was irregular. Gurgly. I wanted to measure what I was and wasn't hearing. Periods of silence, 8 to 17 second gaps with no breathing. She was working hard.

I told her I was back from Michigan. I held her limp hand, arm loose and jangly, while timing those raggedy breaths. She might have made a slight squeeze of my fingers, but it was so faint and fleeting, I wondered if I had imagined it, or felt it only with my heart.

I kissed her cheek, stroked her temple, using touch to hold my calm. I believed she could hear me, knew it actually, but also knew that all her energy was focused on breathing.

I stroked her arm, gently rocking it forward and back in my grasp. I held her hand, willing myself to memorize the feel of her flesh against mine, the softness, the old skin smooth under my fingers. She was working to be in this moment.

But I knew she was nearly gone.

So today really is **October 17**, but it began yesterday, in the middle of an Autumn afternoon.

Her fingers were cool, bluish. Tess said she had been breathing this way since morning. Tess also said that when she had arrived, my sisters were giving Mom liquids, mixing medicine with juice and pouring it into her. Tess told them to stop, had warned them about aspiration and choking. Awful. Unfathomable. Absurd.

Tess reported that care management hadn't heard from them at all. They had come and gone and come back, doing night care shifts on their own terms. It was only at a shift change did anyone see them or observe what was going on. Which was why Tess could describe the medicine and juice episode.

This was exactly what Tee and I had thought might occur, sadly speculating that action such as this might, in fact, be Mom's destiny. Though I had fantasized plenty about their banishment from Mom's life, I faulted neither Mom nor myself for their presence, they were family. But it wasn't lost on me or Tee, that perhaps the twins were destined to be the very agents of a pneumonia that would release Mom from her earthly bounds.

People who knew my fractured family, knew this hurtful dilemma. Tee and I had fretted surely, but understood our sisters had a right to share Mom's remaining time. Mom had never said keep them away, way back or any time since. Nor would I have ever asked such a painful question.

We were here, all of us. The same moral ethic that held me to Mom's plan, kept me from excluding them, even if I thought they were as misguided in end of life care as in everything up to now.

What possibly could be the lesson in that?

For the last 11 days, I had dreaded a phone call, expected to learn Mom had left on her trip. But she hadn't. And I had had a glorious respite. As I sat holding Mom's hand, listening to the battle in her lungs, I was sad, but so gratified. Her final breaths would be in this home. She would be free very soon.

Holding on with what little energy Mom had left, I believed

Mom had been waiting for me, for this, for what I recognized as her last moments.

The end of days. I knew it.

Chaplain Donna, put her hand on Mom's shoulder briefly, asked me if I wanted her to pray. Said she had a favorite prayer for this time, compassionately direct and clear. She affirmed that Mom was where I thought she was--nearly ready.

I felt Donna's soothing voice wash over us, a cadence of comfort, rising and falling like gently flowing water or music. The prayer was for journeyers, filled with calm and faith on that nearly perfect October afternoon. Peaceful. A prayer of transition, Psalms for Mom and her soul, words of intercession and spirit. Donna prayed that Mom's final steps could be as easy as possible, for Jean to get herself, enfolded in love, to the door only she could walk through.

As Donna continued, the prayer saturated everything. Immersed in a gentle murmur in this stillness, I opened my eyes to look around, to hold these moments. Tess also, sitting silently sharing this time, eyes closed, hands folded in her lap. There was a profound sense of movement in the flowing ribbon of words. Perhaps like prayers Catholics call last rights, or how God and Jean describe final instructions on the road of passage.

The cool blue fingers with fresh pink polish were gently folded into my hand as Donna spoke words that embodied love and the tender spiritual link between one world and another. I felt words wrapping around us, sinking into my skin. The air felt soft, clear blue. Comforting. Peaceful. I closed my eyes again, concentrating on my hand clasping her limp one, committing our link to my heart. I embraced a wonderful impression of being exactly in a special perfect place.

Tonight, I want to remember all the Chaplain's words. I cannot, but I want to ask Donna for a written copy soon.

In the middle of that soliloquy of peace, suddenly there was a bolt, an electric tingling, a buzz of something, like putting your finger in an electric socket. It zapped through my hand travelling up my arm, zinging through me, pulling all my awareness. Alive with sensation, my eyes had shot open. I was expecting something, stars, a streak of yellow light, anything to explain what I had just felt. But there was only the continuing song of Donna's prayer, Tess sitting quietly, eyes closed, and Mom's hand in mine.

I wondered briefly if anyone had noticed, but I was in awe, realizing what had happened. An amazing force, a personal burst of pure energy, love from Mom to me, had flared in our joined hands. Strong, pronounced. Here and gone in a flash.

I turned myself back to the rhythm of prayer flowing over me. As Donna finished, my mind clearly saw Mom, with a tiny smile, standing with a hand on her doorknob, waiting to usher us out the open front door.

In the shadow of her finish line, Mom was beautiful. Tess had done her nails and her toes that morning, reminding me how Mom always said she had pretty toes. I watched her face, so still, a disparate contrast to hearing those agonized efforts to breathe past whatever was there.

A scar on her forehead was suddenly clear, almost illuminated. I had seen it before, but never with such brightness, an old fine line like a crack in china, a tiny circle with a spider leg or two, the aftermath of a car crash when she was a young child. It disappeared, and the graying at her mouth disappeared too.

I asked Donna what else was to be done. She had already called for a Hospice nurse to be there around five.

I started talking again with Mom. Close to her ear. Told her I'd get her to the beach when this was all finished. Told her I loved her. Told her I knew she was ready for her trip. Told her I wouldn't stop my sisters from coming that night but that she could help herself get away. Told her I saw her standing at her door, and it was up to her to decide when to walk through it.

***

The sisters walked into Mom's around 7, unhappy to see me. The night Hospice nurse was checking Mom, calling her supervisor, changing meds, trying for last minute comfort. At her urging, the sisters retreated to purchase suppository Tylenol to bring down the raging fever that had begun late in the afternoon.

While they were gone, the nurse told me how we both were well aware we could not control them. She asked if I knew for certain they hadn't tampered with the meds outside the lock box. I couldn't guarantee anything, except that the lock box medicine had been protected from their hands.

When they returned, there was a moment when we all had hands on Mom's fevered body, turning her as X actually did a nursing thing—placing a suppository. The hospice nurse gently put a cool washcloth on Mom's forehead, and I pushed a stray lock of white hair back from her face.

This wonderful nurse, I'll call her Mary, then turned and lectured my sisters, in a no-nonsense tone. She called them out, blaming Mom's noisy labored breathing on the liquids and foods they had insisted on giving her these past few days. The fever was a result of pneumonia caused by the same. I only asked if they had even noticed. Y admitted a small yes, saying the breathing had seemed to worsen last night, but nothing like it sounded right then.

Getting the fever down would be a comfort, maybe give Mom a bit more time, or not, Mary said. She minced no words about morphine. Mary wanted Mom to have it.

It was my turn then, and I looked X in the eye.

"Do you think you would do that? Could you do what's right?" I asked.

"Well, now I could," she said. As in, apparently, not until this very moment.

Mary wondered if she should arrange continuous care (code for imminent death) right now, and X immediately said no, she was a nurse and would handle it. Waiting a beat, I said yes. Continuous care offered the opportunity to put meds and care in qualified hands and freed my sisters to be daughters.

But I consented to a delay, allowing them to care for Mom tonight as planned. We, meaning Hospice and I, could work out continuous care scheduling tomorrow.

The nurse was finished. I kissed Mom and put my hand to her cheek once more. I told her I loved her and said goodbye, turning quietly to follow Mary out, asking that one of them please call me tonight if there was a change. My voice was flat.

In the shadows of the front lawn, the nurse put a hand on my arm. Kind eyes searched my sad ones.

"You know they aren't going to call you until after she's gone, don't you?"

I nodded.

"And how do you feel about that?"

"I'm okay," I said. "I've said my goodbyes a hundred or a thousand times. Mom and I are okay. We've had a long time to say goodbye, a long road. We're good."

It was true. It was nearly over. We had made the journey as best we could, in a manner Mom wanted. I thanked this nurse who I would never see again, for her forthright honesty, her strength and effort, another gift, an angel in the scheme of passage. I knew it was time for Mom to make her own way.

I had gone home and called Tee. We talked about God, Mom, ourselves and our peace. We had already been over this so much, shouldering the sadness of loss over years of disease, living it out within a fractured family of dissent. We had accepted everything to get here. All was only as it could be.

In the waning minutes of Wednesday, Tee and I speak about tomorrow.

Over these last months, Mom had talked about taking that trip, even waking from sleep to ask about getting dressed to be ready to go. The aides, the case manager, a Hospice nurse, me--we all knew about that trip. When Mom and I had spoken of it, she had been definite: Thursday. She would leave Thursday.

For weeks, the care staff and I had watched Thursdays come and go.

Tess and I had spoken about Thursday with Chaplain Donna, but Tess was holding out for Saturday when she would be again on the care schedule. When does Thursday begin? In the dark after midnight.

It was early Thursday when Tee and I hung up and I went to bed.

***

At 5:49 a.m. there was a call from my sister waking me, telling me Mom was gone, that she had died peacefully in her sleep. That Mom's breathing had begun to skip around three. And then just had quit. I was glad it was over, thanked her for calling. Said I would get dressed and come over.

When I got there, I asked if they had called Hospice. X grumbled out a quick, "Yes, Hospice said they would be sending a nurse." Then they left, literally within minutes, X urging Y, saying she "had to get out of there." I hoped they had said their goodbyes.

All these hours later, I view their nearly immediate departure as another gift. I had final moments alone with Mom, her struggle finished, both of us resting, comfortably silent in the quiet darkness before dawn. In her house.

I waited with my hands on a very warm corpse, grateful for the time, and found myself thinking, over and over, how God had been with us all along. Carrying me, carrying us. Showing the way. Giving me good things in good people. Friends and family with sustaining love. The strength of Mom and me. Perseverance. Angels.

Not by chance but by purpose, and it had taken me all those years to understand. Mom's road but my path, to learn, listen and embrace. To affirm for myself, to guide, guard and strengthen myself to be with her. To have courage in loving Mom, putting myself into whatever could possibly be tossed at me, and then, deflecting the worst, finally and permanently, to do what I needed to do in being here with her.

All day my head and heart have been running over with observations. I think mostly appalling that the sister who is a nurse, remained awful to the end—suggesting the strangest things: to be paid to care for her own mother, to allege neglect and abuse on the part of private duty, hospice and me; to insist just last evening, on elevating the bed, not the headrest, but the height of the entire hospital bed, defiantly, ludicrously, stupidly declaring this to be a comfort measure.

I can't make this stuff up.

A miracle in those last weeks—a day Mom wakes up from somewhere between this world and the next, eyes clear, and I *feel* her heart overflowing. She is smiling with pure joy, calling me her "brown eyed beauty," an old, firstborn endearment. Another treasure from the end of her days, giving so much to me.

That amazing buzz of energy we shared only hours past. Her life force surging between us, zinging into me with love.

Another Hospice nurse I would never see again arrived to pronounce the official time of death. Kathleen is comforting, compassionate, honest. The official time of death is her arrival time at 6:55. Later, she and I notice TOD 545 scribbled onto the pad where the sisters had kept track of meds along with a running tally of hours X had "worked" to care for Mom. (yes, LOL).

Kathleen phoned the funeral company and after an hour has passed, I called them again. When they arrived, later than expected, they were somberly apologetic for my loss, and began their movements to ready Mom's remains for the next destination.

Tee called me and we shared how both of us were up in the night—she with hot flashes and wonder, and me twice wakened in the dark stillness. I don't keep a clock in my bedroom, I only knew it was too early to be up. Tee said at one moment she had seen violet ribbons and a purple flash. Days later, a Hospice nurse would explain this as Mom's final walkabout, coming to us. You know, the stuff beyond our human existence.

I called Mom's brother. Sandy arrived--it was her day to be with Mom. Karen texted. Now would be a final opportunity to see her Grammy before the burial company took her. We made a plan for me to sit out in her car with my beautiful grandson, who ate Dunkin Donut holes while Karen went inside to say goodbye and walk thru a house filled with family memories.

Sandy came out to say hello to the two-year-old, he showed her his donut and his blue eyes. Then Karen was back, borrowing a dollar to buy a few more donut holes, a special morning treat for this awesome two-year-old, the newest precious life in our family. Later, Karen would post on Facebook her happy memories of long-gone days with Grammy, a photo of them together, and how moments of prayer this morning encircled their lives in Florida.

When I returned inside, the nurse shared some thoughts, normalizing this death, saying plenty of people die from fever. I told Sandy to take some things—care products for her own mom, maybe some lipsticks because she had always told Mom that their morning time together had officially made Mom, "Sandy's Work of Art."

Waiting, I concentrated on the softness of a cooling cheek, the serene stillness in these last minutes. I could still feel the warmth of her, but rigor has begun to settle in when I finally stepped aside to allow those earthly transporters to begin their tasks. I watched the delicate respectful maneuvers of the funeral team carefully remove the pink sheets. I took a last look at painted toes, the slender profile of her Marilyn Monroe legs, as I memorized the warmth of her body, the magical moments, and the compassionate solemnity of people who understood passage.

They slowly, deliberately covered her, a respectful methodic wrapping of her body. I photographed the frail beauty of Mom carefully shrouded in white. It is for Tee who has asked for an image of what she could not witness for herself.

I helped them ever slightly, to lift and slide a body board, to move her onto a gurney. Joseph, (yes), laid a rich burgundy velvet cloth across her shrouded remains. I think by law, she must be fully covered to depart the premises. The hospice nurse mentioned that sometimes family don't want to witness the covering. Joseph asked if I was okay, and I said yes.

I was gratified by these final motions, thankful to attend the finish, feeling complete as a vigilant carer doing what I had been asked. I sensed the journey's end in these gestures, holding myself present in the moments of my mother's final road trip from Islander Court.

We rolled out to a van at the end of the drive, a tiny subdued parade. Sandy was crying, along with Sandy's sister who remembered Mom from long ago rides to the beach, the Hospice nurse Kathleen, the young men carefully loading the gurney, me, Mom. Sunlight was streaming through live oak branches on this pretty October morning while tiny dry leaves skittered down the street. I heard birds. I hugged Sandy. I shook hands with Joseph and his assistant, said my thanks. They departed. I hugged the nurse, we closed up Mom's house and I delivered myself to a long-standing date, emcee for this year's inaugural Suncoast Hospice Fashion Show fundraiser.

One hundred or one thousand goodbyes later, Mom reached her earthly finish line. All that happened is now history.

A lesson of love and letting go. Hers and mine. One gone and one remains.

I am scheduled to meet with Hospice tomorrow, the protocol of "closure." I already know that a nurse will tell me another soul has taken Mom's place on the roster.

Already midnight again. I am drained and filled again, and at peace. I am good with today.

Epilogue

"And once the storm is over, you won't remember how you made it through, how you managed to survive. You won't even be sure, if the storm is really over. But one thing is certain... When you come out of the storm, you won't be the same person who walked in. That's what this storm is all about." - Haruki Murakami via Empath Health

Fifteen months after Mom has died, and eight since I released her ashes, I thought I had concluded my appraisal of that worldly question: *what does all this mean?*

It has occurred to me that Mom is still here. Not in the corporeal sense, but certainly in spirit, in my mental realm. There are reminders--a drive past her street, a chance browse through my phone's photo book, forwarded mail, a dream, a trinket. I have not forgotten magic moments, Mom's joy at Tee's loving visit, the predicted finale of a Thursday departure, the music of my buddies, Bob Seger and George Harrison, the feather's touch of angelic consolation on a very hard day, the tingle of energy during a chaplain's prayer of intercession. I remain enriched and awestruck by all these things, but especially by that singular jolt passing from Mom to me, on a last afternoon filled with grace.

Sometimes I sense her new freedom—a contrived image of my emotional editorial license—she is a free bird, floating, smiling, enjoying the beach, all pain and disease erased. And sometimes, I "have a moment" when I feel her visit, though this is not often, because mostly I am sure she has moved on.

Loss softens with time. Frustration and hurt are in the past. They no longer haunt my days. But the real lessons never vanish: love between us, the support of so many people, God's hand in it all…and a plan that offered shelter from the storm (thank you, Bob Dylan). I have embraced the ultimate privilege, that Mom and I could share her end of life trail.

There is my expanded fascination, a unique awareness, awe for the steps on that highway. The angels, human and ethereal, who helped me walk with Mom. Incredible moments, miracles only explained beyond our limited human experience. I live fully, with a grander belief in a greater Universe. Once given, this is the gift spiraling into my future.

There are Hospice people who will tell you I grieved throughout Mom's journey, an observation which suggests I had an easier time with closure, with the Stage 6, "end of the plan," (thank you, Dr. Prochaska), by the time she died.

But the revisit to tell our weighty story has brought reminders of grief. I was too exhausted for a long while. Picking up and putting down demons in remembering has not been easy. I've been sensitive to additional insight and understanding in the retelling. The story, and Mom, wouldn't let me go.

Joyous and cathartic, *Walking with Mom* has required a 360-degree view. If grief and relief were partnered up at the finish, sadness was tempered by success, not a word usually associated with death, because Mom finished on her terms.

I share what Mom and I lived through so that others can know our path in order to build and live their own masterful journeys in the natural framework of death as part of life. Mom and I shared the good, the bad and the ugly, but I hear her voice whispering, "pretty good" about our partnership, and what morphed over years and circumstance to the bigger lesson of what we accomplished together.

That age-old wisdom, *Time Heals,* seems to fit, giving me stamina to share our story and get it right. I do wonder about Hospice professionals. Do they withstand grief and hardship in a field of death and dying because it isn't personal? I think this may be only part of it.

From the personal side, I can report that sharing anyone's final road is exhausting on its own. It can nearly deplete you, make you feel crazy. Add in the stress of family dissension and it takes you to your knees.

On your knees is a great place to find grace and divine intervention. Believe me: I'll tell anybody I felt it. More than once. Truthfully, plenty of times.

All that time in Mom's trench, had the ability to transform. Is that what Hospice folks get? Transformation with each passage? A sense of purpose by being there? The miracle of a complete circle?

If you are paying attention, there is NO WAY not to reap the education and awe of the senior highway, especially if you see it to the end. I'm guessing this is what Hospice folks know: each life brings natural order, something to be gained as witness to its passing.

In the Mirror

For a long time, almost forever, I would look in a mirror and see my Italian ancestors staring back. Dad's cheekbones, dark eyes, his height. The wavy full head of hair, the lightly olive skin. Throughout Mom's illness, it was Dad looking back at me, trusting who I was, what I could accomplish. Dad's eyes saying *stay strong* for as long as it takes. Against the wind, (thank you Bob Seeger).

Sometimes that face looked back with despair, deep dark pools reflecting anguish for where we found ourselves—Mom and her denouement, and me as sentinel. The eyes echoed misery, moments when I did not want to be my mother's daughter glued alongside her in that deteriorating limbo.

I didn't want Mom's reflection in that mirror, her poor little evaporating mind at the mercy of such circumstance. I *needed* to be my Dad, to be a soldier.

Today, I recognize that bit of nascent Italian pride for my personal standard of doing best amid seismic moments. I see family history in my face, and know myself better, for everything these dark brown eyes have seen.

Once, in the throes of another crazy brutish episode concocted by my sisters, I told Mom that I was strong, that I could hold on and do what she wanted, but that I *needed* her to know, just *know*, how very hard it was. Mom had no words that day, her eyes simply had held mine.

Just recently, I looked in the mirror, surprised to see Mom staring back. She, who had been there all along. It had been her loving trust to give it all over to me, confident that my determination and honor would see to her plan, to do what needed doing, to do the time, to see it through.

Overcoming minutiae and heart ache, bearing witness and

walking alongside a parent to the end, is second perhaps, to being at the miracle of beginning. Hospice professionals might feel the miracle of passage, too.

My good old friend, Hindsight, has provided a great opportunity for me to embrace and savor the full human experience. I feel very fortunate to have been there, yet also *very* relieved to have stepped beyond the darkest days.

Dawn Hafner, a blogger with a Twitter handle, **#bewhereyouare** described it this way… *"even in the most difficult of times, there is still joy…"*

For a year, local Hospice folks who suggested I had grieved all along the way (true), made check-in calls to see how I was fairing after Mom's death. The tick of quarterly contacts are routine markers of hospice closure, the caring for *she who remains*. Simple, gentle, brief, affirming, "we remember where you've been and what you've done."

I've long since finished Mom's estate work, sold a house, dispersed possessions. The responsibility of caring for Mom has shifted to caring for myself--playing, traveling, welcoming a new granddaughter, looking for my whole self again, gently moving on. I feel the distinct luxury of blessed life.

What remains however, is this cache of memory and accomplishment. Mom's "human tornado" has spun herself out, down a path that swirled to a finish with acceptance and joy for a complete life. Efforts in love, compassion, misery and amazement, I am ultimately enriched by the grandness of spirit and human existence.

Mom's final rocky road through normal human territory was as close as possible to the way she wanted it to. Because of a plan. Couldn't ask for more.

With a nod to the past, the present and the future, I am my

father's daughter, but I am also my mother's brown-eyed beauty girl, and I am greatly OK being me.

That's *pretty good*, don't you think? It's greatly good enough for me.

Resources as Red Bull

*K*nowledge is power, right?

When we began Mom's walk, I was already a lifelong voracious reader. The path broadened my reading list with nourishment, education, validation, satisfaction and careful insight (thank you Dr. Phil!), as I grew into my role.

Fate, faith, experience and circumstance tweaked the reading list. Self-help and tips for my carer condition and our days came from many places, sometimes when I wasn't looking. Bookstore angels knew what to suggest; there were gifts from friends, doctors, hospice. Messages resonated in fiction and memoirs. An OpEd piece would show up in the <u>Wall Street Journal</u>. A collaboration to reorganize my church's 100-year-old library yielded C. S. Lewis. Graduate school social science texts offered intuitive explanations of family dynamics and life cycle mileposts. Social media shared meaningful commentary.

I really lost myself in a purposeful essay of one man's last days (the O'Kelly book), and I looked through windows provided by veteran hospice nurses (<u>Final Gifts</u>). Reading quieted storms, tightened wheels, boosted conviction, and offered a reminder overall, of life's normal rhythm from birth to death. It all helped me cope, allowed me to sleep, helped me lean in against the wind (thank you, Bob Seeger).

This bibliography is not meant to be exhaustive, but simply my own, across a giant learning curve. What doesn't fit right now, might help in a month or a year. And keep looking for that next good read.*

- JG

---

* FYI, the reading bug is genetic. I got it from Mom who got it from her father, and our shared love for books reminds me about love and celebrating life. About seven years into <u>Walking with Mom</u>, I came over and found her comfortably kicked back, lounging with a book in each hand, and three open novels in her lap!

Nobody said we couldn't smile.

Bibliography

Albom, Mitch. For one more day. Hyperion, New York. 2006.

Albom, Mitch. The first phone call from Heaven. Hyperion, New York. 2013.

Alexander, Aimee. Pause to rewind. Kindle Edition, 2014.

Byrne, Lorna. Angels in My Hair. The True Story of a Modern-Day Irish Mystic. Three Rivers Press, New York. 2008.

Callahan, Maggie & Kelley, Patricia. Final Gifts. Understanding the Special Awareness, Needs, and Communications of the Dying. Bantam Book, New York. 1992.

Coehlo, Paulo. The Alchemist. 1988

Coste, Joanne Koenig. Learning to Speak Alzheimer's. A Groundbreaking Approach for Everyone Dealing with the Disease. Houghton-Mifflin, New York. 2003.

Davis, Patti. The Long Good-bye. Alfred A. Knopf, Random House, New York. 2004

Eisen, Armand. Mothers, a tribute. Andrews and McMeel, Kansas City. 1992.

Fishel, Ruth. Wrinkles Don't Hurt. Daily Meditations on the Joy of Aging Mindfully. Health Communications, Deerfield Beach, Florida. 2011.

Gawande, Atul. Being Mortal. Illness, Medicine and What Matters in the End. Profile Books Ltd., London. 2014.

Hafner, Dawn. Six things I learned about life by working with Hospice. Blog post, 03/06/2015. Twitter site: www.twitter.com/bewhereyouare1

Halifax, Joan. Being with Dying. Cultivating Compassion and Fearlessness in the Presence of Death. Shambhala Publications, Boston. 2008.

HuffingtonPost.com. "10 Things that changed Me After the Death of a Parent." November 4, 2015.

Karnes, Barbara. Gone From My Sight. The Dying Experience. Vancouver, Washington. 1986.

Karnes, Barbara. The Final Act of Living. Reflections of a Longtime Hospice Nurse. Barbara Karnes Books, Depoe Bay, Oregon. 2003.

Kubler-Ross, Elisabeth. <u>On Death and Dying. What the dying have to teach doctors, nurses, clergy and their own families.</u> MacMillan Publishing Company, New York. 1969.

Lamott, Anne. <u>Almost Everything. Notes on Hope.</u> Riverhead Books, Penguin, New York. 2018.

Lewis, C.S. <u>A Grief Observed.</u> Harper & Row Publishers, San Francisco. 1961.

Lindbergh, Anne Morrow. <u>Gift from the Sea.</u> Pantheon Books, New York. 1925, 1935, 1975, 1983, 2005.

Mace, Nancy; Rabins, Peter. <u>The 36-hour day. A Family Guide to Caring for Persons with Alzheimer Disease, Related Dementias and Memory Loss.</u> The John Hopkins University Press, 1999, Third edition.

McGoldrick, Monica; Carter, Betty; & Garcia-Preto, Nydia. <u>The Expanded Family Life Cycle, Individual, Family, and Social Perspectives.</u> Allyn & Bacon Publishers, Boston. 2001, Fourth Edition.

McGraw, Phil. <u>Life Code. The New Rules for Winning in the Real World.</u> Bird St. Books, Los Angeles. 2012.

Menten, Ted. <u>Gentle Closings. How to Say Goodbye to Someone You Love.</u> Running Press, Philadelphia. 1991.

Millman, Dan. <u>Way of a Peaceful Warrior. A Book that Changes Lives.</u> H.J. Kramer, Novato, California. 1980.

Normile, Patti. <u>When a Loved One Wishes to Die at Home.</u> Care Notes, Archabbey Press, St. Meinrad, Indiana. 2006.

O'Kelly, Eugene and O'Kelly, Corinne. <u>Chasing Daylight: How My Forthcoming Death Transformed My Life.</u> McGraw-Hill, New York. 2008.

Quindlen, Anna. <u>A Short Guide to a Happy Life</u>. Random House, New York. 2000.

<u>Still Alice</u>. American independent drama film, about early onset Alzheimer's Disease starring Julie Ann Moore. 2014.

Strauss, Claudia J. <u>Talking to Alzheimer's. Simple Ways to Connect When You Visit with a Family Member or Friend</u>. New Harbinger Publications, Oakland, California. 2001.

Welch, Ashley. <u>Emotional Health about Dying.</u> AOL Everyday Health Blogs. April, 2015.

Weiner, Eric. <u>The Geography of Bliss</u>. Hatchette Book Group, Inc., New York. 2008.

<u>www.aplaceformom.com</u>

<u>www.elderhelpers.org</u>

<u>www.marcandangel.com</u> 8 Things to Remember When Everything Goes Wrong.

<u>WWW.N4A.org</u>. An online guide for beginning questions and

considerations.

www.starttheconversation.org Vermont.

www.wordpress.com Alzheimer Blogs.

Final Inspiration & Encouragement

The Universe speaks. Through time or imagination, by faith or fate, an assortment of voices delivered messages on our shared path. These words are the ones I remembered long enough to write down.

Anna, in <u>Anna and the King</u>: *"It has remained with me how such important moments in our lives can take such a few moments of time. They are nearly gone before they have begun."*

Buddha. *"You cannot travel the path until you have become the path itself."*

Charlie Brown, <u>Peanuts</u>. *"Worrying won't stop the bad stuff from happening. It just stops you from enjoying the good."*

Lois Summer Cider, forever friend. *"Don't let yourself fall into that hole."*

Paulo Coelho, in <u>The Alchemist</u>. *"Tell your heart that the fear of* *suffering is worse that the suffering itself."*

Ram Dass, American Spiritual teacher. *"We're all just walking each other home."*

Derek C. Doepker. About motivation: *"…we all can't be up and positive all the time, but the tasks don't go away. What to do? Bypass your feelings and rely on habit to move you on the path."*

Max Ehrmann, Desiderata essay excerpts, 1927. *"Go placidly amid the noise and haste, and remember what peace there may be in silence.… Take kindly the counsel of the years, gracefully surrendering the things of youth. Nurture strength of spirit to shield you in sudden misfortune. But do not distress yourself with imaginings. Many fears are born of fatigue and loneliness.*
"Beyond a wholesome discipline, be gentle with yourself. You are a child of the universe, no less than the trees and the stars; you have a right to be here. And whether or not it is clear to you, no doubt the universe is unfolding as it should. Therefore, be at peace with God, whatever you conceive Him to be, and whatever your labors and aspirations, in the noisy confusion of life keep peace in your soul. With all its sham, drudgery and broken dreams, it is still a beautiful world…strive to be happy."

Ralph Waldo Emerson, poet, transcendentalist. *"What lies behind us and what lies before us are tiny matters compared to what lies within us."*

Ann Hilty, forever friend. *"The bad things cannot last forever."*

Elisabeth Kubler-Ross, author: *"The most beautiful people are those* who have known defeat, known suffering, known struggle, known loss, and have found their way out of the depths. These persons have an appreciation, a sensitivity, and an understanding of life that fills them with compassion, gentleness and a deep loving concern."

Gotthold Ephraim Lessing: "*A single grateful thought toward heaven is the most complete prayer.*"

Haruki Murakami via Empath Health, Clearwater, Florida. "*And once the storm is over, you won't remember how you made it through, how you managed to survive. You won't even be sure, if the storm is really over. But one thing is certain… When you come out of the storm, you won't be the same person who walked in. That's what this storm is all about.*"

Hebrews 13.2 "*Do not neglect to show hospitality to strangers, for by this some have entertained angels without knowing.*"

Lupytha Hermin via Purple Clover. "*One day she finally grasped that unexpected things were always going to happen in life. And with that she realized the only control she had was how she chose to handle them. So she made the decision to survive using courage, humor and grace. She was queen of her own life and the choice was hers.*"

Barbara Karnes, hospice nurse, author, <u>Gone from my sight: The Dying Experience.</u> "*…a time of withdrawing from everything outside of one's self and going inside. Inside where there is sorting out, evaluating one's self and one's life…room for only one……the processing of one's life…. spending more time asleep than awake becomes the norm…. This appears to be just sleep, but know that important work is going on inside…*"

L.R. Knost, via Facebook/the idealist. *"Life is amazing. And then it's awful. And then it's amazing again. And in between the amazing and the awful it's ordinary and mundane and routine. Breathe in the amazing, hold on through the awful, and relax and exhale during the ordinary. That's just living heartbreaking, soul-healing, amazing, awful, ordinary life. And it's breathtakingly beautiful."*

Abraham Lincoln. *"I do the very best I can; and I mean to keep doing so until the end."*

Mary Todd Lincoln. *"What day is so dark that there is no ray of sunshine to penetrate the gloom?"*

S.C. Lourie, <u>Collective Evolution/Facebook</u>. *"BE confused, it's where you begin to learn new things. BE broken, it's where you begin to heal. BE frustrated, it's where you start to make more authentic decisions. BE sad, because if we are brave enough, we can hear our heart's wisdom through it. BE whatever you are right now. No more hiding. You are worthy, always."*

Positive P's Page/Facebook. *"You will find no better best friend than your mother in this world. Believe me. She knows you more than any one does. You are the flesh of her flesh. Respect her, cherish her and love her with all your heart. She could be gone one day and you'd find no one like her."*

The Purple Sherpa/Facebook. *"Caregivers go through more than they will ever tell you. They give up a lot and rarely have a social life. They can get sick and emotionally worn out. It's a lot for one person and you will never know until you have walked the road of a caregiver."*

Sally Quinn, wife of former Washington Post Editor Ben Bradlee, speaking about her husband's worsening health: " ...*the most horrible experience I have ever had but the caretaking part of it has really become something almost sacred.*"

Eleanor Roosevelt: "*A woman is like a tea bag…you never know how strong she is.*" "*Many people will walk in and out of your life, but only true friends will leave footprints in your heart.*"

Unknown, @SuzanneSomers.com. "*Your mother is always with you. She's the whisper of the leaves as you walk down the street. She's the smell of certain foods you remember, flowers you pick, the fragrance of life itself. She's the cool hand on your brow when you're not feeling well. She's your breath in the air on a cold winter's day. She is the sound of the rain that lulls you to sleep, the colors of a rainbow; she is Christmas morning. Your mother lives inside your laughter. She's the place you came from, your first home, and she's the map you follow with every step you take. She's your first love, your first friend, even your first enemy, but nothing on earth can separate you, not time, not space…not even death.*"

Martha Washington: "*I am still determined to be cheerful and happy in whatever situation I may be; for I have learned from experience that the greater part of our happiness or misery depends upon our dispositions and not our circumstances.*"

Wordpress.com, January 25, 2016. "*Truth be told, every person who has watched a loved one suffer through Alzheimer's has times when they wish their husband, sister, grandpa, wife, mom…would die and end their suffering.*"

Made in the
USA
Columbia, SC

81449352R00200